To

Wit

CW00663906

David

6th November 2014

Mosley and British Politics 1918–32

1918–32

Oswald's Odyssey

David Howell
University of York, UK

First published 2015 by
PALGRAVE MACMILLAN

Palgrave Macmillan in the UK is an imprint of Macmillan Publishers Limited, registered in England, company number 785998, of Houndmills, Basingstoke, Hampshire RG21 6XS.

Palgrave Macmillan in the US is a division of St Martin's Press LLC, 175 Fifth Avenue, New York, NY 10010.

Palgrave Macmillan is the global academic imprint of the above companies and has companies and representatives throughout the world.

Palgrave® and Macmillan® are registered trademarks in the United States, the United Kingdom, Europe and other countries.

ISBN 978–1–137–45637–3

This book is printed on paper suitable for recycling and made from fully managed and sustained forest sources. Logging, pulping and manufacturing processes are expected to conform to the environmental regulations of the country of origin.

A catalogue record for this book is available from the British Library.

Library of Congress Cataloging-in-Publication Data

Howell, David, 1945–

Mosley and British politics 1918–32 : Oswald's odyssey / David Howell, University of York, UK.

pages cm

Includes bibliographical references.
ISBN 978–1–137–45637–3 (alk. paper)
1. Mosley, Oswald, 1896–1980. 2. British Union of Fascists. 3. Great Britain—Politics and government—1910–1936. 4. Fascists—Great Britain—Biography. 5. Politicians—Great Britain—Biography. 6. Fascism—Great Britain—History. I. Title.
DA574.M6H69 2014
320.53'3092—dc23
[B]   2014026503

Typeset by MPS Limited, Chennai, India.

Politics is a matter of boring down strongly and slowly through hard boards with passion and judgement together... Only someone who is confident that he will not be too shattered if the world, seen from his point of view, is too stupid or too vulgar for what he wants to offer it; someone who can say, in spite of that, 'but still' – only he has the 'vocation' for politics.

Max Weber, *Politics as a Vocation*, 1919

Contents

Preface and Acknowledgments

Early in 1968 I heard Robert Skidelsky give a paper entitled 'Oswald Mosley, Last of the Radicals'. The presentation developed ideas already raised in Skidelsky's recently published book on the second Labour Government; they would achieve extensive and controversial expression in his biography of Mosley. The debate over Mosley raises significant and contested issues about the character of interwar British politics which extend far beyond the complexities of an individual personality. Matthew Worley through his own research on the New Party stimulated me to attempt an understanding of Mosley's pre-fascist career that might illuminate the topography of party politics in a critical period. I have explored these issues in seminars at the Universities of Reading, Oxford and Durham; the critically supportive responses that I received both in these formal settings and in many discussions elsewhere have been immensely valuable.

I am grateful to the following bodies for permitting me to quote from materials in their possession; material from the Harold Macmillan Archives is used with the kind permission of the Trustees of the H M Book Trust; the Parliamentary Archives for kind permission to quote from the Beaverbrook Papers; material from the Boothby Papers is reproduced by kind permission of the National Library of Scotland; material from the Mosley and Neville Chamberlain Papers is reproduced with permission of the Cadbury Research Library University of Birmingham; the British Library of Political and Economic Science kindly gave permission to reproduce material from the Passfield Papers, the Dalton Diaries, the Lansbury Papers, the E.M.H. Lloyd Papers and the Gerald Barry Papers; material from the Lord Cecil of Chelwood Papers is reproduced with the permission of the British Library; material from an interview with George Strauss in the Nuffield College History Project collection is reproduced with the kind Permission of the Warden and Fellows of Nuffield College Oxford; material from the Stansgate Diaries by kind permission of the Right Honourable Hilary Benn MP.

This book has been written in the context of Coalition, and of broader political uncertainties which suggest uncomfortable parallels with the age of the young Mosley as does a corrosive agenda of austerity which is economically irrational and destructive of social solidarity. My alternative worlds have been crucial, walking in Yorkshire and watching Manchester City's aesthetically compelling version of the beautiful game. I thank all who have shared these trans-Pennine pleasures with me.

York, 13 May 2014

Overture: Guilty Men

All changed utterly in May 1940. The political tectonic plates shifted. The fall of Neville Chamberlain, the formation of the Churchill Coalition and Labour's entry into government for the first time since the disintegration of August 1931, were the visible signs that the political settlement which had dominated the thirties was dead. The new war cabinet debated the option of exploring the prospects for a settlement with Germany. Churchill and his Labour colleagues offered unbending opposition to Lord Halifax's flexibility. The Government's resolve was tested immediately. The British Expeditionary Force, pressed back to the Channel, began a hazardous evacuation from Dunkirk.

Late on that fateful month's final day three journalists, employed by Lord Beaverbrook, debated the crisis in the *Evening Standard* offices. Frank Owen, the *Standard's* editor had been a progressive Liberal in the 1929 parliament. Michael Foot, from a West Country Liberal dynasty, had inherited Liberalism, but experience of Liverpudlian depression had helped to shift him to socialism and to a Labour candidacy at Monmouth in 1935. Peter Howard's previous political involvement had been limited. His time as 'Crossbencher' on the *Sunday Express* had made his reputation as a no-holds-barred sketch writer.

Their late night discussion led to the rapid production of a polemic that would denounce as incompetent and unpatriotic the regime that had presided over military disaster. *Guilty Men* was produced over four days, a weekend at Howard's Suffolk house followed by intervals between getting successive *Standards* to bed. The text was handed over to the publisher Victor Gollancz on 5 June. A month later it was published under the pseudonym 'Cato', a symbol of Roman populist rectitude. In the interval France had fallen and a German invasion of southern England was widely believed to be imminent.

W.H. Smith's and Wyman's refused to distribute *Guilty Men*, yet by the end of the year sales had reached 200,000. Its prose captured and intensified the widespread animosity towards the recently deceased 'regime of little men'. The pre-war political settlement was held responsible for diplomatic and military failures and was vulnerable to a polemic that fused passion with patriotism. For the first time in living memory the right's monopoly on patriotism had been broken. The erosion of credibility was captured in the barrow-loads of *Guilty Men* for sale on London street corners, as Foot claimed, like a minor pornographic classic.[1]

The text began with a cast of 15 'Guilty Men'. Each of the succeeding 24 chapters was headed by a cast list. No pretence of objectivity and balance was intended. Instead, named individuals from Neville Chamberlain downwards were subjected to demolition by polemic. Personal characteristics were mercilessly lampooned; complexities became dichotomies. Truth was pursued through caricature. The heroes were the marginalised and the talented, mostly notably Churchill and Lloyd George. Discretion explained the laundering of Beaverbrook's political record. Ernest Bevin, recently installed at the Ministry of Labour, received a cameo role for his public butchery of the pacifist George Lansbury at the 1935 Labour Party Conference.[2] *Guilty Men* would have made an excellent stage production, performed with the panache that has fired the recent portrait of the seventies downfall of old Labour, *This House*.

In no sense was *Guilty Men* a polemic from the Left. Nor was it a serious historical assessment. Essentially, it captured and articulated in all its ambiguity and anger a seismic political shift. The focus on the culpable 15 provided a collective absolution for the many millions who had sustained them at the ballot box through the previous decade. The future would now lie with the Churchillians within the Tory Party and with Labour. Exactly five years after the publication of *Guilty Men* the electorate returned the first majority Labour Government. The indictment of 1940 had coloured expectations of which politicians could better deliver a People's Peace. Once in opposition, Churchill devoted himself to his authoritative version of what had happened. *The Gathering Storm*, published in 1948, effectively endorsed the verdict of *Guilty Men*, not in a rapidly composed polemic, but in Churchillian periods. An emerging historiography gave a scholarly imprimatur, not just to the explicit condemnation of 1940 but to the underlying characterisation of inter-war politics. Charles Mowat's 1955 classic *Britain Between the Wars* presented the critical moment as the downfall of the Lloyd George Coalition in October 1922. 'And thus ended the reign of the great ones; the giants of the Edwardian era and of the war; and the rule of the pygmies, of the "second-class brains" began, to continue until 1940.'[3]

This emerging orthodoxy not only risked neglecting the complexities of the 'Guilty Men's' predicament and responses; it incorporated significant silences. A week before the Beaverbrook trio embarked on their polemic, Sir Oswald Mosley had been interned by the Churchill Government. He, together with some other members of the British Union of Fascists and a few others, including a Tory MP, were deemed to threaten security. As Peter Howard penned his acerbic portraits of 'Guilty Men' he was perhaps too busy to reflect on his only previous political involvement. In 1931 he had joined Mosley's New Party, what proved to be the latter's bridge from Labour and political credibility to fascism, marginality, ignominy and incarceration. Howard, an England Rugby international, had played a leading and vigorous part in the stewarding of Mosley's New Party meetings and in the sometimes abrasive confrontations with hecklers and disrupters.[4] The emergence of a robust politics of the street had been unwelcome to some within the New Party. They feared it as a harbinger of fascism. Howard's association with Mosley had ended with the dissolution of the New Party.

By the mid thirties, mainstream politicians typically reviled Mosley. Clement Attlee, the personification of the laconic understatement, reacted to the BUF's stewarding of the Olympia rally with a diagnosis embellished with a national stereotype. He accused Mosley of 'the Italian method... the method of the gang... from Catiline to Capone and from Marius to Mussolini... There is a certain megalomania about him. I think there is a streak of cruelty in his character and I doubt whether he is entirely mentally stable.'[5] A victorious war against fascism pushed Mosley even further to the margins. He became the stuff of which graffiti was made. His sparse post-war following would decorate inner-city neighbourhoods with an unappealing dichotomy, 'Mosley or Slump'.

Yet any attempt to locate Mosley within the polemic of *Guilty Men* is ambiguous. In terms of the central arguments about diplomacy, military preparedness and fascism, May 1940 gave a damning verdict. But *Guilty Men* was also about the marginalisation of the talented and discordant. Churchill in 1939 was widely dismissed as an unstable failure with a great future behind him. Lloyd George never regained office after October 1922. Only a national emergency brought Bevin into a partisan politics that he mistrusted. It took May 1940 to free Labour from the electoral consequences of its 1931 failure. Mosley could be viewed as another significant casualty of the 'regime of little men'.

Gradually this assessment left its mark on the historiography. Mowat flavoured his characterisation of inter-war politics with a sympathetic assessment of Mosley's response to the economic choices of the 1929 Labour Government. 'It was easy, afterwards, to say that he had never been a true supporter of Labour or a believer in parliamentary methods; the fact was... that the Labour Party had a great opportunity, in attacking unemployment, to remodel the country; when it shrank from it, he recoiled, disillusioned into bolder and more dangerous choices'. Almost a decade later, A.J.P. Taylor clearly placed Mosley amongst the regrettably marginalised. Within the 1929 Government faced with inexorably rising unemployment, only Mosley 'rose to the height of the challenge'.[6]

The theme of regrettable marginalisation was most thoroughly developed by Robert Skidelsky, initially in 1967 through his study of the 1929 Government, *Politicians and the Slump*, and subsequently in his 1975 biography of Mosley:

> The Mosley of the 1920s seemed to have all the attributes that I wanted from a Labour leader – bold policies, unflinching courage, eloquent language, popular appeal. As the 1964 Labour Government staggered from disaster to disaster under an obviously inadequate prime minister, Mosley took shape in my mind as Labour's 'lost leader'.[7]

This was much more than a one-time Gaitskellite lamenting Harold Wilson's premiership. The rediscovery of Mosley as talented political iconoclast flourished as accepted wisdoms across the political spectrum seemed increasingly vulnerable By the 1960s the beneficiaries of the 'Guilty Men' orthodoxy, Churchillian Conservatism and Attlee's Labour Party were themselves history. *Politicians and the Slump*, with Mosley as hero, appeared just before Labour's devaluation of the pound in November 1967. The sixties are frequently recalled as a decade of emancipation from cultural and sexual constraints and of political radicalism. Yet the ascetic Enoch Powell's populist indictments of immigration policy were the prelude to electoral victory for the right. Anxiety about the need for economic, social and political modernisation raised doubts about the capacity of established institutions and procedures, not least of political parties.

The marginalised inter-war iconoclasts acquired a contemporary resonance. They were presented as challenging the limitations of party doctrine and identities in the interest of creativity. Their defeat could be viewed as the triumph of organisation over flair, but also as the consequence of a specific shift in the character of the party system. Pre-1914 a Progressive Alliance of Liberals and an as yet small and dependent Labour Party had established an electoral majority. Within Britain this majority was small. The Progressives' parliamentary dependence on the Irish Nationalists had dragged them into the quagmire of Home Rule and risked the breakdown of established political procedures. Yet the Conservatives' intemperate response on Ireland expressed a burgeoning alienation from parliamentary decencies and perhaps pessimism about electoral success. In the summer of 1914, Progressives could be cautiously optimistic.[8]

War and post-war crises and challenges transformed the party system. A Liberal Government had become involved in a European war where cherished Liberal principles were confronted by administrative and military pressures. Ministerial responses divided Liberals in an extended overture to the coup of December 1916 and the replacement of Asquith as Prime Minister by Lloyd George. Liberal divisions became institutionalised initially and tentatively between those who held office in the Lloyd George Coalition and their supporters, and those who had been ousted in 1916 or whose sympathies were with the deposed. More decisively, the 1918 election divided Liberals between those who were authoritatively enrolled as Coalition candidates and those who were excluded. The former were generally successful, the latter almost obliterated. Such fragmentation and incapacity in the context of franchise expansion risked marginalisation. Liberal divisions and heightened Labour ambitions combined to destroy any post-war hope for a revival of the Progressive Alliance.[9]

Progressive disarray combined with a major territorial change to improve the Conservatives' electoral position. The Easter Rising, the victory of Sinn Fein across Nationalist Ireland in the 1918 election and the subsequent War of Independence led, by the end of 1921, to the formation of the Irish Free State and the permanent removal of most Irish members from the Commons. This change in the parliamentary arithmetic enhanced the chance of a Conservative majority. Moreover, war had strengthened the Conservative position. Unlike the Liberals, the conflict was not a source of division; from December 1916, Conservatives were the preponderant element in a Coalition that eventually secured the electoral benefits of military victory. Yet, post-war Conservatives had good reason to feel pessimistic. The expansion of the franchise to include virtually all men over 21 and most women over 30 made Britain something close to an electoral democracy. Any party of the right had reason to be fearful. The Hohenzollern and Hapsburg regimes had disintegrated with military defeat. The Bolsheviks believed that survival of the Russian Revolution necessitated its emulation in Western Europe. Events in Berlin and Turin could suggest that such ambitions were credible. Middle-class voters could resent what they saw as wartime redistribution from the frugal and industrious to those who had seemingly benefited from union muscle. In more paranoid moments they could ponder the spectre of the Sevenoaks Soviet, a neurosis that deepened as trade unions, most publicly in mining and on the railways, attempted to capitalise on their enhanced resources, not least the self-confidence of their members.

From 1921, trade depression and industrial defeats eroded trade union resources and limited their expectations. Labour's challenge became defined increasingly as preponderantly political. Despite internal divisions over entry into and conduct of the war, trade union priorities and sentiments of solidarity had maintained the cohesion of the Labour Party. The expanded franchise, an abortive proposal of the alternative vote and the wartime growth of the unions all fuelled Labour optimism that the pre-war limits on the party's electoral growth could be transcended. Labour claims that the 1918 election had seriously understated the party's electoral appeal seemed to be corroborated by municipal and by-election results in 1919. In fact, the party's post-war expansion was limited and uneven, but by 1922 it had established itself as the dominant force in a minority of industrial constituencies. A Labour Government seemed a distant prospect, but the party could not be ignored by its rivals. Conservative doubts about their party's future as an independent force and Liberal disunity and animosities together posed the challenge of an effective response. The electorate contained a clear anti-Labour majority; its effective organisation remained a conundrum. Mosley's political career, from his entry to the Commons in 1918 until his final exit in October 1931, offers a distinctive but illuminating route through these complexities.

Mosley entered the Commons as a very young recruit from a family of country landowners. Rolleston, the family estate of 4,000 acres in south-east Staffordshire, had yielded £10,000 a year in the 1880s.[10] Presided over by his grandfather until his death in 1915, the effective ending of Mosley's parent's marriage led to him spending much of his childhood there. His autobiography portrays Rolleston as a lost world, the memories of which would shape his response to modernity. From the mid nineteenth century the estate could be characterised as a feudal enclave where the family resolutely acted as if industry and economic liberalism could be ignored. In 1846 they had lost their own battle with Richard Cobden and classical liberalism; they had abandoned their manorial rights in Manchester concurrently with the repeal of the Corn Laws. A decaying remnant of feudalism had succumbed to bourgeois triumphalism. At Rolleston an embattled alternative to the new order was celebrated on appropriate occasions. Revelry in August 1873 marked a wedding and the rebuilding of the hall after a fire. The vicar offered his benediction. 'Indeed such a sight as the present is a truly English one for now can be seen at one view the real backbone of our country, the agriculturists and landlords side by side.' Yet industrialisation and urbanisation were undermining any such claim to be the personification of England. Within a few years depression in agriculture would weaken the economic position of many landlords, although at Rolleston the impact would be reduced by a shift from arable to mixed farming. Whatever the wider economic context Mosley could remember his early years at Rolleston, the 1900s, as 'remote from the world, a remarkable truly feudal survival... this really was a classless society'.[11]

This idyll was painted six decades later. It presented an organic community that was hierarchical, involved mutual dependence and lacked corrosive conflict. Yet, an earlier observer of this midlands landed society had had a sharper eye for its power relationships, its inequalities and its condescending patronage. Mosley's elegy should be measured against George Eliot's *Adam Bede* and *Felix Holt*. Inequality and a sense of entitlement were integral to this fondly remembered idyll. Moreover, Rolleston could not be the feudal redoubt that display, ritual and selective memory proclaimed. The Mosley yellow coach with four horses progressing through the village, with women curtseying and men doffing caps, might express the imagined ideal; but when the coach, its passengers and accompanying servants entered nearby Burton on Trent, modernity was inescapable. The products of Burton's breweries were sold nationally and internationally. Beer was transported to London by rail and stored beneath the neo-gothic splendour of St Pancras. Its brewing millionaires personified the commercial achievements and social mobility of the nineteenth century.[12]

Burton's economic rise had meant that the railway had come to Rolleston as early as 1848 – or not quite. The Mosley influence kept the intruder a decent distance from the village. Eventually a station opened in1894 and attracted some suburban development. The original line had linked Burton with Uttoxeter and Stoke, but in the 1870s further construction brought a link with Derby and across the coalfield to Nottingham and beyond. The impact of modernity was not limited to the encroachment of town and trains. Involvement in the modern order was evident within the Mosley family. His paternal grandfather's brother, eventually Lord Anslow, became Chairman of the North Staffordshire Railway. This fiercely independent local company enjoyed a monopoly in the Potteries. Its profits came from local industries, above all ceramics and coal. This Mosley was a political Liberal, a paternalist who was opposed to trade union 'interference' in the company. When many North Staffordshire men backed the union call for a strike in August 1911, he reflected ruefully to shareholders that he and his colleagues had been building castles in the air. Shortly afterwards his sense of vulnerability was confirmed when the 1912 coal strike seriously affected the North Staffordshire economy.[13]

The landed elite's economic strength was in decline, Mosley's fond recollections notwithstanding. By 1912, land sales suggested that the great estates were succumbing to the combination of declining returns and increased taxation. Rolleston would be a casualty of straitened post-war circumstances, and perhaps of Mosley's political ambitions. Attempts to find a single buyer proved unsuccessful. Eventually the estate was broken up and, in November 1925, most of the house was demolished. The old order gave way to suburbia. The political dominance of the landed class had been largely maintained after the abolition of the Corn Laws; the 1906 Liberal landslide heralded a conflict that would challenge this continuity. Progressive Liberalism's distinction between the useful classes and the parasitic was driven by values, policy choices and electoral calculation. The People's Budget of 1909 supplemented by Lloyd George's attacks on parasitic peers combined with aristocratic intransigence and miscalculation to precipitate the constitutional crisis of 1910–11. Its culmination in the curtailment of the powers of the House of Lords demonstrated and intensified the marginalisation of traditional authority. Progressive Liberalism seemed the new orthodoxy. The Conservative Party replaced the aristocratic Balfour as leader with Bonar Law, the Glaswegian metal broker. He would be the first of four successive leaders whose money would come from trade and industry, not the broad acres. His party would remake itself as the defender of all those with property, irrespective of amount and source. Those amongst the landed elite who felt abandoned could fight back, as some did over the compromise on Lords reform or more perilously over Home Rule. They could retreat with varying degrees of equanimity into acceptance of their reduced status; alternatively, they might find merit in projects for national regeneration that were resolutely antipathetic to liberalism and in some cases suspicious or dismissive of democracy.[14]

The young Mosley's response to the crises that shook British politics in the immediate pre-war years is unknown. At apolitical Rolleston there was in all probability little discussion. Aristocratic decline could be masked to some extent by the glitter of formal empire, not least as expressed through military service. Early in 1914 Mosley, after three largely unsatisfying years at Winchester, entered Sandhurst. Within months, cadetship had given way to war. Mosley's service proved brief. Initial enlistment in the Lancers was soon superseded by membership of the Royal Flying Corps and four months as an observer in early 1915. Returning home to take his pilot's certificate, a crash meant a broken ankle and a return to the Lancers. His time in the trenches began in October 1915 and ended the following March. His ankle wound had not healed and had become infected. His active service lasted just under a year. Military experience offered another organic and hierarchical model that had affinities with Rolleston. His time with the RFC demonstrated his fascination with the modern. Both themes would influence his political agenda. Subsequent wartime experience at the Ministry of Munitions and the Foreign Office would supplement these concerns. In a national emergency the wartime state had demonstrated the limitation of liberal procedures and values and the necessity for methods and a culture closer to the organic ideal. Hospitalisation in 1916 had given Mosley time for reading. He read political biographies selectively, not the conformists but 'the great masters of action'. Such reading was intended to guide practical activity. If Mosley was already contemplating a political career, it would be one informed by the heroic and the creative. This aspiration was facilitated yet also hampered by his distance from the enthusiasms and taboos of established parties. Mosley by both inclination and experience was unlikely to be a good party man. [15]

He would present himself as the passionate advocate of the war generation, not just of those who had undergone the distinctive experience of the conflict but of all those who understood that there could be no return to 1914. The new world necessitated not just new policies but new politicians who rejected old methods. For Mosley the new world would mean the sale of Rolleston and the demise of what would become a fondly remembered way of life. Gradually, young men entered politics bringing with them the memories and lessons of the war. Yet the lessons varied. Captain Anthony Eden, from a Durham county family, experienced the rigours and perils of the Western Front. He was awarded the Military Cross and was elected Conservative Member for Warwick and Leamington in 1923. His experience of the trenches with its shared privations helped to form his social Toryism. Major Clement Attlee, from middle-class Putney had lived amongst the East End working class as a social worker; he entered the war as a socialist. Gallipoli, Mesopotamia and France confirmed his politics on both ethical and pragmatic grounds. Elected Labour Member for Limehouse in 1922 he stressed the poverty of his constituents.[16] Too often, the heroes of 1914 had become the post- war unemployed.

Eden and Attlee were conventional party men. In contrast, two weddings in the spring of 1920 prefaced less conformist trajectories. Captain Harold Macmillan had been severely wounded in 1916. Post-war he served on the staff of Canada's Governor-General, the Duke of Devonshire. In April 1920 he married the Duke's daughter, Lady Dorothy Cavendish. The aristocratic guests on the bride's side were complemented by Macmillan authors. Macmillan's political career until 1940 would be characteristically ambiguous. Partisan rhetoric for the activists was accompanied by a deep seriousness on policy that was given an acerbic edge by the economic debris of his Stockton constituency. The plight of the north-east and the indifference and ignorance of many Conservatives led him in the search for allies beyond the parameters of party. He was increasingly hostile to his party leadership, latterly over foreign policy. As a critic of the 'Guilty Men' he would be one of the prime beneficiaries of May 1940.[17]

A month later the wedding of Lieutenant Oswald Mosley and Lady Cynthia Curzon produced an even grander guest list, not least George V and Queen Mary and the King and Queen of the Belgians. Lord Curzon had been Viceroy of India and in 1920 was Foreign Secretary in the Lloyd George Coalition. The economic resources of this 'most superior person' had been strengthened by his marriage to the daughter of a Chicago millionaire. He had assessed Mosley's suitability. They were 'a family well known to me in the old days in Derbyshire where they have or had a big place named Rolleston near Burton on Trent now advertised in *Country Life* as to be sold'. More significant was the state of Mosley's finances. 'He… has practically severed himself from his father who is a spend thrift and a ne'er do well. The estate is in the hands of trustees who will give him £8,000–£10,000 a year straightaway and he will ultimately have a clear £20,000 p.a.'[18] In May 1920, Mosley was an independently minded Conservative Member. Within months he would cross the floor to sit as an Independent. During his odyssey he would meet, amongst others, Macmillan, himself out of parliament following the 1929 election. They would debate the feasibility of an independent initiative. Macmillan's political nonconformity was carefully modulated. Vision, chance, resilience, allied to a certain elusiveness, would bring him eventually to Downing Street. Mosley's contrasting fortunes were captured in his second thoroughly private wedding early in October 1936. His bride, Diana Guinness née Mitford, demonstrated social continuity, but the venue was Berlin. The principal guests were Joseph and Magda Goebbels. The lunch was attended by Adolf Hitler.

1
Apprenticeships

Mosley contested the December 1918 election as the Conservative candidate for Harrow. He had been selected the previous July. His military service and his facility in answering questions with detailed arguments had impressed party activists. In retrospect, Mosley would trivialise his attachment to the Conservative Party. 'I knew little of Conservative sentiment and cared even less. I was going into the House of Commons as one of the representatives of the war generation... I had joined the Conservative Party because it seemed to me on its record in the war to be the party of patriotism.'[1] The 1918 election was fought on novel terrain between combatants whose identities were often ambiguous. The electorate had been transformed. At the previous election, in December 1910, about 60 per cent of adult males had had the vote; post–war, the male exclusions were minimal. Most women over 30 now had the vote for the first time. Franchise expansion was complemented by a radical redistribution of constituencies, the first since 1885. Population shifts meant a notable increase in the number of suburban seats. This expansion was particularly significant in London and the south-east; its impact shaped the social geography of Mosley's first electoral contest.[2]

The political regime, unlike many across Europe, had survived the war and could appear vindicated by victory. In contrast with this continuity, post-war political alignments were opaque and as yet indeterminate. The armistice was followed quickly by the announcement of an election. Most Conservative candidates and 150 Liberals sheltered under the umbrella of the Lloyd George Coalition. They benefited from the formal backing of Lloyd George and the Conservative leader Bonar Law; the so-called 'coupon' confirmed them as the accredited candidates of the 'Man Who Won the War'. Many Liberals remained outside the Coalition Pale and often faced Conservatives who were armed with the coupon.

Arthur Henderson had been Labour's representative in the War Cabinet until his acrimonious departure in August 1917. Thoroughly supportive of the war effort, Henderson had regarded himself as the custodian of Labour's interests at the highest level of government. He reverted to his responsibilities as party secretary and led the party's preparations for what he and many colleagues hoped would be an enhanced position in any post-war party system. The party's structure was reformed; organisational change was complemented by a comprehensive programme, *Labour and the New Social Order*. Henderson's actions in what proved to be the last year of the war perhaps revealed his sensitivity towards nuanced but potentially significant political shifts within the labour movement. Institutional reforms, an ambitious programme and an unprecedented number of candidates expressed the party's heightened expectations. These were fed by franchise expansion, the unrealised expectation of electoral reform and rising trade union membership. Yet Henderson's exit from office and the subsequent reforms had not definitively transformed Labour's position with respect to the Coalition. Some Labour MPs had continued as ministers. The armistice posed a strategic choice for Labour. A special conference decided that the party should fight any election independent of the Coalition. Several Members responded reluctantly to the decisions by the party conference and their own trade unions that they should fight the election as an independent force. A handful refused and contested the election as couponed supporters of the Coalition.[3]

Labour independence involved the suppression of an alternative future that extended far beyond continuing Labour membership of the Coalition. Some Labour politicians and trade union leaders had expressed their support for the war through jingoistic and xenophobic rhetoric. Several were highly respectable union officials who were prepared to limit trade union demands and to suspend workplace practices in pursuit of military victory. They coupled such concessions with support for military conscription and lurid denunciations of German infamy and pacifist cowardice. The highly respectable were accompanied by more colourful characters. Ben Tillett had been a volatile pre-war critic of Labour moderation; as a super-patriot he won a Salford by-election in 1917 with the slogan 'Bomb the Boche'. Such sentiments inspired some on the Radical right to dream of an alliance that could challenge liberal pieties. Alfred, Lord Milner, once the personification of social imperialism in South Africa, had been marginalised by the pre-war Liberal Government. His influence grew after the outbreak of war; as a leading figure in the Lloyd George Coalition he personified the wartime challenge to liberal politics. For him, war offered the prospect of a radical remaking of political alignments; Milner envisaged an alliance between a modernising elite and robustly patriotic Labour in pursuit of a collectivist agenda. From May 1916 several Labour super-patriots endorsed such a programme through the British Workers' League. In 1918 they were forced to choose between Labour Party independence and a cross-class mobilisation for national efficiency that would be implemented by an interventionist state. The BWL became the National Democratic and Labour Party in mid-1918. Almost all supportive Labour MPs reverted to their old allegiance; the NDP became entangled in largely unproductive negotiations with the Conservatives; they sought Tory support in selected constituencies in a post-war election. A few would enjoy the benefit of the coupon. Milner's agenda became no more than an electoral footnote, yet this suppressed alternative would have affinities with Mosley's later response to economic crisis.[4]

The Labour challenge did not extend to Harrow. The pre- war constituency had been a Conservative stronghold. Between 1885 and December 1910 only four out of eight general elections had been contested. The Liberals had been successful only in 1906 when defence of free trade had brought some Conservative votes temporarily into the Liberal column. The recent redistribution had made Harrow even safer for the Conservatives. Kilburn and Willesden, with their Liberal inclinations, had been removed. The new constituency was restricted to Harrow, Wealdstone, Wembley, Alperton and Sudbury. This slice of Home Counties suburbia had begun to expand pre-1914; between the wars it would grow rapidly, stimulated by the profusion of electric train services to central London. In 1918, neither a limited and uncertain local Liberalism nor a barely formed Harrow Labour Party could contemplate an intervention. Mosley's only opposition came from within the Conservative ranks. A.R. Chamberlayne had been a three-times pre-war Unionist candidate . He stood as the candidate of the Harrow Electors' League; he insisted that Mosley had been imposed on the constituency by the national party and was using his wealth to buy the seat. Against such complaints Mosley had a trump card. He was the official Coalition candidate and displayed Lloyd George's imprimatur.[5]

Mosley's first election address included proposals which would be significant elements in his later political agendas. Peace must be preserved abroad as a precondition for effective modernisation at home. The latter would be sustained by full employment at high wages based on buoyant levels of production. Educational opportunities would be extended and there would be provision of decent housing for all. He espoused meritocracy. The House of Lords must be reformed. 'The hereditary principle in legislation was ridiculous.' Mosley emphasised imperial preference as the basis for a cohesive empire that would be able to play an effective role in the League of Nations. His vision of modernity was underpinned by an insistence that the primary purpose of the British state should be the welfare of the British people. 'Aliens' were targeted. In 1918 these were predictably German but Mosley's indictment retailed stereotypes familiar from earlier anti-Irish and anti-Semitic agitations. 'They had brought disease amongst them, reduced Englishmen's wages, undersold English goods and ruined social life.'[6]

His rhetoric wove together idealism, patriotism and the commendation of a state that would act with dignity and effectiveness.

> At this moment when the deeds of their race had surprised the world with their glory, he asked them to regard the future with a world-wide vision. Whoever they sent to Parliament, send him with a national mandate not a parochial one... They had a colossal task before them. This country was seething with unrest, and they must see to it that the Government was a strong one and that the country was behind it, that it had a mandate from the country to reconstruct and build up our empire anew.

Discontent must be canalised, the disaffected must be integrated. Hence the Coalition's programme 'was Radical – some said Socialistic – in its advocacy of social reform'. Mosley used this challenge to justify the continuation of the Coalition. He belittled those outside the couponed ranks, 'a small following of Mr Asquith, a minority (*sic*) of the Labour Party'; within the peculiarities of Harrow his target was Chamberlayne.

> He had heard of some people who called themselves Independent whatever they might be. Men in the stone age were independent. An Independent in the House of Commons was like a lost soul... Surely a man who could find no place in the Coalition Party – composed of all shades of political thought – must be outside all things.

Although, or perhaps because, the candidates had few substantive differences on policy, the contest became personalised; Chamberlayne insisted that it was 'an insult to the electorate to place before them a boy, the son of a baronet, wealthy and able to keep up the party organisation'.[7]

One observer claimed 'a card with Lieutenant Mosley's portrait was to be seen in most windows'. Yet as supposed evidence of overwhelming support the claim was an exaggeration. The same observer noted a lack of polling day excitement and attributed this to the relative absence of 'the party element'.[8] Such assessments were frequent in 1918. In Harrow the turnout was just over 50 per cent. Amongst those who voted, Mosley's victory was emphatic.

Harrow Election 1918
Turnout 50.4%

O.E. Mosley	Coalition Conservative	13,959	82.3%
A.R. Chamberlayne	Independent	3,007	17.7%
		10,952	64.6%

Mosley went from Harrow to become the youngest Member of a parliament that offered a kaleidoscope of political identities. The Coalition administration, headed by a Liberal, included other Liberals in senior positions. The distribution of the coupon meant that the vast Coalition majority was preponderantly Conservative; the Government, whatever its Liberal notables, depended on Conservative votes in the lobbies. Many Conservative Members wished to defend their party's pre-war identity and independence, but they might reflect that the party had not won a parliamentary majority fighting as an independent force since 1900. Others believed that new and urgent challenges meant that a return to pre-war alignments was a fantasy. Instead the Coalition, a product of wartime crisis, could be the basis for a new politics. The Prime Minister and at least some of his Liberal colleagues thought similarly.[9]

The 1918 election had reduced the un-couponed Liberals to a pitiful remnant; senior figures, most spectacularly Asquith, had been defeated. Whatever the wartime record of individual candidates, their lack of the coupon was fatal. Conservative backing for the war had been unambiguous. Unlike some Liberals, they had had no qualms in supporting illiberal policies as necessary for military success. Labour interventions further eroded Liberal support. However the growth in Labour candidacies in response to the extended franchise and the expansion of trade union membership had produced only a small increase in Labour Members compared with December 1910. Prominent figures associated with the anti-war Independent Labour Party, most notably Ramsay MacDonald, had been heavily defeated.[10] The new Parliamentary Labour Party was even more thoroughly trade unionist than its predecessor. To its critics including many within the labour movement, the post-war PLP seemed sectional and unimaginative.

The pre-war Progressive alliance of reforming Liberals and Labour had been shattered. Some Liberal reformers, most notably Lloyd George, insisted that their Progressive credentials survived, despite sharing office with the Conservatives. Other Liberals, including prominent intellectuals and journalists, were antipathetic to Lloyd George. They resented the removal of Asquith from the premiership and damned his successor as unprincipled and unscrupulous. They hoped for an Asquithian revival; any reunification of the Liberal Party would have to be very much on their terms, with Lloyd George as a penitent supplicant. The place of Labour in such Liberal agendas remained unresolved. Some Liberals hoped for a return to pre-war collaboration; many others were more sceptical. Labour ambitions were far greater than before the war; any Progressive Alliance would reflect changed expectations and resources. Moreover, Labour's relationship with increasingly ambitious trade unions made the party unattractive to many Liberals.[11]

Labour's achievement in the 1918 election might have been modest in terms of seats won. However, the potential for Labour growth both politically and industrially preoccupied politicians. Despite the limited parliamentary advance, Labour's vote had shown a significant if uneven expansion. Expectations that in a more favourable environment Labour would increase its parliamentary strength seemed justified by electoral successes during 1919. Parliamentary by-election and municipal victories suggested that this was indeed the forward march of labour. Labour's immediate challenge went far beyond the routines of electoral politics. Trade unionists ,encouraged by economic buoyancy and fuelled by members' heightened expectations, sought initially to advance beyond wartime gains; as the economic climate deteriorated from the winter of 1920–21 they sought to defend their recently achievements against employers' counter-attacks. The challenge of 'Direct Action' was evident in the 'Hands off Russia' campaign, with many within the labour movement proclaiming their willingness to block the shipment of munitions to Soviet Russia's Polish adversary. The prospect of coordinated industrial action by the Triple Alliance of miners, railwaymen and transport workers brooded over unrest in the coal industry. The rhetoric of 'Direct Action' decorated strikes that in reality were focused on wage increases and reduced hours. Advocates could claim legitimacy through a dismissal of the 1918 election as a fraudulent exploitation of patriotic sentiment that had produced an inflated and unrepresentative majority. The ethos of 'Direct Action' had affinities with the verbal and sometimes actual violence of pre-war conflicts; the fact of the Soviet Union and the fear that Red Petrograd might be replicated further west ensured that the containment of Labour, both industrial and political, became a dominant preoccupation. From the beginning of 1919 to the summer of 1921, Conservative, Liberal and many Labour politicians felt compelled to offer an alternative to the rhetoric and sometimes the reality of 'Direct Action'.[12]

The remaking of political alignments became a critical element within any response. One possibility was that the Coalition offered the basis for a Centre Party that would unite all who favoured a strategy that combined resistance to the demands of 'extreme' labour with a programme of 'realistic' economic and social improvement that would offer an attractive synthesis for the expanded electorate. Forty Coalitionists, both Conservatives and Liberals, came together in a New Members' Parliamentary Committee. Mosley was involved as joint secretary along with the Coalition Liberal, Colin Coote. He joined with other ex-combatants to express the hope that the priorities of former soldiers, not least their alleged belief in the need for a new politics, could be expressed through a Centre Party.[13] Such aspirations, shared by some ministers, were suffocated by visceral partisanships. Many Coalition Liberals feared absorption by the Conservatives and preferred the, as yet, illusory objective of Liberal reunion. Many Conservatives from the beginning looked on the post-war Coalition and Lloyd George as temporary expedients. They remained unsure about Conservative prospects within the expanded electorate. Lloyd George might have explored the prospect for a cross-party coalition at the height of the constitutional crisis in 1910, but he was remembered amongst Conservatives as the most partisan of pre-war Liberal ministers. He was not only the man who had won the war; he had been the architect of the Peoples' Budget and the scourge of the House of Lords. For many Conservatives his pre-war Liberalism had been indistinguishable from socialism; his oratory had been a demagogic exhibition of class enmity. As the prospects for a Centre Party withered in 1920, Mosley's disenchantment with the Conservative Party and with significant government policies grew. The Foreign Secretary's son in law was becoming a rebel. Controversy over the Coalition's Irish policy was most decisive in separating Mosley from orthodox Conservatism; the separation brought a closer relationship with opposition Liberals and some Labour politicians.

The decisive Sinn Fein victory across Nationalist Ireland in the 1918 election meant a policy of abstention from Westminster and an attempt to construct alternative institutions that would challenge British rule. By mid 1920, Republican and British forces were increasingly engaged in violent exchanges. The political context was an offer of devolved government to a partitioned Ireland; the proposal was unacceptable to Sinn Fein. Republicans attacked British troops and members of the Royal Irish Constabulary. Nationalist railwaymen refused to carry British troops and munitions. Jurors often refused to serve in politically sensitive cases or refused to convict. Actions by state forces – killings, the burning of houses and creameries, the terrorising of communities – increasingly offered grim evidence of the reality of British rule. Ministers typically characterised such actions as limited, unofficial, understandable and regrettable responses to the killing of comrades. Lloyd George could be less inhibited. In a speech at Caernarfon he welcomed 'taking murder by the throat'.[14]

The Coalition addressed the security situation early in August with the rapid passage of the Restoration of Order in Ireland Act.[15] This permitted government by regulation, the replacement of criminal courts by courts martial and of coroners' inquests by military courts of inquiry. Local authorities showing evidence of disaffection could have their grants withheld. The government also faced a major crisis within the RIC. Once a respected occupation, its officers found themselves targeted by their compatriots. The inevitable consequence was demoralisation. Many resigned; those who stayed faced an impossible task. The Coalition's response was to recruit from across the Irish Sea. The consequence was the arrival of two groups who became notorious in the collective memory of Nationalist Ireland. The 'Black and Tans' were effectively British recruits to the RIC; their sobriquet arose from their makeshift uniform, itself a testimony to the straitened circumstances of the security forces. The Auxiliary Division were ex-military officers and provided a paramilitary force. Both groups were unprepared for service in a country whose passions they could not hope to understand. Isolated from and despised by the population, living often in discomfort, barely under the authority of the civil power, their response to Republican raids and killings was predictable. By autumn 1920 the brittle and qualified legitimacy of the British state across much of Ireland had shattered; evidence of state violence was inescapable. It was not the monopoly of the incomers; beleaguered members of the RIC were heavily involved. Mosley stepped forward as one of the government's most persistent parliamentary critics.[16]

On 20 October 1920 he spoke in support of a censure motion moved by Arthur Henderson, a thoroughly respectable Wesleyan trade unionist whose political formation had owed much to Gladstonian Liberalism. Labour and Asquithian critics were joined by some independently minded Conservatives. Lord Robert Cecil was in significant respects

Mosley's political mentor; Lord Henry Bentinck was a self- styled Tory Democrat. Mosley's own contribution was a forceful denunciation of British policy:

> It might have been said that the method employed in Ireland is the same as that employed in Belgium during the War by the Germans. The method is not quite the same. Germany had a method which was outlined before the War by its leading military authorities... Our method is far more reminiscent of the pogrom of the more barbarous Slavs and it represents a far greater breakdown of law and order and justice... We merely have promiscuous devastation of whole communities.[17]

This indictment placed Mosley in thorough opposition to most Conservatives on an issue which had been fundamental to their party's pre-war identity. Conservative defence of the Union had often used intransigent rhetoric. Many Conservatives remained suspicious of what they felt was the Coalition's excessive liberalism in seeking to meet Nationalist aspirations. Yet, however vehement Mosley's criticisms, they stayed within significant limits. He insisted that he was not attacking British troops. Rather he claimed to be speaking on their behalf. 'Famous regiments that for generations past have performed most magnificent service to this country, are to-day labouring under certain imputations – imputations which I have every reason to believe are unjust'. His assertion was reasonable. The reprisals were the preserve of the RIC, the 'Black and Tans' and the Auxiliaries. Mosley also endorsed an interpretation that was assiduously promoted by ministers. The initial violence had been promoted by a 'murder gang'; by implication their elimination would allow a political settlement. 'There is only one way to break down the murder gang, and no one is more anxious than I to do so, and that is to catch them... You will only restore order in Ireland by catching the assassins, breaking up their gang and bringing them to justice.'[18] In contrast reprisals, whether authorised or not, were counter-productive. Republicans' use of flying columns meant that their units were largely unaffected by collective punishments that served only to alienate the wider population.

Mosley's attack was renewed the following month, this time on a motion moved by Asquith. On the previous Sunday twelve British officers had been assassinated in Dublin. Later that day Auxilaries had opened fire on a crowd watching a Gaelic football match at Croke Park. Fourteen died; they would become martyrs in the fight for independence. The Coalition Liberal Secretary of State for Ireland, Sir Hamar Greenwood, responded to Asquith with imperial paranoia. There was 'a great conspiracy based on Ireland to smash the British Empire'. Mosley indicted the Government:

> In the early days of this controversy certain speeches were made by spokesmen of the Government which slurred over entirely the difference between the right of a man to hit back and to defend himself against cowardly and dastardly attacks, and the right of men to revenge themselves for the sins of the guilty upon the heads of the innocent population of Ireland. It was these speeches of Ministers, the Carnavon (*sic*) speech and others, which conveyed an absolute licence to the police and troops in Ireland to do what they liked.

Mosley did not mention Croke Park, nor did he discuss the appeal and legitimacy of Irish nationalism. Instead his peroration focused on the corrupting legacy of 'frightfulness' for the British Empire:

> No Empire, no Government, has been long sustained except by the power of moral force, together with the impartial justice and beneficence of its role. Our Empire stands alone from the Imperial ruins of history, in its recognition of an obedience to this fundamental law. It is because I am a passionate believer in the destiny and in the yet unfulfilled mission of the British Empire that I am unwilling to sacrifice the inviolate tradition of the ages, even to satisfy the transient purpose of this gambler's expedient, which the Government offers us as their only solution of this terrible question.[19]

Throughout the winter of 1920–21 Mosley harassed ministers on specific incidents and on the broader question of ministerial responsibility for reprisals. Following the truce in mid 1921 he seemed less concerned with the negotiations that culminated in the December agreement. Nevertheless, he had considered a possible route to a settlement even before he began his public opposition to government policy. He had circulated his views to some MPs in July 1920 and published them in his own newspaper, the *Harrow Gazette*, in October. His starting point was at odds with his parliamentary denunciations of the 'murder gang'. He attacked the political settlement offered by the Coalition. The Government had failed to consult Sinn Fein as 'representatives of the Irish people'. Instead Parliament had passed a Government of Ireland Bill to set up devolved parliaments in Dublin and Belfast. The legislation was at odds with political reality. 'Irishmen consider themselves at war with England and the whole civilian population is enlisted in one elaborate system of guerrilla warfare.'

Lloyd George should invite Sinn Fein to a conference which would focus on three points: the status of 'Unionist Ulster', the provision of military and naval safeguards for Britain and, what would be from a British standpoint, appropriate limitations on Irish foreign policy. Acknowledgment of Ulster's distinctiveness would be enforced by world opinion since 'self-determination is an ethnographical and not geographical expression'. Mosley felt that in the last resort economic considerations would override national and religious identities. 'In modern life economic facts transcend atavistic considerations and ultimately it will matter more to Irishman whether they live in plenty or starve than whether they are Ulstermen or Southerners.' He was more perceptive about the early politics of what would become the Free State. 'All the evidence points to the fact that the first Irish National Government would be of a conservative character and these men have already demonstrated their power to establish a certain measure of order and justice in their ranks.'[20]

The complexities of Mosley's response to the Irish crisis were lost on many Conservatives who branded him as a renegade. He crossed to the Opposition benches in November 1920; he sat with, but was not formally attached to the Asquithian Liberals. His criticism of the Government's policy meant discussions with the high-minded and principled left, both Liberal and ethical socialist. Such collaboration revived the politics of self-conscious decency that had characterised opposition to the Anglo-Boer war twenty years earlier. The Irish controversy signalled the start of Mosley's liberal moment. Significantly, this was not limited to Ireland but also would include 'economy', free trade and foreign policy, most notably his advocacy of the League of Nations as a means of preventing another European war. The political novice embraced, in Skidelsky's phrase, 'the marvellous synchronisation of the liberal system'.[21] Everything seemed to inter-connect: economy at home, free trade, the avoidance of unnecessary and financially onerous overseas commitments.

Lord Robert Cecil deeply influenced the young Mosley. Over thirty years his senior, Cecil's Conservatism was inherited. His father, as Prime Minister, had presided over an electorally effective rapprochement between old-style Toryism and the limited post-1885 male electoral democracy. For Lord Robert, Conservatism was fortified and coloured by his devout Anglicanism. A self-consciously progressive Conservative and Free

Trader, he had resigned from the Coalition Government in 1918 over its decision to activate pre-war legislation to disestablish the Church of Wales. This exit, over an issue that had once raised the passions of zealots but now seemed passé, had liberated him. Like Mosley he believed that the War had changed British politics decisively. Labour's increasing strength and the extended franchise meant that Conservatism must be domestically progressive. He insisted on his 'great admiration for the old Conservative Party, or as it used to be called more happily the old Country Party'. But the party's conservatism had withered. 'The great bulk of the Party who have now got hold of the Party machine seem to have moved very far from their old traditions.'[22] They were concerned for little beyond the preservation of their property. They had lost the party's once great ideals of service. Such a lament expressed distaste for the rise of professional politicians, backed by a bourgeoisie who too often lacked any wider social vision, and regret for the consequential political decline of the landed class.

Unpalatable change in Britain was overshadowed by cataclysm elsewhere. The shattering of the old European order had eroded the self-confidence and credibility of the traditional governing class. The consequential potential for anarchy, exacerbated in Cecil's view by the Versailles settlement, necessitated a viable League of Nations as the instrument of a moral international order. His belief in the efficacy of sanctions against transgressors had been strengthened by his experience as minister responsible for implementing the economic blockade against the Central Powers. Such an international order would not mean a victory for left wing critics of the pre-1914 system, but rather the re-establishment of the style and values of that lost world. Lloyd George could personify much that was rotten in its successor; opposition to Irish reprisals could be viewed as a defence of traditional decencies. Cecil's aristocratic idealism could provoke bleak responses. In a Commons debate on reprisals in Ireland, Bonar Law claimed that 'he would make the same sort of academic speech if he were living in a Quaker country where violence was unknown'.[23] Eventually, such moral absolutism would prove a basic difference with Mosley, but in the immediate pre-war years Cecil's influence on the younger man was profound. Sometimes a Mosley speech would read like a recital of Cecil's position.

Early in 1921 both men became prominent members of the People's Union for Economy. The PUE offered a more respectable and less destabilising alternative to the Anti-Waste campaign currently espoused by Horatio Bottomley, wartime xenophobe and fraudster, and by Lord

Rothermere the epitome of the populist press proprietor. Their crude agitation emphasised the resentments felt by many, often relatively well- heeled, voters against the historically high peacetime rates of direct taxation maintained by the Coalition. This sectional appeal was widened through attacks on allegedly profligate levels of public expenditure. Anti-Waste League candidates had been promoted in some by-elections and had been successful in some Conservative seats.[24]. Such raucous campaigns offered a robust expression of sentiments that were increasingly alienating Conservative activists and voters from a Coalition that had been at best a necessary convenience in an uncertain world. The People's Union offered an articulation of anti-waste sentiment free from the politically and culturally dubious associations of the Anti-Waste agitation. The PUE's parliamentary committee had the backing of around 60 MPs. Most were Conservatives but they included some Asquithians and one Labour Member. They were complemented by Tory grandees including Salisbury and Middleton. The PUE offered a discreet, high-minded alternative to the robust agitation of the AWL. The underlying sentiments were shared.[25]

When Mosley insisted that high taxation and excessive expenditure were crippling enterprise, he expressed the angst of his suburban constituents who complained that they suffered from unreasonable taxation. He enthusiastically supported the PUE's campaign against the Coalition Liberal Health Minister Christopher Addison. His housing policy was presented as symptomatic of the Government's economic incontinence. Addison was removed from his post by Lloyd George in April 1921 and subsequently resigned from the Government in July; this represented a decisive defeat for those who had hoped that the Coalition could implement a radical policy of reconstruction.[26] The anti-waste agitation culminated in the appointment of the Geddes committee and its subsequent proposals for heavy cuts in public expenditure. This agitation with its blend of economic orthodoxy and social acerbity contrasted harshly with the modernising agenda that had been expressed by Mosley and many others in the 1918 election campaign.

Most supporters of the PUE were loyal Conservatives who felt that the party's values had been corrupted through involvement in the Coalition. Retrenchment was viewed not just as sound economics but as morally regenerative. The Union reflected and strengthened the sentiments that would lead a majority of Conservative MPs to reject the Coalition in October 1922.[27] In contrast, under Cecil's initiative, Mosley became involved in lengthy discussions about another alternative to the Coalition, the creation of a genteel anti-socialist combination that could transcend the narrowness of existing parties. Cecil characteristically characterised such a project as 'honest and straightforward'. In the first month of the 1921 miners' lockout he wrote to his new party leader, Austen Chamberlain; he commended his own approach as both more ethical and more effective than Coalition confrontation:

> You must remember that I was brought up to think that a class war, whether the class attacked be landowners or Labour is the most insidious form of disintegration... If it becomes inevitable to repeat constantly to the country that the only alternative to Lloyd George is Labour, sooner or later the country will say in that case they will try Labour and I do not know that I should blame them.[28]

Cecil's challenge suggested the antipathy between the outlook of a traditional ruling elite and the style of the industrialists who were increasingly significant amongst the Tory leadership. Mosley had recently made this contrast to his mentor:

> It is evident that our whole mentality and our every sympathy is fundamentally at variance with the elements consolidated under LG and whether he survives is really a matter of detail... We are anathema to the bourgeois profiteer who really *is* the present Government and no true reconciliation could ever take place while that element predominates on the other side.

This assessment came two days after 'Black Friday' when any prospect of sympathetic trade union action in support of the miners had disintegrated. Mosley felt that this failure offered the possibility of a more inclusive alliance. 'I anticipate that you are already inspired with the thought that the psychological moment for an understanding with moderate Labour has at length arrived. They should be a very easy catch on the rebound from this debacle.' His hope was for 'a confederation of reasonable men to advance with a definite proposal for the reorganisation of our industrial system upon a durable basis and a concurrent revision of the financial chaos'.[29]

One personification of moderate Labour, J.R. Clynes, was viewed sympathetically by Cecil. Superficially he could seem a potential recruit. A self-consciously moderate trade union official and an assiduous pursuer of negotiation and compromise, he had emerged as an unspectacular but well-regarded figure within the Parliamentary Labour Party. As a supporter of the War he had held office in the wartime coalitions, eventually becoming Food Controller. He had opposed the Labour Party decision to break with the Coalition in November 1918, but resigned from the Government in accordance with his union's policy. He stood in the 1918 election as a Labour Party candidate; his unopposed return suggested an appeal beyond his party which would only be strengthened by his forceful post-war opposition to 'Direct Action'. Clynes offered much that might appeal to apostles of decency and moderation, but such an appraisal was subverted by one crucial choice, his decision in November 1918 to subordinate his own preference to the demand of his trade union. Impatience and lack of familiarity could generate unrealistic assessments of congenial Labour politicians.[30]

Any proposal for an alternative and high-minded coalition had to address the problem posed by leading Asquithian Liberals, with their cocktail of principle and personalised resentments. Asquith's much heralded return to the Commons after his by-election victory at Paisley in 1920 had proved a disappointment to his political friends. His contributions to debates were often ineffective; he seemed a spent force. C.P. Scott, editor of the *Manchester Guardian*, was struck by Asquith's immobility. The search for an alternative champion of political decency focussed on Lord Grey; the former Liberal Foreign Secretary had been effectively retired from politics since the fall of Asquith in December 1916. Early in the coal dispute, and with sympathetic action by the Triple Alliance as yet seeming credible, Cecil tried to evoke a response from Grey. He recited the Coalition's foreign policy failures; he listed unresolved negotiations with Turkey and Hungary, 'chaotic' relations with Russia and difficulties in Mesopotamia, Persia, Palestine, Egypt and India. The domestic scene was equally bleak. Excessive public expenditure and the Irish calamity were complemented by industrial turbulence. 'The relations between employers and employed are chronically disturbed, while every few months we are plunged into an acute dispute which threatens the very foundations of social order.'[31]

Cecil clarified and developed his agenda to the Liberal benefactor Lord Cowdray. He insisted that the Asquithian Liberals, acting independently, had no hope of a decisive advance at the next election. Pessimism was complemented by optimism. A large body of opinion would not support Liberal candidates, but was supportive of liberal principles and policies. Cecil noted that those Conservatives who had taken an independent line seemed electorally secure. He claimed that the Conservative Party Chairman Sir George Younger, himself increasingly hostile to the Coalition, had acknowledged that Henry Cavendish Bentinck, the self-styled Tory Democrat, would not be opposed in

Nottingham despite his evident dislike of Lloyd George and of the Government's Irish policy. Similarly Cecil emphasised Mosley's security in Harrow. 'They have made attempts to get up opposition... and have completely failed for want of support in the constituency.' The Liberal Party might be electorally weak, but Independents, in which category Cecil included anti-waste candidates, had widespread appeal. The challenge, he claimed, was to ally advocates of such sentiment with the Asquithians. Cecil was explicit about Grey's potential role. 'It cannot be done simply by bringing Grey into the existing Liberal group... Grey reverting to his pre-war position as one of the Liberal leaders would not be attractive to outsiders. Grey as the representative of sane and safe progress on "independent" lines would have a large following.'[32]

Cecil expanded his case to the Liberal journalist J.A. Spender. Grey could appeal to 'the great mass of non-political voters' and to 'non-reactionary conservatives who passionately desire clean government'. Admittedly this option would mean another coalition, but this was unavoidable given Liberal inability to secure a majority. Spender's response was pessimistic; the idea of coalition had been discredited. Any such proposal would 'give the Labour Party the chance of posing as the one and only straight, honest, united party'. The Liberals must retain their independence in a bleak climate.[33]

Eulogies about Grey's decency and sanity were not uncontroversial. Despite his senior position in the pre-war Liberal Party, Grey had never been an aggressive partisan. He could seem a decent alternative to the alleged excesses and corruption of the Coalition. Yet he had been a prime and often secretive architect of the diplomacy that had led Britain into a European war. Many on the left, including former Liberals, condemned him as culpable. Moreover the grounds for his commendation could suggest a restoration of the pre-war virtues rather than a new politics for post-war challenges. Whatever Mosley's acquiescence in Cecil's agenda, he rejected any attempt to return to the world that had ended in 1914. Grey depicted himself as an anachronism. 'As to politics I am not the sort of person that is wanted now; Lloyd George is the modern type, suited to an age of telephone and moving pictures and modern journalism.'[34]

Grey's uncertain health and his diffidence about any return to politics inevitably frustrated his advocates. More fundamentally, his Liberal partisanship, however lightly worn, inevitably posed the question of the contribution that the Asquithian Liberals would offer to such an initiative. Their leading parliamentarians often seemed anachronistic; they pined for an eminence that had been lost and clung to fading hopes that it might yet be recovered. Such dreams were reinforced by activists who had doggedly defended the party's independence and, as they saw it, integrity. Those Liberals who favoured the removal of Asquith, perhaps to be replaced by Grey, saw this as a means of revitalising their party, not as a step towards a broader alliance. Cecil's value for these party loyalists would be as a recruit to a resurrected Liberal Party. C.P. Scott, a sceptic about Asquith's leadership, dismissed any broader project as politically impossible. 'A new Coalition would be the worst fighting flag for an election, for the very name has become a by-word and a reproach thanks to the performance of the present lot.' Herbert Gladstone, one of the architects of the pre-war Liberal–Labour electoral pact, echoed this assessment.[35] Amidst such uncertainties Asquith's determination to remain as leader was never in doubt.

By May 1922 Cecil was acknowledging in private the constraints on his actions:

> For me to advocate the deposition of Asquith would be futile and would cause great agitation in the Liberal Party. Without his deposition, my readiness to work with Grey becomes almost platonic. Do not forget that by the vast mass of county Liberal wire-pullers I am still regarded as a Conservative of a rather rigid type... The announcement that I had joined the Liberal Party would cause an explosion in my constituency and not improbably would result in my losing my seat.

Yet industrial unrest still inspired his search for a middle way. The engineers' lockout in mid 1922 provoked an appeal for conciliation. 'How long are we going to allow headstrong persons on both sides to imperil our national prosperity and make recruits for revolution?' The recipient of this appeal was Asquith ; five months later, in the Coalition's last days, Cecil was still pursuing with him the chimera of a Grey premiership.[36] These protracted and ultimately sterile discussions offered Mosley an early experience of an abortive attempt to break through established party loyalties. Even at a moment of relative plasticity their resilience in the face of pressures for change was significant, even amongst Liberals who had experienced such division and rapid marginalisation.

Yet the complexities and ambiguities of post-war politics meant that Cecil's ideas and perhaps his initiatives could engender a sympathetic response, not least amongst some Liberals who refused to embrace either Asquithian sectarianism or Coalition ecumenism, and who deplored the hostilities between Liberal leaders. Major Cecil Dudgeon was an agriculturist who bred prize winning Ayrshire cattle, had served in the war with the King's Own Scottish Borders, and was thoroughly involved in public affairs in south-west Scotland. In May 1922 this social leader was selected as Liberal candidate for Galloway in succession to the incumbent, who had been returned unopposed as a Coalition Liberal in 1918. Dudgeon had backed the Coalition, until recently, as a symbol of the unity of all moderates. He felt that confidence in the Coalition had ebbed. It had embarked on 'wild schemes'; above all national expenditure must be drastically reduced. This had to be central to any Liberal programme, as did the pursuit of world-wide peace through the League of Nations. Dudgeon's local activities included propaganda work for the League. He proclaimed himself 'a Liberal pure and simple'. He saw 'no necessity for prefixes'. At a meeting he read sections from a manifesto recently released by Cecil. 'He has behind him great Conservative principles, but I think after hearing these extracts you will come to the conclusion that he is a very great Liberal.' What this implied for Dudgeon tactically was unclear. He comforted himself with an assessment that could justify either Cecil's agenda, or optimism about the long term prospects of a revitalised Liberal Party. 'Liberalism in its widest sense had never such a wide following in the country as it has got to-day.'[37] In rural and remote Galloway pre-war political identities proved durable. Dudgeon, with his strong local connections, was successful in all but one of the next four general elections.

Discussions about the means of restoring decency to government were typically restricted to a cloistered few who often seemed insulated from the visceral sentiments and animosities of the activists. Most significantly, they seemed to misunderstand the importance of the escalating and more conventionally partisan anti-Coalition sentiment within the Conservative Party. Eddie Hartington, heir to Chatsworth, explained to Cecil why the latter's strategy had made little headway within the party:

> In the Country the bulk... hate Lloyd George but will support him rather than anyone they consider is even further to the 'left' because they have a very shrewd and right instinct that though L G gives way to extreme Labour and rotten socialists like Addison too much, any alternative Coalition, or any Government composed mainly of Labour and Wee Frees would inevitably be forced to give way to extreme demands even more.[38]

The most fundamental issue remained the prospects for Labour. Debates about the future of the Coalition, Conservative independence and the prospects for and desirability of new alliances – all were concerned with the extent and character of the Labour challenge. Disputes were typically about the most effective response. Mosley made few parliamentary interventions on labour matters. However, the content of the *Harrow Gazette* during his period of ownership expressed consistent hostility towards socialism, and on some major issues criticism of the wider labour movement. He was profoundly and consistently anti -Bolshevik. An article published in October 1920 discussed the Russo-Polish conflict and argued that British and French blunders had allowed the Soviet state to present itself as 'the one enlightened state in Europe assailed by a capitalist conspiracy'. This characterisation offered a plausible excuse for economic chaos. 'It has postponed indefinitely the practical exposition of a Communist state in working order which all sane Economists anticipate as the most potent political factor in the destruction of the Bolshevist regime and principles by a complete revulsion of feeling within Russia itself against the tyrannical negation of democratic ideals.' The 'Hands off Russia' movement would acquire a revered place in labour folklore as a classic demonstration of the effectiveness and morality of 'Direct Action'. For Mosley it was 'a crime that must encounter the condemnation of all rational men'. His justification illuminated his perception of the Labour challenge. 'A general strike to achieve a political purpose can only end in civil war with its concomitant misery, for this country will always resist the attempt of a section to enforce its will upon a majority elected under almost universal franchise... Labour must learn the art of persuasion as opposed to that of violence before it continues to discuss not whether it is fit to govern but whether it has any prospect of exercising that facility.'[39]

The economic and political problems facing the post-war coal industry were distinctive. Nevertheless, the prospect and reality of conflict in the coalfields dominated the Coalition's relations with organised labour from the Sankey Commission in 1919 through the datum-line strike of autumn 1920 to the decontrol of the coal industry and the three-month lockout the following year. The *Harrow Gazette* coverage of the disputes of 1920–21 was through unsigned articles. Mosley as proprietor would not have permitted the inclusion of opinions at odds with his own views on such an important issue, and in at least some instances he might have been the author. In September 1920, and again in March and April 1921, the imminence of a stoppage inspired attacks on the

Miners' Federation of Great Britain. The articles' economic rationale was that of the People's Union for Economy:

> Though we are reluctant to advocate any drastic reduction of wages in these days of high costs of living, it is evident that a start must be made somewhere ... For enormously increased wages, the miners had been giving not even the customary output and the old policy of 'A fair day's work for a fair day's pay' had been entirely ignored. The economic facts of the situation have to be faced. A Government subsidy may have been a desirable expedient when we were in the throes of war, but we must face purely economic conditions now and the subsidy must go.[40]

The Coalition's decision to bring forward the decontrol of the industry to 1 April 1921 precipitated the threat of massive wage cuts in several coalfields; the result was a stoppage that was mostly a lockout, but in a few more prosperous coalfields a sympathetic strike. By mid April, supportive action by the other partners in the Triple Alliance – railway and transport workers – seemed imminent. The *Harrow Gazette* proclaimed its readiness to meet the trade union challenge. The miners were led by 'the extremist faction'; the rapid response to the call for defence units demonstrated 'the determination of all law-abiding citizens to maintain law and order against the forces of disruption, forces which are no less dangerous than those we defeated in the great war'. This rendition of the Enemy Within was complemented by a lament for the hard-pressed Harrow electorate. 'The middle classes of the community, the backbone of Britain are being subjected to a strain which is almost unbearable.'[41] Such anxieties proved groundless. On 15 April, 'Black Friday', railway and transport unions decided not to strike, the MFGB stood alone for three months until the inevitable, and for many miners, devastating, defeat.

Such sentiments might help to explain why, despite his increasing criticism of many Coalition policies and his breach with Conservative organisation in the Commons, Mosley's relationship with the Harrow Unionist Association initially remained amicable. He was an effective campaigner who was highly visible in the constituency. Cynthia Mosley was assiduously involved in a wide variety of local organisations. Mosley backed such activity with abundant funds. The Conservative central organisation had only limited control over local associations; the latter typically stayed loyal to Members who whatever their foibles were generous with their time and cash.

Mosley was aided by the continuing uncertainty over the future pattern of party conflict. Shifting and diverse opinions about the desirability of maintaining the Coalition, rumours of plots and counter-plots to promote new initiatives, debates about how far and in what ways Tories should adapt to the post-war world – such a kaleidoscope could license local activists' toleration of an individualistic Member. When Mosley crossed the floor in November 1920 over British reprisals in Ireland, the Unionist Association President A.K. Carlyon defended him. He had kept both the Association and the electorate informed about his activities. He had never promised, nor had been required to 'follow blindly' the Coalition beyond its official programme.[42]

The Association's own nuanced assessment of the Coalition effectively endorsed Mosley's actions:

> The Coalition may be – probably is – the only form of Government at present available, but in such matters as its reckless and inexcusable squandering of the nation's money and its hopeless mismanagement of Ireland, most of us are glad to know we have a representative in Parliament who has the honesty to form his own opinions and the courage to express them.

Mosley's demands for economy resonated with party activists. This accord balanced his position on Ireland, which was viewed less favourably by the rank and file. When he spoke in the constituency in February 1921 a former Chairman of the Association left the platform in response to Mosley's criticism of the 'Black and Tans'' reprisals at Balbriggan. Mosley seems to have taken the initiative. 'Go down into the body of the hall if you wish to disagree with me.' 'I will too' was the response.[43]

Above all Mosley emphasised the provisional character of existing alignments, but as yet claimed that there was no credible alternative to the current administration. 'Personally I believe that we shall be governed by Coalition of varying forms and degrees for some time to come until the present anomalies and fluctuations of political thought consolidate into definite shape.' This justification inevitably became less persuasive as an election came closer and anti- Coalition sentiment within the Conservative Party strengthened. This feeling was facilitated by rumours that the Centre Party project had been resurrected at the beginning of 1922. Conservative activists insisted that criticism of the Coalition must be made from within the Conservative Party. Mosley was tantalisingly evasive on what to activists was the fundamental question. Would he be prepared to stand as an official Conservative candidate at the next election? By late May the Association President had abandoned his earlier tolerance, and had decided that Mosley's position was untenable. His verdict reflected growing unrest within the Association. 'At the beginning of this year Mr Mosley's vagaries and eccentric conduct in the House of Commons were beginning to cause serious anxiety.' Activists felt that Mosley could well abandon the party in the constituency as he had in the Commons. What had been admired as dexterity in argument in 1918 now seemed mere artifice. 'He could never be persuaded to give a direct answer to a direct question, and developed an unrivalled skill in qualifying any written statement he would be induced to make with some loophole by which, if convenient, he could escape from the obvious meaning of his words.' Negotiations and a meeting in early May between Mosley and the Association members proved fruitless. Eventually, on 24 May, Mosley met Carlyon; he came equipped with a document that precipitated the latter's negative response. Mosley had insisted that his commitment to any party should be determined only by his assessment of its efficacy for the furthering of his principles. He linked his position to that of Robert Cecil and suggested the title 'Progressive Conservative'.[44]

When the Unionist Association met on 7 July it debated a resolution laying down conditions for adoption as an official candidate. A post-Coalition world was envisaged. Any official candidate must 'pledge himself if the next General Election results in the formation of a National Unionist administration to give that administration his loyal support'. Whatever the electoral outcome a Conservative Member for Harrow must follow the party whip and agree to discuss with the association any failure to give support on a major issue. These requirements ruled out any repeat of the association's experience with Mosley. Predictably he objected. 'A gramophone would be more suitable to this requirement than a human being.' He moved quickly to exploit divisions amongst Harrow Conservatives. He circularised party members and secured significant support, not least from the association's former secretary, who became his agent.[45]

The dominant mood in the Harrow Association expressed the increasingly powerful and widespread ant-Coalition sentiment amongst Conservative activists. Coalition policy in Ireland and India, the formation of the Free State and the Government's reaction to the Amritsar massacre seemed to threaten imperial stability. In agricultural areas, the Coalition was attacked as insensitive to rural priorities. The old antipathy towards Lloyd George as a potentially destructive radical was inflamed by allegations of corruption. The claims of extravagant expenditure and punitive taxation remained a potent indictment for many Conservatives. For Conservative defenders of Coalition, their last resort was the need for an effective anti-socialist strategy. They insisted that the dictates of electoral prudence suggested the continuation of coalition; but for others the integrity and unity of the Conservative Party necessitated independence. Evidence that the demands of principle, unity and electoral credibility might point to the same conclusion would destroy the Coalition.[46]

Conservative MPs voted decisively at the Carlton Club on 19 October to end the Coalition. Majority opinion perhaps was based on optimism that the Conservative Party, liberated from Coalition constraints, could be an effective anti- Labour force. The result was to transform the Conservative hierarchy. Austen Chamberlain stood down as leader; he and other Conservative ministers who had argued for the continuation of the Coalition were marginalised. Bonar Law returned to the leadership that he had vacated the previous year, on health grounds. He formed a Conservative cabinet lacking many senior figures. Faced with the consequential election Mosley justified his independent position; the party political world was changing decisively but the change was not yet complete. 'The war destroyed the old party issues and with them the old parties. The party system must of course return in the near future, but it will be a new Party system. The great new issues will shortly create new Party alignments, which will truly divide the lines of men and determine their permanent associations. Then, and not before, I am prepared to form my Party allegiance.' His candidacy, in style, content and visiting speakers, showed the impact of his recent associations with Robert Cecil and with wider liberal opinion.[47]

The backing of the Wealdstone Unionist Association gave some legitimacy to his claim to be a Progressive Conservative. Robert Cecil notwithstanding his status as an official Conservative candidate spoke for Mosley. His parliamentary record, particularly on Ireland and European issues, attracted support beyond Conservative voters. Many Liberal and Labour activists worked for him in the absence of their own candidates. Lord Crewe, a personification of Asquithian rectitude, blessed his candidacy. 'So far as his actions have been concerned and the votes he has given in Parliament there is no reason why any Liberal so far as I am concerned need do anything but support him.' Liberal benediction was complemented by Liberal resources. Lord Cowdray gave Mosley £10,000 towards his expenses. This support was reciprocated in Mosley's insistence that 'Free Trade is the only hope of the country and of the world.'[48]

Bonar Law, in reaction to the allegedly high-risk and flamboyant Coalition offered sombre caution. Mosley, not to be outdone, opposed 'wild extreme government' and anticipated Stanley Baldwin in commending 'safety first'. Unemployment in the long term could be addressed by schemes of imperial development, but, more immediately, European markets must be revived – and this necessitated a secure Europe. Within the complex alignments of 1922 there was little difference between Bonar Law's commendation of tranquillity and the Asquithians' traditional Liberal rhetoric. Both proclaimed and welcomed a return to pre-coalition respectability.[49]

The confusions of the election were evident in the politics of Harrow's official Conservative candidate Charles Ward-Jackson. He had sat in the 1918 Parliament as Member for Leominster. His Association had become unhappy about his support for the Coalition; they had wished him to run in any future election as an independent Conservative. This had led to a breach in 1921. In search of a new constituency, he had been adopted at Harrow just before the Carlton Club vote, and had voted there with the majority against the continuation of the Coalition. In the subsequent election campaign however, he urged co-operation between Conservatives and the disorientated Coalition Liberals. In contrast he presented Mosley as effectively an Asquithian, or in the disillusioned Carlyon's picturesque but hyperbolic image 'a Liberal wolf running about in Unionist sheep's clothing'. Amongst all the confusion the Harrow contest was effectively a plebiscite on Mosley. The verdict was decisive. A leader in the *Harrow Observer* acknowledged, 'Mr Mosley has so far engrossed his personality on the electorate.'[50]

Harrow Election 1922
Turnout 65.1%

O.E. Mosley	Independent	15,290	66.0%
C.L.A. Ward-Jackson	Conservative	7,868	34.0 %
		7,422	32.0%

The vagaries of a complex party competition and of the electoral system gave the Conservatives a comfortable parliamentary majority on an unusually low proportion of the popular vote. The party's bid for independence had succeeded in returning a Conservative Government. Nevertheless, electoral arithmetic and ambiguous party alliances suggested that any success was provisional; whether the Conservatives could establish themselves as the dominant and popular anti-socialist force remained unclear. The election also confirmed that a strengthened

Labour Party would be a durable element in the party system, although as yet seemingly far from office. Labour's increase in seats compared with 1918 was less than some opponents had feared. However, the Parliamentary Labour Party was now much more broadly based. It included some well-heeled former Liberals, a few middle-class social-ists and the return of Ramsay MacDonald and Philip Snowden after their comprehensive defeats in 1918. MacDonald's subsequent victory over the incumbent Clynes for the PLP chairmanship was by a nar-row margin. Nevertheless it was a decisive moment in the party's development. MacDonald became Labour's first real leader as opposed to transitory office holder. He would personify the party amongst the wider electorate; Labour, despite its limited advance, was beginning to establish a claim as an alternative government. Elsewhere, much remained obscure. Leading Conservatives who had opposed the end-ing of the Coalition remained outside the administration. Former Coalition Liberals had often benefited from local Conservative support but were much reduced in numbers. They had lost many industrial seats to Labour and were unsure of their distinctive position in a post-Coalition world. The Asquithians, sometimes labelled the 'Wee Frees', had shown only modest expansion. Their political identity varied between constituencies, anti Tory in some situations, anti- Labour in others. Expectations of Liberal unity remained meagre. Nevertheless its continuing possibility meant that the Conservatives could not be con-fident that they had established themselves as the dominant focus for anti-socialist sentiment.

In the new Parliament, Mosley appeared increasingly as a 'de facto' Asquithian. J.A. Spender, until recently editor of the Liberal Establishment's *Westminster Gazette,* applauded Mosley's victory as 'one of the brightest spots in the election'. Spender's wider diagnosis blended wishful thinking, conservatism and factionalism. 'The Wee Frees were sadly unlucky with their seats and votes. I should have liked them to have 40 more and Labour 40 less, but on the whole I am glad that B (Law) has a majority which prevents Ll(oyd) G(eorge) from command-ing the House.' Asquith came to regard Mosley as effectively a member of his party. Returning to the Commons after dinner he heard 'a bril-liant speech from Tom Mosley who is one of our best recruits and the more welcome to us and hated by the Tories because he is Lord Curzon's son in law'. Similarly, Sir John Simon, often seen as an austere guard-ian of Liberal principles, responded to one of Mosley's speeches on the Ruhr crisis and its implications for European stability as having said 'in the best language what a real Liberal feels'. He thus endorsed his wife

Kathleen's post-poll assessment that Mosley would offer *'great* value to the party in the House'.[51]

Throughout 1923, Mosley's liberalism was typically expressed on international issues. He attacked British involvement in Mesopotamia as epitomising failure both internationally and at home. Against imperial adventures he articulated the liberal ideal of international harmony and domestic wellbeing. He indicted those

> whose eyes are not open to the seething miseries of their cities but are fixed upon the spectacle of Eastern deserts... It is all very well to elaborate these grandiose schemes of Imperial dominance, but these schemes are founded on the degradation of Englishmen... It is better to risk disorder in Iraq than in a city like Manchester.

He spoke on the developing Ruhr crisis, criticising French policy and vowing that for Britain at least, the disaster of 1914 must not be repeated. 'The follies of Europe have been cleansed sufficiently in the blood of our people, and never again will they contemplate or will they tolerate military intervention from this country in the internal affairs of the Continent.'[52]

With Progressive opinion recoiling from the legacy of Versailles, Mosley's speeches strengthened the image of him as a politician of the left. His arguments and rhetoric could strike a response from many within the Labour Party, not least those inspired by the ethical socialism of the ILP. Beatrice Webb's first profile of him dates from this moment, when alignments and prospects on the left remained unclear. A positive endorsement was coupled with a characteristically acerbic ending:

> Tall and slim, his features not too handsome to be strikingly peculiar to himself, modest yet dignified in manner with a pleasant voice and unegotistical conversation, this young person would make his way in the world without his adventitious advantages which are many – birth, wealth and a beautiful aristocratic wife. He is also an orator in the grand old style and an assiduous worker in the modern manner. So much perfection argues rottenness somewhere.

Perhaps his political independence posed a question. 'Is there in him... some weak spot which will be revealed in a time of stress, exactly at the very time when you need support, by letting you or your cause down or sweeping it out of the way?'[53] As yet, Mosley remained an Independent. The Liberals were limited in numbers and divided;

Labour's parliamentary strength was geographically and occupation-ally restricted. The eventual configuration of anti-Conservative forces remained unclear. Equally, the debris of the Coalition posed questions about the future organisation of anti-socialist sentiment. Winston Churchill had been defeated at Dundee as a Coalition Liberal; only his attachment to free trade linked him specifically to a divided Liberalism. Otherwise, his fervent hostility to socialism suggested a rapprochement with the Conservatives he had left almost twenty years earlier. In mid 1923, some Harrow Conservatives canvassed the possibility of Churchill standing as a Conservative in opposition to Mosley.[54]

The Conservative Government had a secure parliamentary majority, but Bonar Law's time in Downing Street was brief. Terminally ill, he resigned in May 1923 to be replaced by Stanley Baldwin, a succession that demonstrated the thorough impact of the Coalition's termina-tion on the Conservative hierarchy. Baldwin as leader would have been unimaginable a year earlier; his leadership in content and style would be central to the fortunes of anti-socialist politics for the next 14 years.[55] He began dramatically; in November he called an election on a Protectionist platform. His motivations have been much debated. Crucially, he was a long-standing Protectionist, as befitted his involve-ment in the West Midlands iron trade; he viewed the policy as a cred-ible response to unemployment and needed emancipation from Bonar Law's pledge not to introduce tariffs. Protection could be offered as an answer to Labour claims to offer a distinctive response to the instabili-ties and inhumanities of capitalism. Hopefully it could attract working-class electors. Conservatives, voters and to some extent politicians, were divided. In contrast, Liberals forged a sometimes tenuous unity, Asquithians, Lloyd Georgians, including Churchill, and the resolutely unattached came together, to defend free trade; they hoped that the passions of 1906 could be rekindled.

Mosley's recent politics made him a credible, if semi-detached mem-ber of the Liberal mobilisation. This identity was strengthened by the new Harrow Conservative candidate. Hugh Morris was a committed Protectionist; appropriately a high priest of Protection, Leo Amery spoke at his adoption meeting and presented Mosley, whatever his per-sona in Harrow, as in the Commons 'something between an advanced Radical and a Bolshevik'. Mosley responded to the alleged hyperbole of his opponents with speeches packed with facts and figures, in the ser-vice of a doctrine that soon he would come to disparage. 'Free imports stimulated the real trade upon which they were dependent – the export trade, and it was the export trade by which this country lived. It was the decline of that export trade owing to the diminution of the total volume of the world trade which was responsible almost entirely for their unemployment.' Although Mosley suggested 'a great scheme of State development' as an immediate response, he insisted that there was only one permanent solution to unemployment, 'the pacification of Europe, the stabilisation of exchanges and the restoration of their foreign markets'. Margot Asquith's telegram on polling day was predictable. 'All thinking of you today and wishing you good luck.'[56]

The peculiarities of Harrow politics meant that the Free Trade–Protectionist controversy was fought between a Conservative Protectionist, and Mosley backed by Liberal, Labour and Mosleyite sections, with the campaign organised through his Constitutional and Progressive Association. A swing to the Conservative, compared with 1922, in an election where that party was often losing support over Protection, suggested that Mosley's local position was becoming more precarious. Perhaps he was nevertheless the beneficiary of a regional move to Liberalism on the Free Trade issue. Two nearby constituencies, Finchley and East Willesden went Liberal. On a foggy evening the commuter trains through Harrow carried electors home to Aylesbury, Wycombe and Hemel Hempstead; all were Liberal gains.

Harrow Election 1923
Turnout 64.5%

O.E. Mosley	Independent	14,079	59.9%
E.H.F. Morris	Conservative	9,433	40.1%
		4,646	19.8%

The Conservatives, damaged by the revival of the appeal of Free Trade, lost their overall majority. The Labour Party made a limited advance, and with 191 seats were 33 seats ahead of an uneasily reunited Liberal Party, for whom the focus on their traditional icon had brought gains in unexpected places. Critically, in an election fought on this most favourable terrain they finished behind Labour. Responses to the new parliamentary arithmetic were debated feverishly within and between the parties. When the Commons met in January 1924 Labour and Liberal combined to defeat the Baldwin Government. A minority Labour Government took office under Ramsay MacDonald. For Oswald Mosley the political options had shifted.

2
Renegade

Rumours abounded about Mosley's likely prospects during the fevered interlude between the December 1923 election and the meeting of Parliament in mid January. He would take office in an Asquith Government; he would become Under Secretary for Foreign Affairs in a Labour Government. In the Debate on the Address he attacked Conservative 'Red Scare' tactics and chastised the Baldwin Government in language reminiscent of his speeches during the previous Parliament. 'They have financed the luxuries of Arab princes by starving physically and mentally the people of this country. They have made remissions of taxation to the rich and they have paid for them by squeezing the poor.' He proclaimed that 'the army of progress has struck its tents and is on the move'.[1]

His own position within the 'army of progress' remained unclear. To his constituents he characterised his attitude towards the MacDonald Government as 'vigilant friendship'. Just before Christmas 1923, as speculation intensified about the possibility of a Labour Government, Mosley had written to MacDonald as 'my dear prospective Prime Minister'. Flattery – 'the issues are immense and will require all your skill and courage' – was combined with characteristically melodramatic rhetoric. 'The mightiest problems and the mightiest opportunities of History combine to present themselves.' The implication, perhaps, was that MacDonald's Labour Party could be the instrument for 'a great policy worthy of a great age'. Yet privately, Mosley expressed disappointment about the new administration's first steps.[2]

The Westminster Abbey by-election in mid March 1924 acquired significance because of Winston Churchill's almost-successful independent campaign, an early step on the brief journey that would take him back from the Liberal Party to his Conservative origins, and into the next Tory cabinet. Mosley, as an elector, voted for the Labour candidate, the pacifist Fenner Brockway. Shortly afterwards, he presented a usable political autobiography to his supporters in the Harrow Constitutional and Progressive Association. He claimed to have been a consistent advocate of social reform who had abandoned the Conservatives when they reverted back to their old ideas and methods. The Irish campaign had brought him new allies. He insisted that the new Labour Government would not pursue 'wild revolutionary methods'. Instead change would come in 'measured ordered steps'.

This speech was an obvious prelude to a formal announcement. He published an 'Open Letter' to his constituents dated 29 March. 'The present Government has now clearly emerged as the effective champion of the forces of progress and sanity in this country. Independence in a period of political confusion is abundantly justifiable but these conditions are now past.' His profession of allegiance to MacDonald, who had been vilified because of his response to British involvement in a European war, was bedecked incongruously with military images. 'The battle array of the future is determined. You stand forth as the leader of the forces of progress in their assault upon the powers of reaction. In this grave struggle... I ask leave to range myself beneath your standard.'[3]

Margot Asquith was predictably unimpressed. Mosley's action in leaving 'our party' was 'an unwise thing at a foolish time'. Robert Cecil's response to the arrival of MacDonald in Downing Street contrasted with that of his former follower. He dissented from Churchill's 'terror of socialism... his belief that a Bolshevik army is going to over-run Europe'. Nevertheless he rejected Labour's claim to govern, since 'it depended for its vitality on the conception that the working class ought to govern, or that at least government should be carried on primarily in the interests of that class'. He dismissed this doctrine as 'disastrous'. On this issue he thought 'many Liberals and Conservatives are agreed'. Whatever the stylistic contrast Churchill had reached the same conclusion. 'It is absolutely necessary now that a Conservative and Liberal Union shd come into being to provide a sound basis for a National Government.'[4]

Even when Mosley's position had seemed virtually indistinguishable from Liberal orthodoxies, Beatrice Webb had suggested that he might join the Labour Party. In June 1923 with Labour seeking to establish itself as the principal opposition party, she noted that 'J R MacDonald is much taken with him and he with MacDonald.' The Labour leader corroborated this assessment to Cynthia Mosley. 'He is filling a difficult position gloriously well. He is one of the redeemers of that dear old place.' In parallel with this increasingly cultivated proximity to a leader susceptible to flattery, Mrs Webb also understood that Mosley appealed to a prominent section on the Labour left. 'Even the Clyde contingent have been fascinated by his personal charm and the wit and wisdom of his speeches.' Mosley, once within the party, would seek both an inside track with the party leader and a rhetorical appeal that could nurture a reputation for radicalism.[5]

On the eve of Mosley joining the Labour Party Beatrice Webb offered a further assessment. She queried whether his evident talents might prove insufficient for practical effectiveness:

> The rhetorical, picturesque and emotional aspect (*sic*) of Labour politics attract him and may become his snare. He is too clever at words and too inexperienced in affairs to be as yet a first-rate statesman. If (he) develops the 'administrative' sense he has got a great future before him as one of the leaders of the Parliamentary Party. He is a Disraelian gentleman-democrat, tall, good-looking, courteous and deferential in manner, open-minded with fervour for the people's cause rather than intellectual conviction. He is the most accomplished speaker in the House and hated with a quite furious hatred by the Tories whom he has left.[6]

Mosley made his Labour debut at the Independent Labour Party Conference in York. He spoke briefly in a debate on European affairs. Hugh Dalton would become an early and hostile critic; he acknowledged that Mosley was 'well received'. Through the spring and summer of 1924 he wrote loyalist articles for the ILP's *New Leader*. He began to socialise within his new party. Wedgwood Benn, an independently minded Liberal who would join the Labour Party three years later, reflected on an evening at the Mosleys. 'The Labour Party at play amidst Mosley luxury is a curious spectacle.' Mosley's Commons speeches concentrated on economic and international issues.[7] Whilst there were significant continuities with his earlier interventions, his arguments were linked assiduously to a defence of the Government's record informed by recognition of its minority status. Above all he began to establish himself as a party campaigner. His platform style, and by extension the basis for his popularity within the party, were captured vividly in an outsider's portrait.

In the spring of 1924 Egon Wertheimer had just become the London correspondent of the German Social Democrats' newspaper *Vorwarts*. He attended his first Labour party meeting on a Sunday afternoon in south

London. He contrasted the 'hilarity' of the audience with the solemnity and earnestness of their counterparts in Munich and Hamburg. In contrast with German Social Democratic secularism this London audience listened to 'a parson in a clerical collar'. But Wertheimer was most impressed by the arrival of the principal speaker-or perhaps-speakers – and their reception. 'Suddenly there was a movement in the crowd, and a young man with the face of the ruling class in Great Britain, but the gait of a Douglas Fairbanks, threw himself forward through the throng to the platform, followed by a lady in heavy costly furs.' Mosley's first London meeting was serenaded by a chorus of 'For he's a jolly good fellow'. Again, Wertheimer proclaimed the peculiarities of the English. 'Unthinkable that in Germany, a man of barely twenty-eight (*sic*) years a recruit, a typical aristocrat, a renegade, should have been so greeted by an assembly of workers or should let himself be so greeted.'

Mosley's speech confirmed Beatrice Webb's emphasis on his emotional appeal. Although Wertheimer acknowledged his own linguistic inadequacies, the style was evident, to an observer accustomed to an approved and contrasting party rhetoric:

> All the more unforgettable was the impression, the visual and oral impression, which the style of the speech made upon me. It was a hymn, an emotional appeal directed not to the intellect, but to the Socialist idea, which obviously was still a subject of wonder to the orator, a youthful experience. No speaker at a working-class meeting in Germany would have dared to have worked so emotionally on the feelings without running the risk of losing for ever his standing in the party movement.

This assessment, as Wertheimer acknowledged, was not just about Mosley; it illuminated the relative ecumenism of the Labour Party compared with the SPD. This proposition requires contextualisation because the precise range of approved identities and styles was arguably specific to the 1920s, the years between the restructuring of the party in 1918 and the trauma of 1931. The period was more or less concurrent with MacDonald's leadership. It involved an attempt to construct a successor to the pre-war Progressive Alliance, but one expressed through a party linked to the trade unions. In pursuing this project, the welcoming of well-heeled recruits from other parties was an important element; for the sceptical it might offer comforting evidence that Labour had transcended the sectionalism of a union-based party. Nevertheless, catholicity came under pressure from the mid twenties as elements that were decreed discordant were marginalised – pro-Communists, feminists and the ILP left. The 1931 split, with the consequential anathema of 'intellectuals' would narrow the approved range further.

Wertheimer's reflections on oratorical style were accompanied by his thoughts about the party's social culture. Cynthia Mosley responded to calls from the audience that she should speak.

> Suddenly the elegant lady in furs got up from her seat, and said a few sympathetic words which I understood because they were simple and came immediately from the heart. She said that she had never before attended a workers' meeting, and how deeply the warmth of the reception touched her. She said this simply and almost shyly, but yet like one who is accustomed to be acclaimed, and without stage fright, to open a bazaar or a meeting for charitable purposes.

The style expressed a hierarchy to which Labour was formally opposed. Wertheimer's portrayal of one party member's response suggested the complexity of party culture. '"Lady Cynthia Mosley" whispered in my ear one of the armleted stewards who stood near me, excited, and later, as though thinking that he had not sufficiently impressed me, he added "Lord Curzon's daughter". His whole face beamed proudly.'

As Wertheimer understood, in those early weeks of the first Labour Government party members and supporters were understandably proud that 'by men of their class and in their name, the mightiest empire of the world was ruled'. The advent of Oswald and Cynthia Mosley could be seen not as diluting that achievement but as its confirmation. Labour had arrived. The contrast with the SPD was again apparent to Wertheimer. 'Where I had come from a Mosley would have had to serve for years in the darkness because he was Curzon's son in law.' But in Britain this connection with a former Viceroy, Tory Foreign Secretary and 'most superior person' was no handicap. 'The crowd seemed to revel in his confession and conversion.' They did not appear to feel patronised; privilege personified apparently provoked no hostility. 'How strange that, amongst those two thousand working-men and women, none appeared to resent the furs of the woman, or to feel as a provocation her air of cultivated, easy well-being that radiates from her like an aura.'[8]

Pride could shade into deference, yet it would become evident that those sentiments that struck Wertheimer so forcefully were strands within a complex culture. New recruits were expected to endorse codes of conduct – respect for particular kinds of experience, established institutional practices, and the acceptance of a necessary solidarity in the face of hostility. The Labour Party saw itself as an instrument through which the poor and dispossessed could emancipate themselves by their own efforts and creativity, a usable understanding of the past that could offset pride in affluent recruits. Long service to the movement and status as the representative of a major interest offered routes to party eminence. In the eyes of the impatient with a sense of their own talents, such an ethos could be criticised as elevating mediocrity. But in 1924 with the novelty of a Labour Government such battles were for the future.

Wertheimer's portrait highlighted Mosley not just as the product of a ruling class, but as someone who brought to the political platform the glamour of Hollywood and in particular that new phenomenon, the male film star as sex symbol. Douglas Fairbanks was viewed widely as the silent screen's masculine ideal. He was the star of *Robin Hood* and *The Mark of Zorro*; he had played the swashbuckling D'Artagnan in *The Three Musketeers*. Ellen Wilkinson, from October 1924 the vivacious Labour Member for Middlesbrough, drew another Hollywood parallel. She saw Mosley as 'the Sheik, a Valentino in real life'. The reference was to the film starring Rudolph Valentino in 1921 and seen by an estimated 125 million people. The film had been based on a 1919 novel of the same title, written by 'Edith Maude Hull' (Edith Winstanley) in wartime rural Derbyshire. Savaged by some critics and ignored by many others, it had been reprinted 108 times in Britain by 1923. Ingredients included racism, sado-masochism and sexism in a story of sexual dominance by an exotic male. Yet it has also been argued that *The Sheik* offered sexual experience as a liberalising of identity. Sheikh Ahmed is ultimately revealed as the son of an English aristocrat and a Spanish woman, a racially acceptable ending, similar to the aristocratic pedigree of Tarzan. Ellen Wilkinson's representation of Mosley drew on a familiar cultural icon. She insisted that Mosley was not 'the nice kind hero who rescues the girl at the point of torture but the one who hisses "At last we meet."'[9]

Whatever Mosley's oratorical skills he could not ignore one urgent issue. He needed a new and winnable constituency. From the standpoint of Labour – even 'Mosley for Labour' – Harrow was clearly hopeless. He did not lack invitations from hopeful local parties. On 21 July 1924 Mosley was selected as candidate for Birmingham Ladywood. His first speech to the Ladywood party featured an appropriately revised account of his career. His 1918 programme had been 'not very far removed from Labour's policy of to-day'. His Liberal period became invisible. 'Within a year he crossed the floor, took his place in the company of his Labour comrades and co-operated with them for five years before joining them last (*sic*) year.' He attempted to still doubts about his reliability. 'He was a strong party man, he believed in working through his party. His experience as an independent had strengthened his conviction to be a strong party man. Don't quarrel with your party... don't attack it, don't make it more difficult for your leaders.'[10]

The vacancy had occurred because of the Ladywood party's refusal to readopt their previous candidate, Dr Robert Dunstan. A pre-war Liberal, Dunstan had fought Birmingham's Moseley constituency in 1918 and Ladywood in 1922 and 1923. He visited the Soviet Union in April 1924; two months later he left the ILP for the Communist Party. Communists were still eligible to stand as Labour candidates, a practice which would be banned by the party conference that October. Such candidacies had become more contentious because of the recent Glasgow Kelvingrove by-election. There, the Labour candidate, Aitken Ferguson, was a Communist and had attacked the Labour Government. The consequential acrimony provided the context for Dunstan's removal.[11]

Mosley justified his choice of constituency in terms of electoral strategy. 'Labour had to break fresh ground and shatter the strongholds of the opposition. That was why Birmingham had drawn him like a magnet.'[12] By 1924 the city stood out as a deviant case. Labour's postwar advance had involved the establishment of some presence in almost all industrial cities. Even in Liverpool, with its maritime economy and religious sectarianism, Labour held two seats by mid 1924. Labour's failure to win any Birmingham seat, and its consistent weakness in municipal contests, were increasingly anomalous, not least within the West Midlands, The party had captured some Black Country seats in 1918; in 1923 Labour had won Coventry for the first time.

Labour failures in Birmingham must be understood in the context of the dominance of the city's politics by the Chamberlain dynasty. This ascendancy is sometimes seen as harmonising with the culture of the local economy where the dominant metal trades were conducted typically in small workshops. Workplace relationships were usually informal, and industrial conflict was rare. However, the city's politics were not simply the consequence of a distinctive economy. Political choices mattered. The Chamberlain dominance went back to the 1870s, the growth of the city's Liberal organisation, and the mayoralty of Joseph Chamberlain. When the dynasty's founder broke with Gladstone over Irish Home Rule in 1886, the City's Members and many electors followed. Their politics were expressed through the medium of Liberal Unionism. Birmingham loyalty remained solid through Joseph

Chamberlain's subsequent vicissitudes. He served, as Colonial Secretary, in Lord Salisbury's essentially Conservative cabinet from 1895; the Anglo-Boer War was labelled as Joe's war and his blend of populism and patriotism helped to secure a landslide victory in the 1900 election. His resignation from Balfour's cabinet to pursue a campaign for tariff reform in 1903 divided the Conservatives and reunited the Liberals. Even in the disastrous 1906 election Birmingham remained monolithically loyal to Chamberlain. 'We Are Seven' affirmed a solidarity strengthened by a belief that tariffs would benefit the Birmingham trades. Only in East Birmingham, where railway employment was significant, was there a credible challenge even in this bleakest of elections. This came, significantly perhaps, from a Labour trade unionist. When a much expanded electorate and redistribution increased the city's representation to twelve Members in 1918, the monopoly of representation was maintained; the twelve victors included two of the founder's sons, Austen and Neville.[13]

This durability rested on and in turn resourced a formidable party organisation which when necessary could take a robust line with opponents. Crucially, its politics in both style and substance were not translatable as conventional Conservatism. Joseph Chamberlain's political trajectory had injected a radical ingredient, not least evident in the extensive municipal activities promoted by a council where the Labour presence was usually slight. Yet in the early 1920s Labour's vote in some inner-city seats was growing. In Deritend and Duddeston, in Austen Chamberlain's West Birmingham seat, and in Neville Chamberlain's Ladywood, the old order was under pressure greater than anything experienced pre-war. In suburban King's Norton the Austin plant at Longbridge was a world apart from the informal consensus of the small workshop.

The discarded Dunstan had given Neville Chamberlain a scare in the 1922 election, and a year later had reduced his majority to 1,554. Neville Chamberlain saw his position as vulnerable. Mosley planned an autumn campaign to expose the reality of the incumbent's policies and to attack 'the notorious Birmingham caucus whose wooden effigies had been set up like images'. In contrast with Mosley's precocious entry to Westminster, his opponent's parliamentary career had begun belatedly. His brother Austen had been designated as Joseph's political heir. In 1921 he had become leader of the Conservative Party. Neville had had successful careers in business and in municipal politics and a disastrous interlude as Lloyd George's Director of National Service before his election for Ladywood in 1918. He was fortuitously absent from the Carlton Club meeting in October 1922 and therefore had no part in his brother's deposition from the leadership. Neville Chamberlain, like Baldwin, was a prime beneficiary of the Carlton Club decision. He put aside any political attachment to his deposed brother to enter Bonar Law's government. Beginning as Postmaster General, he became Minister of Health in March 1923, and the following August under Baldwin moved to the Treasury. Mosley was attacking not just a personification of a powerful dynasty but a rapidly rising star within the Conservative Party.[14]

Yet, Chamberlain's stellar quality was less obvious in Ladywood. His reserved personality was not readily adaptable to the mores and expectations of an impoverished working-class district. His brother claimed that 'N's manner freezes people. His workers think that he does not appreciate what they do for him. Everyone respects him and he makes no friends.' On his own admission, Neville Chamberlain found constituency socialising uncongenial. The contrast with Mosley glad-handing his way around the densely populated streets and playing the full range of the emotional scale is telling. Chamberlain's frigidity was compensated by the assiduous involvement of his wife, Annie. She came down from leafy Edgbaston, cycling around the constituency, calling on constituents, offering a sympathetic ear to their problems. She organised help for the needy and sent flowers on appropriate occasions. Christmas cards from the Chamberlains arrived through Ladywood letter boxes. Mosley had employed similar methods in Harrow; he and Cynthia had the resources and the style to counter this a-political appeal.[15]

Chamberlain shared Mosley's diagnosis that the war had transformed political allegiances and identities. 'Parties will be disrupted, new cries and new men very likely will be coming to the front... The old shibboleths have gone for ever and it may be that when the war is over, we shall find new groupings of parties on new lines.' His wartime treatment by Lloyd George as Director of National Service had distanced him from the Coalition; he felt much more comfortable in the post-Carlton-Club Conservative Party. He believed that the party must respond effectively to the challenging consequences of franchise expansion that were all too evident in Ladywood. 'The new electorate contains an immense number of very ignorant voters... whose intelligence is low and who have no power of weighting evidence.' Labour had 'exploited the sufferings of the poor, setting class against class, and particularly appealed to the out-of-works who were in such a hapless state that they were ready to believe that their sufferings were due to political causes'.[16]

Customary deference was eroding; Birmingham Unionists complained of organised disruption by their opponents. After the 1923 election they claimed to be the victims of 'unfair and malicious propaganda'. The local political rivalry was already abrasive before Mosley arrived. He could articulate the prejudices of Ladywood Labour in the accent of Winchester and Sandhurst. Perhaps it was this apparent incongruity that Birmingham – and other – opponents found disturbing. Neville Chamberlain referred to him as 'that viper'. An allegedly sympathetic cleric would complain in 1926 that Ladywood Labour was distinguished and discredited by 'drunkenness, foul language and entirely unprovoked rowdyism preventing reasonable freedom of speech'.[17]

The 1924 election revolved around the issue of Labour's fitness to govern. The dissolution of Parliament followed the Government's defeat in the Commons over the Campbell Case, which fuelled the claim that Labour was susceptible to pressure from the left. Together with the tortuous negotiation over an Anglo-Soviet trade treaty, the affair licensed claims that Labour was unpatriotic and a Trojan horse for Bolshevik influence. Conservative rhetoric sought to mobilise the apolitical and to recruit Liberal voters in defence of national decency. The campaign culminated in the Zinovieff Letter a coping stone on Conservative Red Scare tactics, a forgery published in that paragon of political objectivity, the *Daily Mail*. The abrasiveness of the Ladywood campaign was fed by both local and national passions; the denouement was high drama. The initial count gave Chamberlain a majority of seven; a checking of the votes gave Mosley a majority of two. A further protracted recount produced a majority of 77 for Chamberlain. The interminable process was interrupted from the galleries by Labour claims of errors, incompetence and malpractice. These demonstrations and Mosley's involvement fuelled the Conservative image of an unscrupulous manipulator who traded on the emotions of the uninformed. Neville Chamberlain presented him as 'beside himself, walking up and down the tables and bullying the officials'; Leo Amery, victorious in Sparkbrook, claimed that Mosley had revealed his true character. 'Mosley behaved very badly, accused everyone of cheating etc. A hairy heeled fellow.' The established order was fracturing. Chamberlain, bruised by the affair, reminded the party faithful that 'the Gallery had been full of Socialist supporters, who constantly created disturbances and also the public on the Floor had been allowed to make speeches and insolent remarks. The whole proceedings had been scandalous.' Mosley's verdict was characteristically dramatic.

Only the hundreds of Unionist motor-cars and the downpour of rain enabled the Unionists to retain the seat. A downpour from Heaven washed back to Westminster the lifeless body of the last of the Chamberlains, dead as mutton, running away from public debate, beaten in argument, a flood of rain carried home a corpse. In the course of six weeks the Labour campaign in Ladywood has killed a tradition of sixty years.[18]

Birmingham Ladywood Election 1924
Turnout 80.5%

N. Chamberlain	Conservative	13,374	49.1%
O.E. Mosley	Labour	13,297	48.9%
A.W. Bowkett	Liberal	539	2.0%
		77	0.2%

The rhetoric, the allegations and counter-allegations, the drama of Ladywood diverted attention from a less spectacular but more success-ful challenge to the Chamberlain monopoly. Robert Dennison of the Steelworkers captured King's Norton from Sir Henry Austin. This victory of a trade unionist over a major local employer articulated a significant theme in the politics of the twenties – claims and counter-claims about which life experiences best qualified someone to be the representative of a community. Within Birmingham, Mosley's performance in psepho-logical, as opposed to theatrical, terms was not outstanding. Leaving aside West Birmingham, where the discarded Dunstan stood as a Communist and there were many Labour abstentions, Mosley achieved one of the lowest pro-Labour swings in the city. Rather, the impact of his campaign was to raise turnout to over 80 per cent, a level exceeded only in King's Norton where Dennison's victory depended on much less flamboyant methods.

The comparison raises the issue of how far Mosley's style and resources were vital for the effective challenging of the Chamberlain dominance. Mosley could be understood as reviving a populist, and sometimes scur-rilous, politics that had been personified in Joseph Chamberlain, and had been locally effective, but which had not been maintained at the same intensity by his heirs. Perhaps the Ladywood clash personified the growing challenge of Birmingham Labour, but too much focus on that drama obscures the basic point that Labour's advance in Birmingham was led by men characteristic of Labour's local leaderships elsewhere. Across the 1924 and 1929 elections Birmingham returned seven Labour Members. Three, Dennison, Gosling and Sawyer were trade unionists. George Sawyer, a ticket collector at New Street station, was a quintes-sential representative of his own community. Another three, Longden, Simmons and Whiteley were ethical socialists, heavily involved in the ILP but loyal to the broader Labour Party and unsympathetic to the ILP's late-twenties radicalisation. Only John Strachey, born 1901, the son of the editor of *The Spectator* and educated at Eton and Magdalen, was intellectually and socially close to Mosley.[19]

Birmingham Labour in the Mosley years was not a deviant case in the social and political character, as opposed to the timing, of its Labour representation. Sheffield seemed by the late twenties the epitome of a solid Labour advance. The steel mills of the city's East End and Labour control of the city council expressed the party's forward march in centres of heavy industry. Yet Sheffield numbered amongst its Labour Members from 1922, a pacifist local employer Cecil Wilson, and Arthur Ponsonby, the son of Queen Victoria's private secretary, born in Windsor Castle. Such variety was congenial to MacDonald, with his vision of Labour's future as a broad-based Progressive movement.[20] In his view, the party's credibility was strengthened by the recruitment of those 'with the face of the ruling class'. Some, but not all of them, would financially support their local parties to a degree conventionally associated with the Conservative Party. Mosley would remain as Ladywood candidate until late in 1926. During his final year he spent £1,700, paying the Agent's salary, buying a house for him and funding floral gifts and dispensary notes for medical treatment.[21]

Mosley's Ladywood campaign must also be located within the broader context of the 1924 election. Although Labour had a net loss of 40 compared with 1923, the party made 23 gains. Only seven were from the Conservatives, one of which had been first won in a by-election, and another, Motherwell, which had been Communist in 1922 and Conservative the following year. Labour's principal achievement was to take 16 seats from the Liberals, ending much of their presence in industrial seats in northern England, Scotland and London. However, these Liberal losses were overshadowed by their losses to the Conservatives. Their parliamentary representation in the new parliament had fallen from 158 to 40, as Liberal voters both short-term and long backed Baldwin. This allegedly consensual leader had benefited hugely from the Red Scare. In 1923 he had led the party unsuccessfully as the party of protection; a year later he won decisively leading a party of anti-socialism flavoured by appeals to idealism and a programme of 'sensible' social reform. Labour was clearly the second party; to that extent the complexities of the immediate post-war years had been resolved. But Labour faced a full term in opposition and the challenge of constructing an effective electoral strategy.

3
Elect

After his Ladywood defeat Mosley was, more than ever, a young man in a hurry. He proclaimed his continuing commitment to Ladywood both in rhetoric and in funding, but he was eager to return to the Commons as quickly as possible. After six years in Westminster, electoral defeat risked marginalisation, not least in terms of the Labour Party hierarchy. The lengthy wait until the next general election made the prospect of a winnable by-election attractive. However compelling Mosley's platform appeal and however seductive his money, any attempt to secure such a nomination faced personal and institutional obstacles. Several aspiring young recruits to Labour were looking for winnable constituencies. More seriously, some who had spent many years in the party had lost their seats in October 1924 and were keen to return. In several constituencies local notables had parliamentary ambitions. Trade unions were keen to protect and if possible expand their parliamentary holdings. The complexities of industrial and communal identities, the hopes of the ambitious, the need for local funds, the tension between deference and robust egalitarianism, all would shape Mosley's experience of local Labour.

The first prospect of an early return arose in June 1925. The Forest of Dean on the west bank of the Severn had a progressive political pedigree, in part the consequence of the Forest's coal miners. Pre-war it had been represented for many years by the Radical Sir Charles Dilke who had enjoyed decent relations with the local labour movement. From 1918 a considerable section of the electorate expressed their radicalism through the Labour Party. James Wignall, a Dockers' official subsequently sponsored by the new and ecumenical Transport and General Workers' Union, won the seat in 1918, and held it narrowly through the next three elections. His death in June 1925 meant a vacancy in a seat that offered relative security to the lucky nominee. When the Divisional Labour Party Executive met on 16 June, its first choice was Margaret Bondfield. She had been the Member for Northampton in the 1924 parliament and a junior minister in the Labour Government. An official of the recently formed and impeccably moderate National Union of General and Municipal Workers, she was a member of the TUC General Council and had had a lengthy and effective career as an organiser of women workers. Her record left no doubt as to her roots in the labour movement. Once a campaigner for the adult suffrage, she had suppressed her feminism as she sought to establish herself in an organisational culture where distinctively women's issues were often seen as divisive of the labour cause.[1]

Four days later the selection process shifted to a full meeting of the Divisional Party. Delegates were presented with a short list of five candidates. Some strongly queried the wisdom of a woman candidate. The Executive recommendation was not accepted. Bondfield was demoted to second place; Mosley was preferred. He visited the constituency on 22 June and agreed to stand. The Labour majority had declined in the 1924 election; the choice of candidate was important both locally and to strengthen the party's electoral credibility. Other than prejudice there was no ground for doubting Bondfield's effectiveness as a campaigner. A year later she would prove an impressive and successful candidate in Wallsend, a seat that combined heavy industry and mining. Perhaps money mattered more than sexism. Mosley would have funded the local party generously and arguably to a greater extent than Bondfield's cautious trade union.[2]

The choice of Mosley was approved by the Party National Executive Committee's Organisation Sub Committee on 23 June in readiness for the full NEC meeting the following day. NEC members arrived ready to endorse his candidacy, only to be informed that Mosley had withdrawn. He said that his decision to stand had been strongly opposed by the Birmingham party and that he had responded to their sentiments. He explained his withdrawal to the NEC in person, a gesture that apparently met with approval. This version is recorded in the NEC minutes; it differs from the account given by Mosley to the Birmingham party and publicised in its weekly newspaper. In this version he denied that he had ever accepted the Forest of Dean nomination. Rather he had received and refused a unanimous invitation; he had suggested Margaret Bondfield. Nevertheless his name had still gone forward to the selection conference and had been supported unanimously. Despite pressure to accept from the national party, he had consulted both the

Ladywood and Borough Party Executives on the evening of 23 June. As a result he had definitely refused the candidacy. However attractive the Forest of Dean offer might have been, Mosley's commitment to Birmingham was not just financial. In 1925 he was hoping to use the party's local organisation and enthusiasm to resource the campaign for his economic programme, the so-called Birmingham proposals.[3]

Mosley's refusal did not mean a reversion to Bondfield. Following her apparent demotion she had indicated her lack of interest. The choice moved to the third name on the short list of five, A.A. Purcell of the Furnishing Trades' Association. He, like Margaret Bondfield, sat on the General Council; in 1925 he was its chairman. Their politics contrasted. Whereas Bondfield was, like her union, a dedicated supporter of political and industrial sobriety, Purcell spoke unapologetically from the left. His enthusiasm for assertively socialist agendas went back to pre-war Salford, where he had campaigned for socialist unity in contrast to the alleged political ambiguity of the Labour Party. His more recent sympathy for the Soviet Union and support for Communist initiatives were undisguised. His politics had proved compatible with a brief spell in parliament as Member for Coventry. Like Bondfield he had been defeated in October 1924. His emergence as the Forest of Dean candidate concerned some within the party leadership, but whatever the individual doubts, the seat's marginality demanded the commitment of significant resources. Enthusiasm within the local labour movement was strengthened by a mining crisis that posed a threat to the already low wages of local miners. The publication of the coal owners' terms during the election served only to strengthen Purcell's position. The Divisional Labour Party, frustrated in its choice of Mosley, mounted a muscular campaign. Turnout rose by over 10 per cent to almost 81 per cent and Purcell won decisively. The victory proved expensive. The Labour Party National Agent estimated the cost at nearly £1,000. Whilst part of this expenditure would be met by Purcell's small union, it was hoped that a fund-raising effort would fill the gap.[4]

The mining crisis that had shaped the Forest of Dean by-election was postponed by the Baldwin Government's provision of a six months' subsidy to the industry, and the appointment of the Samuel Commission to investigate its problems and make proposals for its reform. The Commission's report became the prelude not to a settlement but to the General Strike and the seven-month miners' lockout. Although, or perhaps because, the eventual outcome was a disaster for the miners, by late 1926 the Labour Party was electorally more popular than at any time since October 1924. Against this dramatic backdrop, and encouraged by the electoral auguries, Mosley made another attempt to re-enter parliament. The Smethwick constituency was contiguous to Birmingham, but had been shaped by a contrasting politics. The Black Country extended from the edge of Birmingham northwards to Wolverhampton, and westwards into urbanised north Worcestershire. The politics of its industrial towns and villages was significantly shaped by the economic fortunes of its diverse metal trades. The Black Country lay largely outside the gravitational pull of the Chamberlain citadel, and Liberalism achieved some success after 1885. This was most evident in 1906 when Black Country Liberalism contrasted with Birmingham's 'We are seven'. However the vulnerability of many Black Country trades to foreign competition made tariff reform attractive, and through the 1910 elections the Liberals lost much of their Black Country presence.[5] This political decline was followed by a rapid expansion of trade unionism, both pre-war and during the war. The combination of Liberal decay and trade union growth gave Labour its opportunity. Black Country Conservatism offered no equivalent to the Chamberlain blend of patriotism, empire and municipal enterprise. In 1918 on new constituency boundaries and with the wider franchise, Labour won four Black Country seats – Kingswinford, Smethwick, Wednesbury and West Bromwich. Bilston added a fifth in 1924. Although the margins of victory were normally slender, the cluster of seats contrasted with the Chamberlain monolith next door. Every Black Country Labour Member was a trade unionist, some had local associations. All presented a political identity that was Labour rather than socialist.[6]

The Smethwick Member from 1918, John Davison, epitomised this politics. A Sheffield-based official of the Iron Founders, he had been a junior Whip, perhaps contributing to the alleged incompetence of the Whips' Office during the 1924 Government. On 19 November 1926 the Smethwick Trades and Labour Council Executive met to select a candidate for a Board of Guardians' election. After they had completed this municipal business they were informed that Davison wished to resign as MP on health grounds, with immediate effect, and that Mosley had made it clear that he would be prepared to stand. The Executive met Davison two days later. The Member commended Mosley in terms that combined the partisan and the deferential. 'Mr Mosley was endowed with great qualifications as a politician; he had seen him in the House of Commons with the Tory Party fretting at the mouth. Then there was educational attainment.'[7]

Mosley subsequently met the Executive. The miners' lockout was in its final days. He spoke in customarily apocalyptic rhetoric. The contest would be 'a struggle quite vital to the future of their Movement in the whole of the midlands and the whole working class movement of the country'. He emphasised the miners' imminent defeat and the Baldwin Government's proposed legislation to reduce trade union powers. He reassured delegates that there would be no repeat of the Forest of Dean confusion. Neville Chamberlain had recently expressed his intention to leave Ladywood for Edgbaston at the next election. Mosley claimed therefore that he had accomplished his mission and Ladywood would release him. 'He undertook to go there and to break the Chamberlain tradition. When Chamberlain ran away that tradition was broken.' The attraction of Smethwick to Mosley was obvious. It offered a secure parliamentary base adjacent to the city in which he had invested much. Some within the party's upper echelons felt that Davison's resignation had been encouraged, if not engineered, by Mosley. There were rumours that Davison was often drunk for weeks on end. The Smethwick Executive did not seem too concerned about indecent haste and procedural propriety. They recommended him as candidate to the full Trades and Labour Council. Egerton Wake, the Party's National Agent, was informed by letter.[8]

The Labour Party NEC's monthly meeting was scheduled for 24 November. Wake responded to the Trades Council's letter by informing them that the NEC's constitutional rights must be preserved. The Smethwick TLC had acted precipitously. They had not informed the NEC of the pending by-election; they had not initiated a selection conference nor invited nominations. The TLC had broken the rules. However the NEC's critical response was fuelled by individuals' resentment against Mosley, his style, his money, his recent entry into the party; above all Mosley evinced what could appear as a sense of entitlement. Some NEC members had developed a dislike for Mosley that would endure. Herbert Morrison, aged 38, was already a party veteran. He had won a seat in 1923 only to lose it in 1924. For such a talented and ambitious figure there could be no Smethwick-type fix fuelled by personal wealth. Morrison had a passion for procedural propriety anyway but that Mosley, almost nine years his junior, was the transgressor added to his zeal. Hugh Dalton, like Mosley, was an expensively educated recruit to Labour who had fought a succession of difficult elections before winning Peckham in 1924. He characterised Mosley as young, unscrupulous and on the make. Along with his money Mosley allegedly was adept at caressing the susceptibilities of credulous party activists. Older trade unionists on the NEC might share Davison's respect for Mosley's talents; they were happy to see their opponents riled by one of their own. Some saw Mosley as a prime recruit to Labour who should be met with understanding and perhaps indulgence. Against such tolerance was a trade union concern to protect their parliamentary representation against erosion by wealthy and plausible incomers. Rennie Smith, a high-minded ILP Member discussed the controversy with Dennison, the party's sole Birmingham MP. He reflected afterwards that Mosley 'had done much wire-pulling' and had shown 'indecent haste... He seems to throw a lot of money about.' The NEC's reprimand, in Smith's view, was deserved. There was also some disquiet within the Birmingham Labour Party. A few thought that the move would seem opportunistic. 'To the general public there was not much difference between Neville Chamberlain leaving Ladywood in order to be sure of *keeping* in Parliament and Mosley leaving Ladywood in order to be sure of *getting* into Parliament.' As so often with Mosley such protestations were 'all to no purpose'.[9]

Whatever their prejudices, all NEC members could agree that the rules must be kept. The National Agent and the NEC chairman, coincidentally F.O. Roberts, the Member for neighbouring West Bromwich, discussed the muddle with Davison. He confirmed his decision to retire and denied the rumour that he had made a deal with Mosley. They met the Smethwick executive and found them insistent on their position. Over the following weekend the NEC and their Smethwick counterpart exchanged claim and counter-claim. The NEC met Mosley but continued to oppose the TLC's actions. The sensitivity of the NEC was evident in a resolution repudiating claims that it had been influenced by 'any personal feelings' towards Mosley.[10]

George Lansbury was widely seen as a high minded veteran of the left. A member of the NEC he spoke in Birmingham during this deadlock. He insisted that he wanted Mosley back in the Commons, but not at the cost of violating the party constitution. Mosley must accept the imperative of unity. Appropriate respect for his talents must not marginalise the contributions of the many. 'He would not say anything about Mr Mosley's sacrifice, but he and his wife had done no more than many a humble man and trade unionist when in the teeth of his employer he had held up the flag of trade unionism.' Lansbury could appeal as an idealistic ethical socialist rather than as one who emphasised the constitutional question. In the twenties he represented a force for unity in the party. His high-minded reputation could be a valuable resource for the party leadership.[11]

The need to contest a by-election with a united party proved paramount in resolving the impasse. The Smethwick Executive telegraphed

Wake seeking advice on how to regularise Mosley's candidature. On 1 December the NEC decided, although not without acrimony, that the problem could be solved if the TLC held a special conference of affiliated organisations that could consider nominations for the vacancy. This decision was taken only by six votes to four. This episode is probably the one noted by the implacably hostile Dalton. 'Shindig on National Executive Committee over Mosley and Smethwick. In the end the peace party wins by one vote, I voting in the minority.' The lengthy special conference held on 4 December included contributions from two Smethwick Aldermen who regretted that no local members had been considered for the nomination. However the dominant sentiment was for unity behind Mosley. The mover of his adoption, a foundation member of the Independent Labour Party in Smethwick, insisted that 'he was against the Labour Party accepting any narrow class distinction. Their opponents would very much like them to restrict it to the working class representative.' F.O. Roberts, speaking as Party Chairman, not as a constituency neighbour, insisted that the contributions of older members were respected but that 'it would be a bad day for Labour when they refused to welcome men and women into its ranks whose views were somewhat ahead of local men'.[12]

The Smethwick campaign became the epitome of the Mosley legend. Mass meetings were fanned by oratory, most notably that of the candidate. MacDonald spoke to a vast open air meeting on a frosty evening. Jim Simmons of the Birmingham ILP recollected how 'it seemed that the whole of the Labour world and his wife were there as supporting speakers, and the greatest aggregation of organising staff I have ever seen was assembled. Mosley's own private "menagerie" moved down from London "en bloc"; his secretaries, private research man (Sutton), a vanload of filing cabinets and press-cuttings.' This carnival was symptomatic of the private enterprise funded by private wealth that so concerned custodians of the rule book. So might another claim made retrospectively by Simmons. 'No one challenged his return of election expenses; I should not like to be the election agent responsible for compiling them, but then Mosley had the staff capable of finding all the loopholes.'[13]

The Conservative press contrasted a fantasised Mosley life style with the reality of life for Smethwick voters. The proletarian credentials of the Conservative candidate M.J. Pike added further combustible material to hyperbolic assertions of grandeur. Mosley's platform act included theatrical references to Cynthia as 'My Missus'. Sensational rumours included a claim that the Soviet mint would strike a medal in Mosley's honour if he won. As in Ladywood there were assertions that the Labour campaign had a dark aspect. Pike complained of 'systematic riots'. More significantly the *Birmingham Post* emphasised the inadequacies of the Conservative campaign – insufficient canvassing, poor stewarding at meeting, and a lack of outside speakers. This mouthpiece of respectable West Midlands Conservatism noted how the excesses of the anti-Mosley press campaign had proved counter-productive. 'They flung against Mr Mosley a torrent of abuse-much of it altogether irrelevant... This produced a reaction in his favour... As it was, he reaped advantage from the extravagance of his opponents.' Nevertheless the *Birmingham Post* drew on a common Conservative theme of the twenties. Labour oratory, usually described as 'socialist', was linked with incitement to disorder. Such outbursts by working-class speakers were perhaps excusable. Mosley however was culpable. 'When a man who has had such opportunities of culture used his invaluable gifts of oratory for no clear purpose than to stir up class against class and cause ill-thinking and bitterness he was doing a very great disservice to the country.' Conservatives through the twenties remained anxious about the spectre of the irrational mob as a legacy of mass electoral democracy and post-war dislocation. Ladywood 1924 and Smethwick 1926 were two intense instances of an extensive neurosis.[14]

Smethwick By-Election 21 December 1926

Turnout			78.6%
O.E. Mosley	Labour	16,077	57.1%
M.J. Pike	Conservative	9,495	33.7%
E. Bayliss	Liberal	2,600	9.2%
		6,582	23.4%

Beyond the hysteria and the high poll, the result, a swing of over 9 per cent from the Conservatives compared with the 1924 election, was typical of Labour by-election performances in the 1926–7 winter. As the coal crisis had dragged on, the Baldwin Government had lost support particularly in working-class districts. This indicated in all probability not so much a strengthening class consciousness as the shortage and rising cost of a basic fuel. Yet as so often with Mosley, mythology mattered most. His victory could be seen as the triumph of a heroic fighter against the forces of darkness. Amongst the party's leaders, doubts remained. When the NEC met the day after the poll, satisfaction at the result was tempered by concern about Mosley's statement that in the light of the selection controversy, 'he had no confidence in the Head

Office and had no intention of working or communicating with them'. This dismissal fed a more thorough concern that Mosley, with his private funds and campaigning appeal to the party membership, was a potentially destabilising loose cannon. The NEC set up a sub-committee 'to review with Mr Mosley in a frank and friendly manner, the whole situation in the Midlands, more particularly as it had arisen in connection with the Smethwick By-Election'.[15]

The sub-committee included at least one member, Dalton, who was hostile to Mosley, but others were more concerned to reach a compromise. As a trade unionist, Dennison was doubtless concerned to protect union interests against well-heeled recruits, but his position as a Birmingham Member complicated his relationship with Mosley. Arthur Henderson, a member of the same trade union as Davison, was concerned that the union had only learned of Davison's resignation from the press. Yet, against this apparent slight, Henderson, as party secretary, was keen to attract a socially broad range of talent to the party. As so often, he was an agent for compromise, seeking a settlement that would maximise unity. MacDonald and Lansbury likewise favoured conciliation, while Roberts had been thoroughly involved in the Smethwick negotiations. Mosley, having re-entered the Commons, was keen to consolidate his position and had no reason to be adversarial. Discussions were harmonious; he produced a memorandum that committed him to make all future contributions through the Party's Head Office. He rejected as 'a fantastic and malicious lie,' the allegation that many Birmingham and other Midlands candidates were on his 'pay roll' and, if successful, would become his 'kept men' in the Commons.[16]

Nevertheless some influential figures were not prepared to abandon their criticisms. While the sub-committee was engaged in its act of reconciliation Morrison was using the ILP's *New Leader* to attack Mosley. He began with a typically Morrisonian disclaimer. Personal feelings were not the issue. His concerns were 'policy and procedure and... the proper rights of the rank and file and of the National Executive'. He itemised the breaches of rule. Behind such constitutional concerns, however, lay the social issue. 'One cannot exclude from consideration a fact which should have made Mr Mosley more careful than he was. Mr Mosley happens to be a well-to-do man, and it was inevitable that such a procedure would involve him and the Party in the suggestion that a Labour constituency could be bought over the heads of the rank and file. The dangers of such a situation and such an atmosphere are not to be solved by Mr Mosley threatening poor men with slanderous actions.' Morrison's conclusion combined self-righteousness and myopia. 'It all goes to show how careful well-to-do people should be in their relations with a Political Party which cannot and will not have its constituencies handled in the way the Liberals and Tories handle the constituencies which they control.'[17]

Dalton characteristically made the point more directly: 'How the fellow stinks of money and insincerity.' The Smethwick embers continued to smoulder and at least for him could readily burst into flames on the NEC. 'Row with Lord Oswald all about nothing, arising out of my remark that it was abominable how some seats were simply auctioned to rich men.'[18] Criticism was not limited to ambitious young rivals. Sidney Webb had predicted Mosley's endorsement as the Smethwick candidate but noted that this approval had been reluctant. He emphasised 'the utmost discontent of the leaders who think he has behaved very badly and who are apparently highly disgusted with him'.[19]

Some Labour activists were not averse to the stink of money. Early in 1926 Wilfrid Whiteley, an ILP member from Huddersfield, became Mosley's Ladywood agent. Mosley paid Whiteley's salary of £350 a year, and bought a house for him. The new agent found the Ladywood finances confusing. Mosley was characteristically buoyant about the debts. 'Please do not worry about the past muddle in Ladywood. It is largely my own fault for being abroad so much during the past 18 months. The only thing now is to pay for the mess and to start again with a clean sheet.' This involved Mosley contributing £1,700 for 1926. This included the house purchase and £288 to cover pre 1926 liabilities. Once Mosley had been elected for Smethwick he started paying £337.10.0 a year for that agent's salary, but the party premises were funded through the Trades and Labour Council. Mosley had promised the Ladywood executive that he would continue his commitment there until the next general election. This amount was agreed as the agent's salary plus £100 a year.

The Ladywood Divsional Labour Party selected Whiteley as its new candidate early in 1927. This choice, in preference to a union sponsored candidate, necessitated a continuation of Mosley's money. The candidate could offer no financial help; he doubled as agent and was himself dependent on Mosley's money for his own income. This situation was likely to generate tension, and by January 1928 Mosley was expressing irritation with Ladywood's financial demands. He cited his post-Smethwick agreement with the NEC in his defence. 'I should like it to be clear at once that I have neither the power nor the inclination to increase my contribution of £450 per annum to the Ladywood Division. I have not the power because I have given an undertaking to the National Executive not to make any fresh expenditure on politics without their permission. I have not the inclination because I think it entirely wrong to spend any more money than I have done, or am doing on this one Constituency, when urgent demands for assistance are coming in daily from all over the country.' He felt that his generosity had damaged the local organisation. 'Like nearly every other local Labour party, Ladywood must make some effort to be self-supporting... I can see no record of money having been raised locally during the last two years – except by the letting of the Assembly Hall for dancing.'

In fact the finances of the Assembly Hall had contributed significantly to the local party's budgetary difficulties. The party had taken a seven-year lease on this former chapel in September 1924; the commitment was indicative of the optimism that had accompanied Mosley's arrival. The annual rent was £140; Mosley was a guarantor of the lease. The investment in the Assembly Hall expressed the expectation that Labour could establish a vibrant social presence in Ladywood. Like many such hopes this one was unfulfilled. The project was always a financial drain and by early 1928 the situation had deteriorated, not least due to a collapse in income from dances. The party vacated the building, leaving Mosley responsible for the rent. A new tenant was soon found and the lease was transferred, but Mosley had already used his liability for the rent as justification for a cut of £100 in his funding of the Ladywood Party.

Acrimony continued until the eve of the 1929 election. Whiteley relayed the grievance of the party activists. 'To us it is just simply a question of expecting that a comrade's word shall be his bond.' Mosley responded by making no promises about funding for the general election. In the event £150 was earmarked for Ladywood within Mosley's donation to the national party, but by then Whiteley had deposited copies of the increasingly acrimonious correspondence with the party's National Agent.[20] Perhaps a crucial factor in this deteriorating situation was the relative weakness of local trade unionism. In many centres, branches of affiliated unions reinforced and funded much of the party organisation. In Birmingham, such trade union resources were limited. Individual benefactors could become more significant but they could be alienated by what could appear as the heightened expectations and passivity of often impoverished party members.

In contrast, Mosley's relationship with the Smethwick organisation seemed harmonious. The cash nexus underpinned the attempted construction of a social order which was not so much a socialist counter-culture, but more a case of Rolleston's hierarchical community adapting to modernity. On a July Saturday in 1928 two special trains left Smethwick on the Great Western route south. 'God's Wonderful Railway' carried these Smethwick Labour activists past affluent Solihull and across the south Warwickshire and Oxfordshire countryside. Leamington Spa, Banbury and Bicester were milestones on a journey to a world far removed from Black Country grime. They alighted at Denham, rural but accessible from London. Their destination was Savehay Farm, Mosley's Buckinghamshire retreat. In all 3,000 were given lunch in the barn and later tea on the lawn. MacDonald arrived from London and insisted, appropriately and perhaps persuasively, in these surroundings that Labour was 'not a miserable petty-fogging small class movement'. Which made the greater impression – MacDonald's oratory or Harrods' 'arrangements' and the catering by Lloyds of Maida Vale – is not recorded.[21]

Amongst the pilgrims to Savehay were 500 from Stoke-on-Trent. By mid-1928 Cynthia Mosley was well established as the Stoke Labour candidate. The Potteries were just a short train journey from the Black Country; both had proved fertile territory for Labour since 1918. Yet the patterns of Labour expansion differed. Black Country Labour, buttressed by a growing trade unionism, had benefited from the relative brittleness of pre-1914 Liberalism and from a subsequent decline in the appeal of Conservatism for the working class. In contrast, Edwardian North Staffordshire had become a Liberal bastion, with potters and miners providing vital support. Even after the Miners' Federation of Great Britain affiliated to the Labour Party in 1909, North Staffordshire miners remained largely unmoved by an independent Labour alternative. When a local miners' official stood on the Labour platform in the 1912 Hanley by-election, most working class electors supported a radical Liberal land reformer.[22] Yet by the late 1920s North Staffordshire was becoming a Labour stronghold. Its parliamentary representatives were not as homogeneously trade unionist as their Black Country counterparts. Some personified locally dominant industries. Successive members for Hanley, Samuel Clowes and Arthur Hollins were officials of the National Society of Pottery Workers; William Bromfield, the Member for Leek was secretary of the local textile workers' organisation. But in Burslem the first Labour Member Samuel Finney, a Miners' official, had been succeeded by Andrew McLaren, a single-tax land reformer and former Liberal. Another land reformer, Josiah Wedgwood, was immovable in Newcastle-under-Lyme, a permanence guaranteed by his family's eminence through all the shifts in his formal political position. A Liberal Member from 1906, he had joined the Labour Party in 1919 and had sat in the 1924 cabinet. Thereafter his individualism often estranged him from party orthodoxy. This coalition offered a Potteries variation on the complexities of Labour under MacDonald; its loyal trade unionists were complemented by sometimes idiosyncratic former Liberals whose enthusiasms were redolent of an earlier radicalism.[23]

The Stoke constituency was an exception. For Labour it became the 'Black spot' of the Potteries. The party did not contest the seat in 1918; in the three subsequent elections it was defeated. The successful candidate, John Ward, was thoroughly proletarian. A navvy at 12, he had helped to form the Navvies' Union in 1889. He had joined the Social Democratic Federation in the 1880s, but his socialist attachment proved brief. Prominent in the National Democratic League, a radical initiative for labour, by the early 1900s his commitment to radical Liberalism was such that, in contrast to most trade union officials with political ambitions, he refused to sign the constitution of the Labour Representation Committee. In 1906 he won Stoke as a Liberal with strong local trade union support. Pre-war his Liberalism was expressed in radical terms, although by 1914 his position as a trade union Member outside the Labour Party was increasingly anomalous. The war brought new alliances. He took the rank of lieutenant colonel in the Middlesex Regiment and raised five labour battalions. He saw service on the Western Front and subsequently with the anti-Bolshevik forces in Siberia. Standing as a Lloyd George Liberal in the 1918 and 1922 elections he increasingly became the candidate of a local Liberal–Conservative alliance whilst insistently proclaiming his labour credentials. He argued that the interests of labour had been corrupted by socialists who manipulated trade unions for their political purposes. In the 1924 election Ward stood as a Constitutionalist, the label employed after nine months of Labour Government by some Liberals who sought to attract Conservative support on an anti-Labour platform. This one-time navvy was backed by the Duke of Sutherland. A prominent Stoke Liberal insisted that Ward was 'the only bulwark between them and the "Red Menace"'.[24]

Ward's position nevertheless rested on weakening foundations. By late 1928 a local Liberal described his party's organisation as defunct, and its Conservative counterpart as limited largely to women and publicans. Ward hoped to secure support from the Lloyd George fund and also from the Conservatives. The underlying issue was his political position. One supporter was pragmatic. 'If the Tories will find all the money without demanding any pledges or compromising in any way your absolute independence and if essentially such financial support could be kept *secret* I would just accept it.' Ward's strongest card was that on his past record he could claim a breadth of support unavailable to any mainstream Conservative and thus offered the most credible defence against a well-funded and highly personal Mosley operation.

When Ward characterised Cynthia Mosley as 'a beautiful society lady with plenty of money' he denied that she was politically serious. Rather, she could be portrayed as essentially frivolous and devoid of ideas, a privileged socialite who had entered politics only at the behest of her husband, a decorative spectator as he pursued his ambitions. One sceptical observer felt that her charm was essential 'to undo the harm which Mosley's brusque manner did to his future'. Yet such condescension missed her essential appeal to Labour voters and activists who responded to her spontaneity and authenticity, a contrast with the theatricality of her husband. Whatever their reasons, Ward's supporters were pessimistic. 'Nothing but a superhuman effort can keep Lady Cynthia from winning Stoke.'[25]

Such pessimism was not complemented necessarily by Labour optimism. Oswald Mosley's Smethwick success was not the overture to a decisive national swing to Labour. The party's by-election record in 1927–8 was mixed. When Labour regained Northampton early in 1928 Mosley reacted cautiously. 'I am not very satisfied at the moment with the way things are going in the country. Northampton was not too good.' He hoped that 'the new programme may make a difference, but that is in the lap of the gods'.[26] Mosley had sought an early return to Westminster in order to influence the political debate. His position as a campaigner was secure but any impact on policy and strategy necessitated influence within the party. The Smethwick controversy had demonstrated some of the obstacles.

4
Networker

Mosley's entry into the Labour Party inescapably posed the issue of his relationship with the trade unions. At every level of the party union influence was significant. Union delegates were central to many divisional parties; they provided much needed organisational resources for campaigning. Sponsored candidates came with funding. Union votes, if not oratory, dominated the party conference and provided a majority of the electorate for every seat on the National Executive Committee. Many of the party's safest seats were held by union-sponsored Members. The trade union presence in the Parliamentary party to which Mosley returned after his Smethwick victory was numerically predominant. Any Labour cabinet necessarily included prominent trade unionists. Arthur Henderson was a consummate reconciler of political differences, a senior, long-serving parliamentarian and party secretary. He also was sensitive to the limits of trade union tolerance, and thus was pivotal in moderating differences between the industrial and political wings of the labour movement.[1]

Such centrality did not mean trade union domination. Effective management of the party necessitated an appreciation of the complex mosaic of interests and identities that had come together under the Labour umbrella. Any claim of a single trade union interest was often misleading. The occupational priorities of individual unions were not always compatible, and the political differences that marked the wider party were often present within and between trade unions. Several unions pre-dated the effective emergence of an independent Labour politics. They had already established industrial and political identities that adjusted only slowly to involvement in Labour politics. This chronology posed a challenge for those socialists who had committed themselves to an alliance with the unions. To upper- and middle-class recruits from other parties, the complexities of union politics constituted a foreign country where they did things differently. Trade unionists could feel overawed by the oratorical and journalistic skills, and social self-confidence, of the incomers. They could react with a visceral anti-intellectualism that allowed for no distinction between the principled and the careerist. In turn, their targets could despair at what they saw as the narrowness and complacency of union officials.

When Mosley entered this labyrinth in 1924 his political record showed minimal involvement in trade union issues. Like several other recruits to Labour, his progressive credentials rested on international questions and, in his case, Ireland. Those Liberals with whom he had worked closely from late 1920 yearned for a progressive politics in which the unions were at most a junior presence. Insofar as Mosley had addressed issues that were of interest to the unions, his attitudes towards public expenditure, subsidies to the mining industry, and Direct Action were unsympathetic. Yet, his early years with Labour were dominated by industrial issues, notably in mining. Unlike several of his parliamentary colleagues he did not take refuge in prudential pieties.

Mosley's consideration of the Forest of Dean candidacy in June 1925 coincided with a crisis in the coal industry. An attempt by the employers to cut wages, especially but not only in the less profitable districts, met with the threat of sympathetic action by the transport unions. Conflict was postponed through the Baldwin Government's granting of a nine-month subsidy, offering an interlude where a commission could investigate the industry and make proposals for its reform and recovery. The Samuel Commission, in membership and findings, reflected the Progressive Liberal agenda of rationalisation humanely administered. The failure of the employers and the Miners' Federation of Great Britain to reach agreement on the Report's proposals meant the posting of heavy wage reductions in several coalfields. From 1 May 1926 coal production stopped; the Trades Union Congress called a General Strike from 4 May.[2] The consequence was in reality not a General Strike but a sympathetic action by some trade unions; it evoked a complex response from Mosley. The opponent of the 'Hands off Russia' movement and of the proposed sympathetic stoppage in similar circumstances in 1921 felt that industrial battles were incompatible with ordered decision making and could not produce effective solutions. Such a conflict promised the antithesis to Mosley's insistence on a Revolution by Reason. His doubts would have been strengthened had he been aware of the lack of any meaningful strategy within the TUC General Council and the lack of rapport between the General Council and the leaders of the MFGB.

Whatever the confusion and anxiety at the top of the trade union movement, the strike in many places was solidly supported and provided an occasion for the flowering of creativity and a dogged resilience in pursuit of a principle. Mosley responded vigorously and sympathetically to this vitality. He was active on the Birmingham strike committee; he spoke regularly and funded a strike bulletin under the editorship of John Strachey. Cynthia Mosley was active in Stoke-on-Trent, speaking daily to large crowds and persuading tramway men, some of whom appeared to be wavering, to stay solid. This victory was crowned by an intervention dramatised by Strachey. 'Outside, an angry crowd, faced by mounted police, with drawn batons was just about to rush a tram which had already started with a blackleg driver. She hurried out from the meeting, and jumping on a lorry, told the crowd that the tramway men were not going back, and appealed to them not to wreck the tram. Thus, what might have been an exceedingly ugly riot was averted and the solidarity of the strike maintained in the Potteries.' Once the General Strike had ended in defeat after nine days Mosley spoke widely across the coalfields through the long months of the miners' lockout. Rhetoric was complemented by cash as Mosley supported fund-raising efforts on behalf of the increasingly desperate miners. Gone were his qualms about the General Strike. The miners were enduring a lone war of attrition that was not of their own choosing. Any credible solution must be political and would necessitate a change of government, but that was for the future.[3]

When the Labour Party conference met at Margate in early October the miners' resistance was crumbling. In the more prosperous Midlands districts a majority had returned to work. There, the dispute had been less a lockout and more a sympathetic strike in support of those faced with devastating wage cuts. A refusal by the rail unions to implement an embargo on coal movements had led a few weeks earlier to a scene at the TUC. The Locomotive Engineers' leader John Bromley had been a bizarre choice to move a resolution in support of the miners, and had been shouted down by some of the MFGB delegation.[4] Predictably, the party conference debate on the coal dispute was a relatively brief affair introduced with deliberately undemonstrative speeches. Despite the stage management, the debate revealed the differences even between a cautious Miners' leader, the Durham official, W.P. Richardson, and Jimmy Thomas, the Railwaymen's leader, who had always been hostile towards any proposal for sympathetic action. Thorough criticism of cautious leadership came from Communist members of trade union delegations; Mosley's contribution was distinctive. He spoke as an ILP

delegate. He emphasised that the solution to the coal industry's problems could only be political; the commitment and passion that he had
seen in the mining communities must be directed to a political target.
The crisis was too acute for the customary calendar of electoral politics:

> Conference should challenge the Government to a General Election,
> and they should use the strength of the Movement, political and
> industrial, in the fight. We should not be passing resolutions and
> looking with confidence to elections two or three years hence. But
> we should realise the vital struggle of the age is upon us here and
> now, and we should sit down to the hard concrete work of devising
> measures for taking part in this struggle and driving this government
> from power.

Their shared emphasis on a political solution notwithstanding, his
speech contrasted with MacDonald's characteristic blend of sentimentality and prudence.[5]

The conference's organisation and overall ethos suggested that, con-
trary to Mosley's clarion call, many Labour politicians saw the coal
dispute not as inspiration and resource, but as a potentially damaging diversion from the serious business of winning the next election.
MacDonald was vehemently critical of what he characterised as the
inflexible and naïve leadership of the Miners' Federation Secretary
A.J. Cook. 'In all my experience of Trade Union leadership... I have
never known one as incompetent as yourself' was his verdict once
the miners had been comprehensively defeated. This condemnation
was shared by several of MacDonald's close colleagues and by some
Miners' officials who hoped for a return to the structured and stable
negotiating culture within which they felt comfortable and valued.
Such criticisms neglected the determination with which employers in
the unprofitable coalfields sought to reduce wages, increase hours and
worsen conditions. The critics misunderstood Cook, an inspirational
orator who spoke for, rather than to, the vast crowds that listened to
him in mining communities. He was acerbically caricatured by Beatrice
Webb as 'an inspired idiot, drunk with his own words, dominated by
his own slogans'. She compared him to a celebrated American revivalist
preacher; he was the miners' 'Billy Sunday'. His oratory was like 'the
gangrenous gas of a badly wounded body'. Wertheimer, as a dutiful
Social Democrat, was equally dismissive, albeit in more measured tones.
'For all the violence of his invective he is a weak man, and he is weak
because he is without consistency of conviction. Intellectually far below

the level of the average miner's agent, he was early fascinated with the half-baked Marxism he picked up at Labour College classes, and mixing the Communist dialectic with that of the Nonconformist evangelical preacher, he became a powerful propagandist. He is a man of words, not deeds.' Cook, vilified by many who were powerful, and idolised by many who were not, articulated the passions that fed the miners' resistance. Mosley admired him for his vivacity and authenticity. Moreover, despite appearances, Cook combined these virtues with a tough practicality. In July 1926 he had attempted in private to negotiate a settlement using Seebohm Rowntree, a conciliatory Liberal, as an intermediary. This blend of passion and pragmatism reflected his syndicalist roots and had affinities with Mosley's own political style.[6]

Mosley's support of the miners was not forgotten in the coalfields during the bleak months that followed the end of the lockout in November 1926, The Durham miners went so far as to formally reject the employers' final terms. Their inevitable return to work meant wage cuts, longer shifts and short-time working. Several pits never reopened. Activists were refused work. In 1927, as they attempted to come to terms with this catastrophe, the Durham Miners' Lodges voted for Mosley to be one of the guest speakers at the Durham Gala. The 'Big Meeting' dated back to the formation of the Durham Miners' Association. For one day in the year Durham City was transformed, or perhaps more accurately, turned upside down. The city's traditional Anglicanism and conservatism expressed in the stonework and accents of cathedral and university gave way to another world. The coalfield came to the city. Miners paraded through the centre. As they passed the County Hotel they were greeted from a first floor balcony by the dignitaries of the labour movement. Down by the River Wear, where all came together, extended families sat down to picnics, children were introduced into the folklore of their coalfield and discovered a litany of heroes and villains. DMA officials and invited speakers spoke from two platforms. In such a setting rhetoric rather than rigour was essential.

Lodge banners presented the diverse inspirations that had shaped the DMA. Religious themes, symbolic depictions of the struggle between labour and capital, local and national labour leaders, all were affirmations of village identity. A handful proclaimed their admiration of the Soviet Union; three banners included images of Lenin, in one case accompanied by Marx and, rather incongruously, MacDonald. The precariousness of the miner's work was evident in those banners that were decked with black crepe; they indicated fatalities at work in the past year. Some banners came from small and old collieries in the Pennine foothills, others the large recent coastal pits where coal was won under the North Sea. Together the identities had come together to make the solidarity that was the DMA and had been expressed in the long months of the lockout. Recollections of the Gala emphasise its vitality, its colourful spectacle, the villagers' day out in a city that was both the home of an unsympathetic clerical establishment often critical of the miners, and the site of the DMA headquarters. These portraits typically stress the decency, the rule-governed character of this invasion. Such images present partial truths. The respectable outing cohabited with a ribald sometimes bawdy and hedonistic culture. Durham's bars had a profitable day; many never made it to the speeches. The life-affirming rituals of the Gala could not disguise a sombre reality. In the 1920s the coalfield experienced a decline that would prove to be permanent. The crisis could be charted in the Gala's cancellations in 1921 because of the lockout, the following year because of the depressed conditions following the miners' defeat, and again in 1926. In the most recent case this might have reflected anxiety about public order. A well-attended unofficial meeting at Burnhope found Cook attacking the Durham coal owners and the Dean of Durham, J.E.C. Welldon. Mosley would claim later that his experience of the Gala would inform his appreciation of the significance of colourful spectacle for political movements. The procession of banners past the County Hotel to the uninformed might suggest British Union of Fascists parades and mass rallies, but any superficial similarity masked a profound difference. The Gala was not a regimented top-down mobilisation, but a coming together of communities with diverse histories. Participants expressed solidarity as DMA members but the Lodges enjoyed considerable autonomy. Vitality came from the villages; this meant a solidarity that permitted differences within a generally accepted code of behaviour.[7]

The harsh post-lockout conditions meant that in 1927 this solidarity was under pressure. The DMA leadership were concerned about the threat of breakaway non-political trade unionism in emulation of the Spencer Union's success in Nottinghamshire. They also faced a threat from the left. As the miners' resistance had fragmented, relationships between DMA officials and the Communist-influenced Miners' Minority Movement had deteriorated. Officials attacked MMM activists for an intransigence that they deemed futile and divisive. The MMM alleged a lack of backbone on the part of many officials. The Minority Movement had secured some footholds in Durham and hoped that in post-lockout conditions they could expand. The DMA leadership fought back, branding both the MMM and the non-political movement as equally disruptive of a necessary solidarity.[8]

The effectiveness of the officials' response demonstrated how firmly the DMA was embedded in coalfield society. The union was at the heart of a patronage network which dominated local government and controlled several Divisional Labour Parties. One consequence was the phalanx of DMA sponsored Members at Westminster. Undeniably, the domination of communities by a partnership of DMA lodge and local Labour party afforded advancement for a few. Crucially, it offered a degree of material protection to the many, the achievement of some decency within the uncertainties, deprivations and indignities of coalfield capitalism. Yet the DMA leadership that greeted Mosley in August 1927 faced an uncertain future; for James Robson, Peter Lee and W.P. Richardson, all with many years' service in the union, a rule-governed and predictable world had been lost.

The most tragic figure that August afternoon was A J Cook. Worn out by his exertions through the lockout, defeat had brought intensified criticism, not only from Labour politicians from MacDonald downwards, but also from within the MFGB. The Federation's right now felt free to express disagreements with him that previously had been hidden under the rhetoric of a necessary solidarity. Increasingly, the criticism of MFGB policy by the Miners' Minority Movement attenuated his links with a Left that was increasingly vulnerable to the vagaries of Comintern policy. Cook at Durham was unapologetic. He insisted that he would not take responsibility for a situation that he did not create. Durham would face a choice when the existing wage agreement ended. His advice was unequivocal. 'I make a call for Durham not for patience but I am going to organise revolt.' Revolt however required organisation; the DMA was much weaker in membership and finances than before the lockout. Elsewhere, the decline in membership and sometimes the rise of breakaway unions made a collective response unlikely. Cook was a would-be radical in a world where radical hopes seemed to have died.

Mosley offered a different response to the coalfield's miseries. Flower in lapel, 'a striking and imposing figure, a voice like a bell,' he praised the Durham miners, 'the shock troops of the labour movement'. They and their wives 'have still as fine hearts and as fine spirits as when the fight began last year'. The crucial lesson was that industrial action offered no solution. 'The struggle of 1926 was the first round. The last round will come at the general election.' His strategy was a hyperbolic variant on that enunciated by MacDonald. Thus Mosley indicted the Baldwin Government. 'They won their power by fraud and forgery and are using that power to establish slavery in the free land of Britain.' No doubt the audience also enjoyed another guest, Jack Jones, an established Commons turn, with his swipe at 'cantankerous canons, dismal deans and bilious bishops'.[9]

Whether such rhetoric offered the audience more than passing entertainment is doubtful. Some were impatient, not with the guest speakers whose task was perhaps to enthuse not least with humour, but with the fatalism of the DMA officials:

> On Gala day we trudged to Durham with bands and banners. We looked for something new and relevant to the coming crisis. Not a word! Instead the General Secretary and President recited to us all the reforms granted during the last fifty years, and the 6s 8d men got impatient and shouted for Cook, because they felt Durham leaders had no message for men getting thirty shillings a week as wages.

When the Durham employers applied for wage reductions early in 1928, the arbitrator compromised with smaller reductions than those demanded. The Minority Movement inspired local stoppages but the DMA Council, representing every lodge, rejected calls for a strike ballot. Radicalism had been contained. Mosley in all probability would have been perturbed had he known of MacDonald's pessimistic response to the lament of a Durham official. 'Things seem to get worse and worse and what the way out is going to be goodness only knows.'[10]

Whatever the stylistic disparity between Mosley and the more cautious Miners' officials, his reputation in the coalfields meant that he enjoyed MFGB support in the election to the Party NEC at the 1927 conference. Placed fourth out of five successful candidates, he repeated the success the following year. His defeat in the 1929 NEC election would be attributable to the halving of the Miners' affiliation to 400,000. This support was significant in securing Mosley's entry into a significant position during an important pre-election period. His friendship with Cook, however, proved of diminishing value. Cook's position within the Miners' Federation weakened as left–right factionalism became increasingly polarised around a Communist–anti-Communist dichotomy. He was vilified by former allies as they articulated the sectarianism and unreality of the Comintern's 'Class against Class' line; he was never close to the coterie of respectable officials with their networks in the District organisations. Within the wider trade union world his influence had always been limited. Recriminations over the termination of the General Strike and the subsequent self-conscious 'realism' of a majority of the General Council marginalised him further. His opposition to the Mond–Turner talks on industrial co-operation underscored his isolation. He could offer Mosley no access to the wider trade union leadership.[11]

Most leading trade union figures were at best distant from, and sometimes hostile to, those categorised as outsiders. Some upper- and middle-class recruits idealised the 'common sense' of trade unionists. These included Clem Attlee; his thorough commitment to the party, and his respect for its conventions facilitated a viable if distant understanding with trade unionists that was informed by his years in London's East End. Mosley lacked such experiences. The fondly remembered Rolleston hierarchy offered no equivalent to social work and residence in Limehouse. Mosley appears to have had little contact with senior trade union figures other than Cook. Henderson and J.R. Clynes, characterised by Wertheimer as 'safe homely men', seem to have been tolerant if distant from the glossy recruits to Labour.[12] For Mosley, however, perhaps the most significant lack was any rapport with Ernest Bevin.

The architect of the Transport and General Workers' Union was, in the mid twenties, still a relative outsider within the TUC. His early life in rural Devon had been insecure and impoverished; his formal education had been limited. A Bristol carter, he had joined a trade union only in 1910 at the age of 29. Little more than a decade later he was architect and head of the TGWU. The debacle of 1926 made and damaged trade union leaders' reputations. Whether merited or not Bevin was a beneficiary. As an aggressive realist, he supported the Mond–Turner talks; the unions were too weak to challenge the existing order and socialism, lacking sufficient support, was not a credible prospect. Rather, employers and trade union leaders should construct an agenda for modernisation which could benefit from state help. His commendation of the strategy commended a 'scientific' approach, a characterisation that Mosley typically applied to his own proposals. Both men had opposed the return to the Gold Standard in 1925. Bevin predicted wage cuts, declining demand and rising unemployment. He and Mosley agreed that the bankers had too much power. There seemed scope for collaboration.

Whatever the affinities, Bevin had minimal tolerance for those he dismissed as intellectuals. 'The difference between the intellectuals and the Trade Unions is this: you have no responsibility, you can fly off at a tangent as the wind takes you.' Mosley, in background, style and substance readily qualified. Bevin was dismissive of the ILP's Living Wage proposals in 1926. This agenda proposed that politicians intervene within the unions' core activity, wage bargaining. Mosley was not involved in its production but could be dismissed as close to those who were. Bevin's antipathy towards intellectuals was such that in retrospect he could misrepresent a past controversy, whether accidentally or deliberately. After 1931 all those named could be damned as renegades. 'I particularly asked that we turn our back on the Gold Standard Theory of Snowden and recognise the price we were paying for orthodox finance. You will find I was not listened to, the intellectuals like MacDonald, Mosley I believe and others held sway.'[13]

Mosley's distance from most trade union leaders contrasted with his initial association with the Independent Labour Party. He spoke at the party's 1924 conference and wrote for its newspaper, the widely acclaimed *New Leader*. As the Ladywood candidate he committed himself to the ILP, describing the party as Labour's 'advanced wing'. For two years, 1927–9, he was a member of the ILP's National Administrative Council, the party's executive.[14] Yet the ILP had severe limitations as a political base for Mosley. These constraints were rooted in the ILP's distinctive position within the broader Labour Party and became more acute from the mid twenties. Within the pre 1918 Labour Party the ILP had been the principal organisation through which individuals qualified for membership of the Labour Party. It attracted those whose occupation or lack of one made membership by trade union affiliation impossible; more significantly it was the home of committed socialists, often also trade unionists, who saw the ILP as the socialist inspiration within the Labour alliance. The pre-war ILP had been shaken by conflicts over the limitations of such an alliance with unions who showed little interest in socialism and over the formally unacknowledged, but obvious, electoral understanding with the Liberals. Despite these controversies, these earlier years were fondly remembered by many in the twenties as a golden age of socialist propaganda. This partial and usable history was employed, not least by MacDonald and Snowden, to eulogise an imagined past in order to indict an allegedly less high-minded present. The intended moral was that the ILP should concentrate on 'making' socialists rather than advocating policies which could be controversial.

A further layer of myth was provided by characterisations of the wartime ILP. The perilous advocacy of internationalism before patriotic crowds, opposition to military conscription, the gaoling of party members who refused military service – all provided material for memories of a heroic age when the party could claim its martyrs in the cause of international socialism. But many party members, not least MacDonald, were not anti-war, whatever the fevered claims of the jingo press. They had opposed British entry into the European conflict; once they had failed to prevent this, they concentrated on defending liberal decencies against their invasion by a predatory wartime state. They campaigned with disenchanted Liberals through the Union of Democratic Control, demanding that foreign policy must never again be the preserve of traditional elites. They opposed press censorship and highlighted the erosion of civil liberties, not least under military discipline. In 1918 this record proved electorally disastrous, but as disenchantment with the Versailles settlement grew and cynicism spread about the post war treatment of returned soldiers, the ILP's ethical socialism enjoyed a revival. Party members celebrated in 1921 when the Caerphilly by-election returned Morgan Jones as the first conscientious objector to enter the Commons. The 1924 Government was headed by a man who doubled as Foreign Secretary and who personified the ILP's wartime record.

This rich inheritance of experience and myth was central to the culture of the ILP. In contrast Mosley's formative years had been in France, and then in London as an ex-combatant whose early discharge had possibly saved his life. His forceful championing of the war generation put him potentially at odds with the ILP's ethos and myths. However some shifts within the post-war ILP seemed more promising from Mosley's vantage point. The 1918 Labour Party constitution challenged both the ILP's position and its purpose. The party forfeited its guaranteed representation on Labour's National Executive; its status became that of a small contestant for a seat in an Affiliated Societies section dominated by the trade unions. More fundamentally the new constitution's provision for Divisional Labour Parties that included individual membership sections ended the ILP's near monopoly of individual access to the Labour Party. The inclusion within the constitution of a socialist objective could suggest that a basic mission of the ILP, the conversion of the Labour Party to socialism, had been achieved.

Although these changes threatened that the ILP could become redundant, the party was not immediately damaged. The new Divisional Labour Parties often grew slowly; in some localities, most notably Scotland, the ILP remained organisationally powerful and often dominated local Labour politics. Within the NEC, the ILP benefited from trade union acquiescence in an arrangement where significant affiliates were usually guaranteed a seat. Many prominent Labour figures carried ILP cards and, whenever appropriate, emphasised the attachment.

When MacDonald was elected PLP Chair, and, in effect, Labour's first leader, in November 1922, the ILP network within the expanded post-election Parliamentary Party was crucial to his narrow victory. Despite this vitality some ILP members recognised a basic vulnerability. They responded by attempting to carve out a new and distinctive role for the party. This agenda involved much more than a prudential response to constitutional changes. The war had radically reshaped Europe – the collapse of empires, democratisation, and, with qualifications, self-determination, the survival of the Soviet Union as an inspiration for would-be revolutionaries and the exploited. Given such dramatic changes these ILP members believed that a reassessment of socialist strategy for Britain seemed imperative. Established socialist principles remained relevant, but their dutiful repetition was insufficient. The ILP could be envisaged as a socialist think tank for the wider labour movement. This modernising agenda had affinities with Mosley's priorities.[15]

The principal ILP moderniser, Clifford Allen, at first sight personified an ILP that was remote from Mosley's experiences. An Edwardian Cambridge Fabian, Allen had been involved with Labour's short lived and self-consciously respectable newspaper, the *Daily Citizen*. His absolutist stand against conscription, consequential imprisonment and permanent damage to his health guaranteed iconic status within the ILP. This hard-earned eminence co-habited with an enthusiasm for planning and scientific organisation. A steel-like purpose, Machiavellian deviousness and sensitivity over abrasive exchanges could precipitate difficult political relationships. His enthusiasm for the ILP as a potential modernising instrument was accompanied by scorn for the emotional rhetoric that marked its culture and contempt for the alleged intellectual limitations of several prominent ILP personalities. As party Treasurer he was an impressive fund-raiser, demonstrating an ability to charm well-heeled progressives. Consequentially, ILP organisation flourished; under H.N. Brailsford's editorship the *New Leader* attracted talented contributors from beyond the ILP circle. Summer Schools were established; study groups were formed to develop socialist policies on specific themes.[16]

When Mosley entered the Labour Party Allen was at the peak of his influence. He was ILP Chairman; his address to delegates at the 1924 conference focused on the challenge posed to socialists by the arrival of a minority Labour Government. Allen acknowledged the constraints facing a minority administration, but insisted that a more radical approach was feasible. Any effective socialist advance necessitated careful preparatory research, for example a thorough investigation of British industry. Detailed studies could lead in Allen's view to a credible and creative radicalism; what he characterised as 'a new form of extreme policy in contrast with catastrophic revolution'. The prescription could have been characterised as a 'revolution by reason'. Mosley responded sympathetically to Allen's soliciting of funds, but emphasised that his priority was Birmingham. 'It is impossible to see much of the appalling suffering in this community and the harsh tyranny of the Conservative machine without becoming a little parochial in one's views and wishing to devote every resource to the struggle immediately at hand.'[17]

The opening of Mosley's autumn 1924 campaign in Birmingham Town Hall offered a more emotional venue than an ILP Summer School for the gestation of a credible and radical programme. The venue inspired a parallel not with any socialist exemplar but with the 1880s radicalism of Joseph Chamberlain and its encapsulation in the Unauthorised Programme for the 1885 election.

> He would like to see the Birmingham Labour movement developing a programme of its own. Birmingham had heard of 'unauthorised' programmes before. Why not start another? He wanted to see Birmingham selecting what it regarded as the most essential things in Labour's programme, concentrating on them, and sending a 'ginger group' of Labour MPs to Parliament to help get them placed on the Statute Book.[18]

Eventually Mosley's ideas were published in an ILP pamphlet *Revolution By Reason*, based on his presentation to the ILP Summer School in August 1925. The basic work had been completed by March, and was the result of collaboration between Mosley and John Strachey. Who contributed what is obscure; Strachey clearly saw Mosley as the politically vital figure. When he later published his own longer version under the same title he would dedicate his book – 'To O M who may one day do the things of which we dream'.[19] A second apostle had also emerged. Allan Young had grown up on Clydeside. After war service he had become a Labour Party organiser and had been party agent for the Wrekin constituency when Labour gained the seat in 1923; he arrived in Birmingham at the same time as Mosley as assistant organiser and agent for the Borough Labour Party. His organisational talents were complemented by intellectual interests; he was an ILP member who took Allen's vision seriously. Intellectual ambition cohabited with distaste for quotidian politics. 'There is such a vast untapped field in Political research. Politics is a hell of a life anyway, ungracious, ugly, dull'.[20] A dedicated researcher and enthusiast for the rational reorganisation of a chaotic capitalism, he would become Mosley's full- time political secretary in 1927.

A retrospective assessment across subsequent political differences acknowledged Young's achievement. 'He had the necessary tact to deal with the varying circumstances in the twelve divisions, a pleasant personality that got over many difficulties and altogether he was the man for the job... He laid the foundation of political organisation in the borough.' Yet this observer felt that Young had aspirations that jarred with the 'hard grinding work' integral to his post. 'He was for ever building up schemes of organisation that were splendid if only they could have been carried through! The lack of finance was a continued source of annoyance to him.' Young's frustrations, for this observer, were responsible for his resignation and subsequent employment by Mosley. Yet this account perhaps fails to give proper weight to Young's intellectual interests and his sense of an affinity with Mosley.[21]

The core of *Revolution By Reason* addressed the connected issues of post-war depression and working class poverty, not through the ILP emphasis on redistribution from rich to poor, but on radical reform of the banking system. The banks should be socialised, not just as an element in the transition to socialism, but in order to alleviate workers' conditions during that transition. Within a socialist framework, therefore, the proposals could be seen as a contribution to a strategic challenge; a peaceful transition necessitated decisive and beneficial action. A socialised banking system would selectively expand consumer credits to the poor. These would be 'a special expedient in a time of industrial stagnation and collapse to stimulate effective demand in the right quarter and to re-start the dormant mechanism of production'. This 'special expedient' would be supplemented initially by producer credits paid by the state to industry.

Critically, Mosley presented thorough economic planning as essential for the strategy's effectiveness. An Economic Council would have statutory powers to plan production, wages and prices. Redistributive taxation would have a secondary place; the crucial proposition was that once credits had revitalised the economy, the bulk of improvement in working-class standards would come from economic growth. 'Prosperous industry, producing to full capacity, must then shoulder its own wage bill, without further assistance for this purpose from State credit.' Having begun by locating his proposals within debates about the transition to socialism, Mosley seemingly envisaged a solution to poverty and stagnation composed of publicly owned banks, state planning and private industry. The crucial division lay not between capitalist and worker, but between finance and the productive classes, the parasitic and the useful. The compatibility of this agenda with socialism depended on definition. For Mosley socialism seemed not to be about the redistribution of power, or greater economic equality. Rather it was 'the conscious control and direction of human resources for human needs'. From this standpoint Labour's financial 'experts' were mistaken in their endorsement of the return to the Gold Standard:

> How can we afford to place the supreme instrument of exchange and purchasing power at the mercy of these blind hazards of fortune? Is the employment of the British worker to be dependent upon a nigger digging up a lump of glittering metal in far-away Africa, or upon the gold jugglery of foreign statesmen and international financiers? Surely a gold-standard Socialist is a contradiction in terms!

The casual racism, including the suggestion of rootless cosmopolitan financiers, was commonplace. More fundamental was the relationship between Mosley's presentation of socialism in terms of science and rationality and the underlying national focus of the argument. The old parties were politically bankrupt. Their 'small minds and small policies' were irrelevant. Rather, national salvation could only be achieved 'in the safe hands of the workers of our land'.[22]

Mosley was ready to present his basic ideas to the ILP conference in April 1925, but the difficulties with the conception of the ILP as a socialist think tank were becoming apparent. Its credibility depended on a consensus within the party not just over specific proposals but over the priority to be given to this exercise. Moreover, its effectiveness necessitated that relationships between significant ILP figures and the wider Labour leadership remained mutually sympathetic. Criticism of the Labour Government during its later months from within the ILP, and the evident dissatisfaction, not least over MacDonald's leadership that followed electoral defeat, had demonstrated the brittleness of any such expectation of harmony. MacDonald had become increasingly dismissive of ILP critics who had claimed that the Government was too cautious. The most outspoken critics had been attacked in turn by ILP members loyal to the Government, and particularly to MacDonald. The disagreements continued through the 1924–5 winter and were expressed with some acerbity at the 1925 ILP conference. With the increasing division of delegates into loyalists and critics Allen's project for a thoroughly researched socialist strategy ran the risk of marginalisation. Mosley's intervention on his central concern, the control and scientific use of the credit system, was precisely that. His speech was followed, not by a debate, but by the moving of the Previous Question.[23]

Mosley subsequently won approval for his proposals from the Birmingham Borough Labour Party. Considerable attention was given to the proposed banking reform as central to any meaningful socialist strategy.

> The success of the Socialist attack is dependent on the early Socialisation of the Banks and the use of the national credit resources, not for the benefit of the few, but for the benefit of the nation; and that during the period of transition to the Socialist Commonwealth, the credit of the nation should be used to break the vicious circle of poverty and unemployment by securing a minimum wage for the workers.

Mosley justified the policy as both expediting progress towards socialism and offering a rapid alleviation of workers' conditions. The brief experience of office had provided a salutary lesson:

> Most of the Socialist doctrine was written in the days before the Labour Party had any experience of the working of the Parliamentary machine. The Party had learnt from its experience in office that it was difficult to force great Labour principles through Parliament quickly and that even with a majority it would not be possible to get more than two or three big things through in one Parliament.

This self-consciously tough realism about the constraints on reform through existing institutions was balanced by an optimistic claim for Mosley's priority. 'The socialisation of banking and the use of the nation's credit in order to raise the whole standard of the workers would make it impossible for Capitalism to retrieve its position.'

The Birmingham Party adopted Mosley's proposals by 65 votes to 14; the minority came from contrasting viewpoints. Some argued that the proposals were 'tinkering'; others that they would mean radical change that was inconceivable without a dictatorship. How far the vote indicated serious support for the policy as opposed to backing for Mosley is unclear. Perhaps many activists remained uncertain about the substance of the programme. In September 1926, one Birmingham ILP Branch wanted to discuss 'the Mosley–Strachey credit scheme'. They requested an informed speaker. 'At present our opinions are rather hazy.'[24] The parallels between Allen's and Mosley's strategies were evident when each presented his case to the ILP's 1925 Summer School. Yet, as the Birmingham experience suggested, such detailed agendas struck only a limited response within a party where many saw their objective as the making of socialists in accordance with familiar precepts. This ethos and the deepening factionalism combined to threaten the viability of the ILP as a socialist think tank.

The increasing dominance within the ILP of critics of MacDonald's leadership meant the marginalisation of Clifford Allen. His distaste for the critics reflected his sympathy for MacDonald and also his belief that such antagonisms threatened the destruction of his modernising agenda. He quit the chairmanship following a row within the ILP delegation at the Labour Party's Liverpool conference in September 1925. His successor from April 1926 was James Maxton. Under his chairmanship the party would shift gradually to the left and would become increasingly the focus of opposition to MacDonald. Brailsford would resign from his outstanding editorship of the *New Leader,* financial backing from those whom Allen had courted would decline, party organisation would become less elaborate. Opponents of the increasingly adversarial style would either lapse into inactivity or increasingly quit the party. The ILP would become less credible as a political base for Mosley.[25]

Ironically, Allen's marginalisation coincided with the most significant achievement of his strategy of new, well researched and relevant policies. The 1925 ILP conference had authorised a commission to develop a programme for the abolition of poverty within the context of progress towards socialism. J.A. Hobson, the radical economist, was in the chair, Brailsford was secretary. They were joined by Frank Wise a former civil servant and subsequently Member for East Leicester, and by Arthur Creech Jones, an official of the Transport and General Workers' Union. The commission's discussions rapidly produced publications. An interim report, *Socialism in Our Time,* appeared early in 1926. The definitive document, *The Living Wage,* followed later in the year.

Its argument was based on Hobson's under-consumption thesis – that economic depression resulted in significant part from economic inequality, and could be addressed by a policy of redistribution, thereby shifting resources from those with a relatively high propensity to save to those with every reason to spend. Proposed measures included a combination of government and trade union initiatives. The former included public ownership, taxation and a system of family allowances. Mosley and John Strachey suggested that *The Living Wage* marginalised the role of credit policy. The criticism was exaggerated. The document did address the issue, and Brailsford's journalism regularly insisted on the need for the 'scientific management' of credit. Whereas Mosley claimed the centrality of credit policy to working-class wellbeing and industrial modernisation, *The Living Wage* emphasised redistribution as the more significant element.

Such differences did not determine the fate of *The Living Wage*. The programme became entangled in the deepening antagonism between MacDonald and the ILP left. The leader's rapid condemnation reflected dislike of its advocates and their associates rather than a reasoned assessment of the proposals. Such animosity predictably produced abrasive responses. The controversy connected with disputes around the defeat of the General Strike and the leadership of the Miners' Federation. *The Living Wage* became increasingly presented under the title 'Socialism in Our Time', itself widely understood as the shorthand for an as-yet-undeveloped alternative politics that symbolised hostility to MacDonald's cautious leadership. The ILP offered diminishing space for the development of policies that might provide a credible strategy for the wider labour movement. The wider reception of *The Living Wage,* despite initial ILP attempts to be accommodating, suggested that such initiatives would gain little support, particularly from the trade unions. Most union officials, especially after the disasters of 1926, were committed above all to the return of a Labour Government. Some had to suppress their doubts about MacDonald's leadership. Almost all could agree that the ILP was an increasingly divisive force and must be prevented from harming Labour's electoral prospects.

Despite deepening hostility towards the ILP left, the party as yet offered a political space that Mosley could find attractive. His relationships with prominent party figures illuminated the diverse experiences that shaped the party's ethos. Jim Simmons, a leading figure in the Birmingham ILP, worked closely with Mosley in the mid and late twenties. He had been born into a Gladstonian Liberal family in 1893, by then very much a minority politics within the city. Nurtured on Liberalism he had shifted into the pre-war ILP. His political style was at one with the radical Nonconformity to which he was devoted. He was also influenced by the *Clarion* socialism of Robert Blatchford, whose own evocations of 'Merrie England' and socialist comradeship were coloured by his earlier army experience. Simmons joined the Territorials and, following the outbreak of war served at Gallipoli and on the Western Front. He lost a foot at Vimy Ridge.

Although, like Mosley, he was self-consciously of the war generation, his political response was very different. Whilst still in uniform, he began speaking on ILP platforms as 'Private Simmons' arguing for a negotiated peace. Arrested and discharged, he was subsequently arrested for a second time and gaoled under the Defence of the Realm Act for a speech that criticised the severity of field punishments. From 1918 he became involved in struggles over the political organisation and allegiance of returned soldiers. He became a vigorous, if intermittent, presence on the Birmingham City Council and an ILP propagandist, with a growing reputation as 'Ex-Private Simmons'. Nevertheless war service offered a shared experience which Mosley and Simmons were ready to exploit on the political platform. At an ILP meeting following the abrasive Ladywood campaign Simmons responded to their opponents' claim to possess a monopoly of patriotism: 'What right had these people, most of whom had never faced a German on the battle field to use a flag which was not a party flag but the flag of the country? If anyone had a right to use the Union Jack it was the ILP candidates... all of whom had seen service in the Great War.'[26]

Despite Simmons's retrospective reservations about Mosley's melodramatic platform style they seem to have worked together effectively within Birmingham in the late twenties. They vigorously attacked established authority: Mosley's anti Chamberlain fusillades were matched by Simmons's scenes within the city council. The 'Ex-Private' would defeat a cabinet minister, Sir Arthur Steel-Maitland, at the1929 election with the help of Mosley's money. Yet such sympathies had decisive limits. Mosley's response to the ILP's deepening factionalism was to try to avoid taking sides; Simmons's conception of the ILP was as a vehicle for socialist propaganda. Policymaking was at best a lesser concern. This was the task of the Labour Party to which Simmons had a thorough loyalty that would ultimately determine his relationships with the ILP and with Mosley. His politics were informed by a religious sensibility far removed from Mosley's outlook. Whilst Mosley was lampooning the Chamberlain tradition during the Ladywood election, Simmons was speaking at the Nechells Wesleyan Church. His topic was 'Christ's Kingdom and the Doing of His Will upon Earth'. He concluded with an appeal for internationalism and peace. A political alliance between Simmons and Mosley might have been viable in the short term, but Simmons's orthodoxy in ILP terms and his loyalty to the Labour Party imposed firm limits.[27]

John Wheatley was a much more prominent ILP figure; he was also in ILP terms much less conventional. Forty years later, Mosley would remember him fondly as 'the only man of Lenin-like quality that the English left has ever produced'.[28] Whatever Wheatley's Leninist propensities might have been, he was definitely not English. Born in Bonmahon County Waterford, his family had moved to the west of Scotland in 1876. Leaving school aged 11 he had joined his father down a Lanarkshire pit. Seemingly destined for a life within the diasporic Irish working class, shaped by poverty, insecurity and prejudice, he became part-owner of a grocery store and eventually owner of a profitable printing business. This individual social mobility meant a house in a middle-class Glasgow suburb and a reputation for smart clothes. For this self-educated former miner and devout Catholic it never meant political conservatism. Wheatley shifted from Irish nationalist politics to the ILP. His ethnic and religious identities led him to play a major role in the formation of a Catholic Socialist Society. The burdens of the past generations mattered. The exits from Manchester and County Waterford could both be debited to classical liberalism. Like Mosley, and unlike Simmons, Wheatley had little reason to genuflect before this orthodoxy.

Whilst Wheatley's emergence as a prominent figure within the Glasgow labour movement was based primarily on his municipal activities, he had links with the radical industrial movements that had made some Coalition Ministers fear that Glasgow had the potential to be another Petrograd. Elected for the East End seat of Shettleston in 1922, his politics combined pragmatism and assertive radicalism. As Minister of Housing and Health he was a notable success within the 1924 Government. Whereas many of his colleagues were content to continue inherited policies and to use the excuse of intractable parliamentary arithmetic, Wheatley's Housing Act showed an ability to act effectively within this constraint. He expressed through his actions Clifford Allen's plea for audacity in office. Once more in opposition, he moved further to the left, at least in part as a response to what he saw as the Labour Party and TUC leaderships' betrayal of the miners in 1926.

Mosley was attracted by Wheatley's pragmatism and toughness, and by his interest in policy. Although Wheatley welcomed the Birmingham proposals, he endorsed the ILP emphasis on redistribution rather than credit policy. His concern with economic policy and industrial reorganisation meant that he trespassed into the sensitive territory of Free Trade. In this critical area, at least in public, Wheatley anticipated Mosley. By 1926 he was envisaging a global system increasingly dominated by rival trading blocs. In this context Protection should not be dismissed as heretical. Trade unions were in practice protectionist, even when their rhetoric suggested otherwise. Concern for jobs and living standards pointed inexorably to the exclusion of imports produced by sweated labour or facilitated by the subsidisation of export industries.

Such suggestions provoked conventional ILP members to dismiss 'the Wheatley school of national socialism'. One critic, Fenner Brockway, a rising figure on the ILP left, deprecated 'a reaction from international idealism to concrete schemes for social betterment in this country'. This preference pinpointed what would prove an unbridgeable divide between Mosley and many within the ILP. Yet the deprecation indicated that a leading member of the ILP did not share the 'international idealism' that was widely viewed as integral to the ILP's identity.[29]

The ILP could still seem a viable political resource for Mosley, and he decided to seek election to its National Administrative Council in 1927. Two paths were available: he could seek election to one of the four national seats – the poll was held at the annual conference; alternatively, he could secure one of the divisional places – in his case this would be the midlands seat. Early in 1927 he was considering both options. He eventually went for a national seat and was successful. Mosley had been keen that the sitting, and in his view inadequate, Midlands member, Fred Longden, be removed. This task fell to Frank Wise who was able, as a prospective parliamentary candidate, to draw on the sizeable Leicester vote. As yet the NAC membership contained diverse viewpoints. The Left were not yet thoroughly dominant; Emmanuel Shinwell, for example, was a strong supporter of MacDonald. The election of Wise meant a strengthening of those who took policy seriously. A Cambridge-educated meritocrat and an ex-civil servant, he had been one of those responsible for *The Living Wage*. Despite such developments Allan Young's assessment of the subsequent ILP conference in April1928 was bleak. 'One thing is quite clear-we will never get anything as the result of the courage of our leadership. Because those who have courage have no brains and those who have brains have no courage.' He responded ironically to his own pessimism. 'The only thing that puzzles me about the Conference is why they had sufficient intelligence to elect Tom to the NAC. There is still hope in the rank and file'.[30]

James Maxton, the chairman, increasingly personified the ILP's politics. Widely liked, insisting on socialist rectitude, largely uninterested in the minutiae of policy, his political style and initiatives increasingly alienated those within the ILP who hoped for a more inclusive party. In July 1928 the Cook–Maxton Manifesto Campaign embarked on a series of meetings. Their centrepiece was a pamphlet, *Our Case for a Socialist Revival*. The initiative was an attempt by the marginalised to regain influence in a labour movement that was increasingly hostile to their politics. Maxton had planned and initiated the campaign without informing the party. The result was a row on the NAC, where positions in part reflected political differences and in part concern over procedural propriety. Significantly, Mosley took a conciliatory position: 'He wondered what all the fuss was about... It required all types and personalities to make a great Movement, and the duty of leadership was to blend them... MacDonald made an appeal to one section of the community with incomparable skill, and Maxton and Cook appealed to the working class as no one else could.' As yet, he still hoped to avoid a destructive polarisation. Similarly, an attempt by pro-MacDonald ILP parliamentarians to rescue the party from the Left failed comprehensively in December 1928. Many MPs felt bemused or exasperated by what they saw as a destructive and intolerant quarrel. Once again, Mosley's was a conciliatory voice.[31]

At Easter 1929 the ILP conference demonstrated the strength of MacDonald's critics. Mosley was defeated in the NAC election by Fenner Brockway, a thorough advocate of the ILP's shift to the left. The defeat was not a serious setback for Mosley. He no longer saw the ILP as a significant political base within the Labour Party, a judgement shared by many colleagues.[32] His assessment not only indicated his dislike for the ILP's leftward shift; his priority was to strengthen his position both within the Parliamentary Party and on the National Executive Committee. This mattered both in terms of his standing within the party and in the preparation of policy for a future Labour Government.

Once Mosley had returned to the Commons early in 1927 he spoke regularly on a wide range of issues before falling ill. He again became a contributor through much of 1928. Already his speeches began to chart a distinctive course on economic issues. In the debate on Winston Churchill's 1927 budget he expressed scepticism about the 1925 return to the Gold Standard. 'Every producer by hand or brain was penalised, not only the workers, but also the productive capitalists, in order to benefit one economically useless section of the community, the rentier class.' In November 1928 he distanced himself from the orthodox response to decline in the staple industries:

> Do not let us make a fetish of the export trade. Do not let us think it is the sole criterion of British prosperity. It is to the home market therefore, and to the raising of wages and purchasing power that we must increasingly look, and we must of course anticipate some transfer of production from the export to the home trade.[33]

Commons speeches, no matter how polished and informed, offered no basis for election to Labour's Parliamentary Committee. The election for twelve places was in part a popularity contest, in part a statement of who should be within the leadership group. When Mosley first stood in December1927, he secured 19 votes, 59 fewer than the weakest successful candidate. A year later, he increased his poll by just one vote. The Parliamentary Committee represented the variety of interests, both occupational and cultural, that had shaped the Labour Party. Since 1924 it had stabilised in membership and had become more thoroughly supportive of MacDonald. The founding generation remained dominant. Henderson, Snowden, Lansbury, Thomas and Adamson had all sat in the pre-war Commons as had MacDonald, the Chair, and Clynes, the Vice-Chair. All but Lansbury had held cabinet office in 1924. So had Trevelyan, who had served in the Asquith Government and had resigned over the decision to enter the European war in 1914. Tom Shaw, a cotton trade unionist, had sat in the Commons since 1918 and had been in the 1924 cabinet. Sidney Webb's record within the labour movement was lengthy and distinctive and similarly had been rewarded with office. Willie Graham and Tom Johnston were younger, gifted and Scottish. They had held junior posts in the Labour Government. In reputational terms Dalton was the most marginal, entering the Commons in October 1924. Mosley was almost a decade younger than any of the successful candidates and in party terms was an infant. It may well be that, within the closed world of the PLP, something of the marginalisation that Wertheimer failed to detect was effective. The Parliamentary Party was a relatively small body; many members were rule-governed trade unionists. Fidelity and long service should be rewarded; 'Serving your time' was a fundamental precept. Against this ethos, Mosley's initial reception within the party could alienate the unspectacular and the dutiful; their doubts could be inflamed by the gossip of the ambitious. Beatrice Webb noted soon after his return to the Commons; 'Mosley, brilliant but without weight, deemed to be a political adventurer by many left- as well as right-wingers'.[34]

Charles Trevelyan, himself very much a Labour grandee, noted the Mosleys' high expectations at the 1925 party conference. 'I had tea with the Mosleys. Lady C is a very jolly person. She regards the whole thing as a lark, though I feel she also intends to be in a subsequent Labour cabinet with him.' 'Larks' were not limited to Labour politics. MacDonald, frustrated at his inability to reach Mosley by phone, exclaimed that the latter's house seemed to contain some 'peculiar people'. He secured 'no reply or a rude one'. Mosley did not abandon his affluent and ostentatious life style when he took out a Labour Party card. Ladywood and Smethwick cohabited with the Rivera and Venice.

Mining communities during the 1926 lockout were complemented by Mediterranean beaches. Within the upper reaches of the Labour Party, Mosley, for all the admiration of his abilities, could seem an outsider. A rival class renegade could take comfort from his alleged shortcomings. Dalton responded with the condescension of the insider to a revised appraisal from Beatrice Webb. 'She thinks Lord Oswald with his connections and wealth has(?) a sure and early future with the Tories and might have become their leader, a prospect very remote, she thought, with us, though I point out that he was still very young. But we all agree that he is very uninstructed.'[35]

A few months later, Oswald and Cynthia Mosley stayed with the Webbs. Their hosts felt that there had been a change since their early optimistic days within the party.

> It struck us that he and she had changed – partly from his long illness last autumn and winter, partly from the ups and downs of electoral failure and success; also from social boycott by their own set and an uneasy position in the Labour Party. He is disillusioned. Labour politics for an aristocrat are not attractive – current and cross-current from left and right and very little real comradeship. 'Labour people' said Cynthia 'especially the better sort and the intellectuals are shy of us except the few snobs amongst them are subservient.'

The paucity of networks was significant, but an experienced parliamentary observer detected a more fundamental and destabilising malaise:

> In his new political surroundings he was much less successful from the Parliamentary point of view than when he was playing the part of a critic within the Conservative Party. He was still polished, ample and ornate; he could still speak in the great style, but it seemed much less natural. Much of its impressiveness had been lost; it suggested not as before the spontaneous outflow of a powerful mind, but the highly cultivated artifice of a skilful mind accommodating to new conditions.

The declension seemed to have gathered pace once he had returned to the Commons. This observer saw someone 'induced to join a party with which his mind is not in natural harmony'.[36]

This verdict would be compatible with Mosley's reflections on two overseas trips during his period out of Parliament. At the end of 1924 he visited India. His assessment placed less weight on the achievement of independence than on economic development. The priority was not so much political liberalisation as a 'mogul with a tractor and a deep plough'. A similar distance from the established wisdom of his new political allies was evident in his response a year later to the economic and social character of the United States. He and Cynthia were lionised by a broad range of Progressive American opinion. Eugene Debs was still the icon of the Socialist Party of America; his 6 per cent poll in the Presidential election of 1912 had been followed by internal feuds and wartime and post-war persecution. Perhaps the marginalisation of the SPA demonstrated the structural limits to socialist growth in the United States; perhaps failure was to some degree the result of contingent factors, not least the complex internal politics of major trade unions. Yet, in 1926 Debs, despite the collapse of his dreams, professed optimism. He felt that the Mosleys' visit had aided the revival of the socialist spirit and the reorganisation of the Socialist party. They were, in his view, 'royal people'.[37]

Debs's hope was expressed despite Republican dominance. Warren Harding's geniality and corrupt administration had been succeeded by the puritanical frugality and economic orthodoxy of Calvin Coolidge. Republicans controlled both Houses of Congress. The Democrats' incompetence had been demonstrated in the 103 ballots needed to agree on a Presidential nominee at their 1924 convention; they were no more than a sectional party based on a disparate coalition of Southern segregationists and some urban ethnic networks. The Democrats' future as a party that would reshape American society was as yet unanticipated, with the exception of the hopes of some progressive intellectuals. When Mosley enjoyed a fishing trip with Franklin Roosevelt, this was recreation with Woodrow Wilson's one-time Assistant Secretary to the Navy and the unsuccessful Vice-Presidential nominee in 1920. Although Roosevelt was canvassed as a future Governor of New York, and some hinted that he might one day become President, the likelihood and political significance of such eminence remained opaque. Only two post-Civil War Presidents had been Democrats; any Roosevelt agenda remained unknown. Republican hegemony seemed unchallenged, not just by the Democrats but by any third party. Robert La Follette had headed a Progressive ticket in the 1924 Presidential contest. He had been backed by some labour and farmers' organisations and had won the support of just over one in seven voters, captured his own state, Wisconsin, and scored credibly in some others in the west and the north-west. Whether this strength indicated the potential for progressive radicalism or ethnic antagonisms resulting from entry into a European war is debatable. La

Follette had died in July 1925; his former significant backers were few in numbers and politically diverse. Coolidge had secured 54 per cent of the Presidential poll; the obstacles to a third-party candidate, even when aided by the weakness of a Democrat challenger, were obvious.[38]

Trade union weakness accompanied the Left's political marginality. Membership had slumped heavily since 1918, a result of employers' attacks supported when necessary by state coercion. Throughout the twenties the courts worked assiduously to undermine the ability of unions to organise. The result was that many industries were open shops; elsewhere unions struggled to retain their negotiating rights. They accommodated as far as possible to employers' agendas and marginalised any hint of radicalism amongst their members. This decade of weakness and passivity was epitomised by the American Federation of Labor. It continued its long-established policy of political neutrality, denied any hint of what might hint at socialist sympathies, and disavowed any ambitious organising objectives to better protect its existing membership.[39]

Mosley encountered American industry most dramatically in the Ford plant in Detroit. He saw mass production, a car completed every ten seconds. The experience, for him, offered an epitaph for a free trade system. The division of labour into simple tasks subverted the accumulation of traditional skills in established industrial economies. Insulation was the only credible response to a future alliance of modern technology, scientific production and cheap labour. As well as a warning, Detroit offered a vision of a future that could work. Scientifically organised mass production was possible under capitalism. Mechanisation, the standardisation of tasks and the scientific utilisation of labour facilitated efficient production, not least by denying the relevance of the skilled craftsman. The production of cheap consumer goods for a mass market could yield high wages. Ford had introduced the five day week; across the industrial sector real wages rose by 25 per cent in the 1920s. If American vitality could be complemented by appropriate collective organisation through the state, here was a viable future. Mosley proclaimed in the *New Leader* that 'high wages is the thinking medicine with which we must dose British industry'.[40]

This understanding was the view from the top, that of the visitor to Ford who was accompanied by company publicists. There would certainly be no union representatives present. Mosley would hear nothing of experiences on the production line. The speed-ups with their neglect of safety, the monotony and long hours, the seasonal shifts in demand that led to high-tempo production alternating with lay-offs, the tyranny of the company's rules and the capricious dictates of fore-men and officials – this was the world of Ford that workers tolerated because the alternative could be much worse. Yet, life on the line bred its informal groups with their strategies for mitigating the monotony of the shift. Workers were often recruited from the countryside and from ethnic communities; they had to be socialised into the company culture and this integration was not guaranteed. The turnover was high despite the initial appeal of employment at Fords. Crucially, Mosley was attracted by the language of science, rationality and efficiency, but for the assembly line worker these might not be the obvious characterisa-tions. Too often, the appropriate terms would be insecurity and tyranny. Such a lack of empathy towards the experience from below was perhaps exemplified, also, in Mosley's understanding of the Labour Party.[41]

Despite this limitation Mosley hoped that the party that he had joined could be an effective instrument for policies that could address economic decline. His quest for influence necessitated allies in high places. Most significantly he courted the party leader. He was MacDonald's guest at Lossiemouth, they travelled abroad together. Mosley's letters to MacDonald were studiously deferential. Some colleagues found this courtship blatantly self-serving. One Conservative aristocratic observer, Lord Crawford, saw Mosley as exploiting the leader's vulnerabilities. 'He has been a parasite on… MacDonald, they have gone about together, and Mosley perhaps gives MacDonald just those things which MacDonald may fancy he lacks – a companion with a certain smartness in costume, conversation and address – a showy, talkative woman versed in the soci-ety side of diplomatic life.'[42] In all probability flattery hid doubts about the effectiveness of MacDonald's leadership – at least as a protagonist for the kind of agenda that Mosley favoured.

MacDonald opened the key debate at the 1927 party conference. He moved a resolution on behalf of the National Executive; the resolu-tion called for the preparation of a programme 'setting forth the broad proposals which have from time to time been approved by the Party Conference and which would constitute a Programme of Legislation and Administrative Action for a Labour Government'. The conference was organised to project MacDonald as the leader of a party prepar-ing for office. The resolution was carried. Mosley was elected to the National Executive with the support of the Miners' Federation, displac-ing Dalton and doubtless deepening the latter's antagonism towards the ambitious outsider. Mosley's hope that he could influence the content of the programme increased when he was elected to the sub-committee charged with the preparation of a draft.[43]

The sub-committee had six elected members. Two were from the NEC's trade union section – C.T. Cramp of the National Union of Railwaymen and F.O. Roberts of the Typographical Association. Both were loyal to the party leadership and suspicious of any proposal that emanated from what could be categorised as the Left. Such predispositions had been strengthened by the unions' post-General Strike predicament. All differences between the political and industrial wings must be subordinated to one objective, the return of a Labour Government. Despite the reservations of some union officials this necessitated the defence of MacDonald's leadership. This loyalty would be endorsed by Herbert Morrison, a thoroughly professional working-class politician, assiduous in his preparations for meetings, procedurally adept and dedicated to MacDonald. His vision of the Labour Party was as a coalition of all useful and progressive sections. Fashionable nostrums should be avoided as superficial and divisive. The remaining three elected members were more likely to offer dissenting voices. Mosley was joined by the one-time Liberal, C.P. Trevelyan and by Ellen Wilkinson, a former Communist. Any political disagreements would be complemented by social contrasts. These two affluent recruits and a socially mobile graduate could be characterised and if necessary, dismissed as intellectuals. This group of six were joined by three *ex officio* members. MacDonald would use his position to prevent the endorsement of unwelcome proposals. He would be backed by Henderson and by the new party chairman. Lansbury, despite his reputation as a critic of Labour caution, in the late twenties was firmly committed to the party's strategy. His emotive socialist rhetoric could be a force for unity whilst obscuring the substance of a proposed policy for an initially sceptical audience.[44]

Tensions on the sub-committee had been pre-figured at the 1927 conference. During a debate on a proposal to replace Labour's policy for a Capital Levy with a surtax levied on property and investments Mosley had moved an amendment on behalf of the ILP. This had insisted that all the resulting revenue be directed to the social services. None of the revenue should be used to reduce the National Debt. 'Would they not prefer to assist the miners in their period of reorganisation rather than repay the bondholders in order they could invest the money in any speculation that they chose?' Once in office Labour must move quickly to address working-class poverty. The takeover of key industries and the construction of a Socialist Commonwealth would be 'a long and arduous process', but redistributive taxation could be implemented in the first budget. Morrison had responded with hostility. He was 'getting sick of new stunts'. The 'unproductive parasitic' National Debt must be removed and resolutions must not tie down a future Chancellor of the Exchequer. Backing for this dismissal had come from one of the party's financial experts F.W. Pethick-Lawrence. By 1927, that the proposal came from the ILP was sufficient to condemn it for many delegates, but, more fundamentally, discomfort at too much specificity foreshadowed later disagreements. The conference resolution incorporated the potential for such disagreement within the sub-committee through its references to both 'broad proposals' and 'a Programme of Legislative and Administrative Action for a Labour Government'.[45]

Mosley rapidly made his position clear in a memorandum to MacDonald. Socialist reconstruction would be a lengthy process, yet there must be a rapid improvement in the condition of the working class under a Labour Government. Failure to achieve this could mean that 'the cause of Labour might be retarded for a generation'. His suggested measures included children's allowances, the offer of £1 a week extra on their pension to those remaining in employment after the age of 65, a tax on luxuries, an embargo on capital exports and the bulk purchase of foodstuffs and raw materials. An Economic Council should be formed and a commission established to examine the banking system. The level of unemployment was relatively high compared with the immediate pre-war years, but it was concentrated in specific industries. Mosley was accordingly optimistic, not least because of the example of Calvin Coolidge's United States:

> If the aged were removed from industry, a very slight change in monetary policy would suffice to absorb most of the remaining 250,000 unemployed. With no appreciable surplus of unemployed, Labour would then be in a very powerful position to struggle for higher wages on a rising market. The position would be in many ways analogous to the situation which has brought high wages in the United States.

An insistence that socialism provided the permanent solution was allied with a concern for national solidarity. 'A final draft must be vividly written throughout and should conclude with a concise summary of the problems of our age, and a rousing appeal for national unity in their solution.'[46]

Discussions on the sub-committee were fretful. Trevelyan noted that an early meeting immediately after the submission of Mosley's memorandum was 'rather unsatisfactory. It is going to be a long business and a struggle between MacDonald's indecisiveness, and Henderson's dullness of exposition and some others of us.' In the New Year, Dalton gleefully recorded a welcome rumour, 'MacDonald and Mosley still hostile to one another'. The leader reacted with characteristic sensitivity to Mosley's claim of procedural irregularity. MacDonald threatened to withdraw from the committee and pronounced on the impossibility of leading the Labour Party.[47]

Whatever the acerbities, MacDonald and his supporters held the initiative. Harry Snell, the Member for East Woolwich, showed Sidney Webb three drafts, a long one written by MacDonald and shorter ones produced by Mosley and Wilkinson. The tensions within the committee had not prevented a significant level of consensus. Sidney Webb reassured Beatrice. 'I presume these drafts have emerged from some meeting as they all agree substantially. Of course JRM's is by far the best and will no doubt be made the basis. It is literary and well phrased and properly vague and comprehensive without anything new to you and me.' Webb considered that 'the programme *will be* constructed and adopted without undue strife'. He was proved right. At the end of February the full NEC decided that MacDonald's version should become the working draft. A month later, MacDonald announced that the draft, now rewritten by the economic historian and socialist writer R.H. Tawney, was being reworked. His proposal that this process continue was countered by Mosley's suggestion that the existing draft be considered immediately. Mosley's defeat was by the narrow margin of ten to eight. The further the reworking went, the more the NEC would be faced with a *fait accompli*. Given the need to present a document to the 1928 conference, significant amendment would become impossible.[48] When the NEC eventually considered a draft early in May, Trevelyan and Mosley urged recognition of a minority position. They expressed this through a shorter draft that presented 'in unmistakeable terms, the actual measures upon which a Labour Government could at once embark'. Their appeal to the previous year's conference resolution for legitimation was weakened by that resolution's ambiguity. The NEC majority offered the concession that the minority opinion would be included in the report to conference. This genuflection left the draft untouched. Whilst this was essentially Tawney's work, its political significance was that it expressed the perspective of MacDonald and his allies.[49]

The outcome was *Labour and the Nation* presented to the October 1928 conference. The document offered a combination of the moral case for evolutionary socialist transformation and specific proposals. The latter offered an extensive menu but without any sense of priorities or immediate strategy. The conference was tightly controlled. Lansbury's chairmanship gave this dominance an ethical additive. The concordat between political leadership and the major unions was indomitable. Dissenters on the left, especially from the ILP, were humoured, threatened and marginalised into irrelevance. Mosley sat silently on the platform, bound by the collective discipline of the National Executive, an observer of the hostility that greeted John Wheatley's criticisms. In contrast, MacDonald enjoyed the moment of his greatest dominance as party leader.[50]

Labour and the Nation offered an authoritative expression of the Labour leadership's economic orthodoxy and political timidity wrapped in socialist rhetoric. Yet, in the political circumstances of 1928 plausible political justification could be offered for its content and style. An overall Labour majority in an election due at the latest by autumn 1929 seemed unlikely. To be the largest party in the new Commons seemed the most credible objective. Too precise a document could handicap the party in a tight struggle for votes and limit its flexibility in an unpredictable post-election situation. Yet in the pre-election period even the most orthodox amongst Labour's leadership seemed briefly to consider a more adventurous agenda. This initiative came from within the Parliamentary Party leadership. A sub-committee considered the issue of an immediate programme. Its membership included Snowden and seemed unlikely to suggest any radical policies. Yet the sub-committee envisaged a large-scale, publicly funded scheme to reduce unemployment. This would involve large public loans. The sub-committee was optimistic that the implementation of such a policy need not be dependent on a parliamentary majority. Here was a hint of the boldness for which Mosley and others had argued in the making of *Labour and the Nation*. Yet, Labour's election manifesto showed no trace of this suggestion. Perhaps this expressed Labour's unwillingness to compete with Lloyd George's similar pledge on unemployment, a reluctance informed by an assessment that Labour would fare better if it separated itself from Lloyd Georgian 'stunts'.[51]

Such 'stunts' benefited Labour in the May 1929 election. Liberal electoral support revived from the disaster of 1924 but the party's gains were limited. Rather, in many constituencies the Liberals damaged the Conservatives much more than Labour, thereby ensuring a Labour gain. In Birmingham, Mosley funded the Labour campaigns in Ladywood, Erdington and Sparkbrook. He also financed the four-page election sheets that circulated across the city. One set-piece of the campaign pitted Mosley against Locker Lampson, the right-wing Tory Member for Handsworth. They debated in Birmingham's Rag Market under the auspices of the *Daily Express*. Mosley used the patriotic card against Locker Lampson's incessant conjuring of Bolshevik bogeys. 'The men who came out on strike to protect the miners and themselves from wage cuts were the "heroes" who fought for "their" country in the "Great War."' He attacked the Baldwin Government, and especially the Foreign Secretary, for its international friendships. 'The Tory Party were the fawning friends of every reactionary Government in Europe. Sir Austen Chamberlain shook hands with Mussolini and in so doing "shook hands with murder" as foul as any done in Russia.' Mosley's election platform also foreshadowed future controversies. Stressing the need to reduce unemployment he emphasised the need to remove both the aged and the young from industry and to embark on a major programme of public works. His understanding of the American economy informed his future vision. 'Higher wages and greater purchasing power are the basis upon which permanent industrial prosperity must root.'[52]

Mosley in a rhetorical flight had prophesied nine Labour seats out of twelve in Birmingham. Although the results fell short of this target, they were, by past standards, sensational. Dennison lost very narrowly in King's Norton but elsewhere in the city six seats were won for the first time. Jim Simmons defeated Arthur Steel Maitland, the Minister of Labour, in Erdington, John Strachey won in Aston, Wilfrid Whiteley had a majority of 11 in Ladywood. Austen Chamberlain survived in West Birmingham by just 43. Mosley pronounced the epitaph for a dynasty. 'The father's fortress has been seized from the nerveless grasp of the sons. Birmingham once followed a man and has now dismissed his plaster effigies.' The Mosley tradition of abrasive contests was maintained in Stoke. The pessimism felt by the incumbent, Ward, about the result perhaps precipitated desperate measures. Cynthia Mosley claimed that canvassers were spreading the fiction that the Mosleys owned a works where the wage was 18 shillings a week. Ward emphasised the incongruity of a Labour candidate who was an aristocrat. Moreover it was alleged that the fortune of this 'Dollar Princess' was the result of sharp American business practices, the manipulation of the wheat market and much else. Ward's agent suggested that a proposed leaflet include 'a little touch of ridicule for Lady Cynthia and her hypocritical aspirations to represent labour'. These attacks were ineffective against the well- funded Labour campaign and the appeal of the candidate. Compared with 1924, Labour's share of the vote increased by over 16 per cent, significantly greater than in the other two Potteries seats. The Stoke constituency had fallen into line with its neighbours. Stoke and Smethwick both seemed safe seats.[53]

Stoke Election, 1929
Turnout 81.2%

Lady Cynthia Mosley	Labour	26,548	58.7%
J Ward	Liberal	18,698	41.3%
		7,850	17.4%

Smethwick Election 1929
Turnout 78.9%

Sir O.E. Mosley Bt	Labour	19,550	54.8%
A.R. Wise	Conservative	12,210	34.2%
Miss M.E. Marshall	Liberal	3,909	11.0%
		7,340	20.6%

In Smethwick, the acrimony of 1926 had given way to expressions of mutual regard. After the declaration Mosley emphasised what united them. 'I am sure now it is all over we can all settle down together quite happily as members of one great nation: they were English men and women before they were party politicians.' Such a claim was made just as the expectation of early office became credible. A profile in the *Birmingham Town Crier*, headed 'The Man Whom the Tories Hate', presented his journey from the trenches through political independence, Ladywood, and Smethwick. Here was the Mosley who had become a hero for many Labour activists.

The personal charm of Oswald Mosley is natural, spontaneous. One can call him comrade and mean it. I have seen him in all moods. He can flame with anger as quickly as the rest of us. But his anger is short-lived, and his smile predominates. He is ambitious and rightly so. His ambition is to serve the common people, to do all that one man can do to abolish poverty and bring gladness and hope where there is now sorrow and despair. He is a gentleman in the highest sense of that much abused term... Sir Oswald Mosley is destined to play a big part in the affairs of the nation.[54]

5
Minister

Mosley was widely expected, not least by himself, to be given a significant post in a Labour Government. Some even speculated that he
might become Foreign Secretary. J.L. Garvin, editor of *The Observer,* was
one. Lord Crawford expressed his horror at the prospect. 'It is almost
incredible that a sane journalist could make such a suggestion-it is
all the more sinister in consequence, the idea that this cad should be
at the F.O... I really feel that Garvin may be right in suggesting that
this toady is designed for high office; but if this be true Ramsay MacD
stands condemned as a judge of men, and his party would be justly
incensed at such an appointment.' Crawford expressed a widely held
distaste for Mosley's style, but this Tory Peer's empathy with Labour's
ethos was understandably limited. The party hierarchy was constructed
out of length of service, reputations for competence and the diversity
of party interests. Long-established figures took the senior positions;
those prominent within Labour's successor generation were allocated
secondary posts. Morrison took over Transport, but outside the cabinet;
Dalton became Under Secretary at the Foreign Office. Garvin lamented
Mosley's marginalisation. 'The FO I very much wished you to have.
More youth is necessary. Gerentocracy is too much amongst us.'[1]

Mosley was perhaps disappointed to be offered the Chancellorship
of the Duchy of Lancaster, a honorific title which left him free to
focus on a specific problem. He became one of a quartet designated to
address the challenge of unemployment. Labour's election appeal had
made much of the long-term unemployed in the staple industries of
coal, steel, shipbuilding and textiles. The heart of the unionised working class and the core of Britain's pre- war economy, they had become
by-words for stagnation and insecurity. Labour had urged voters 'The
Works are closed! But the Ballot Box is Open'.[2] Now the ballot boxes

had given their verdict. However constrained Labour's parliamentary position, principle and political survival required a ministerial response. Mosley had emphasised this necessity ever since his proclamation of a 'Revolution by Reason'. In opposition his proposals had aroused interest but had secured little support; in office he needed to persuade both his ministerial colleagues and professionally sceptical civil servants.

The formation of the ministerial quartet was a statement of intent by MacDonald that the intractable million were a priority. Yet the diversity of this team raised problems about their suitability for the task and the likelihood of a harmonious working relationship. The senior figure, Jimmy Thomas, as Lord Privy Seal, had been given overall responsibility for unemployment. He had sat continuously in the Commons since 1910, a prominent member of the Parliamentary Party, a vivacious debater who had been Dominions Secretary in the 1924 Government. More significantly, he had been leader of the National Union of Railwaymen since 1916, and the union's dominant figure since the resignation of Richard Bell at the end of 1909. He was a consummate negotiator, a fixer who was adept at constructing compromises out of seemingly intractable situations. His oratory blended pathos, passion and, when appropriate, character assassination. His dominance within the NUR rested on substantial achievements. As a young official, he had faced railway companies almost all of whom were unrelenting in their opposition to union recognition. He had attempted, with considerable success, to canalise the militancy of some members to win concessions from the employers. War had meant recognition. The post-war grouping of the companies into the Big Four had brought a complex system of wage bargaining that had maintained real wage standards until 1928. Such stability was maintained despite the significant invasion by road transport into some sections of the industry and the impact of economic depression on some railway business, most notably coal. Thomas could claim that this prudential strategy had protected the incomes and conditions of railway workers, in contrast, so he sometimes suggested, to the intemperate and self- destructive policies of other unions, most notably the Miners' Federation.[3]

Thomas's critics within the institutions of the NUR were few; within the wider trade union world some could be more vocal. He had played a significant part in the events of 'Black Friday', April 15 1921, when, amidst much ambiguity and harsh recriminations, the transport unions had not proceeded with their expected industrial action in support of the Miners. Five years later he had been involved thoroughly in the termination of the General Strike. On both occasions the Miners stayed out, their prolonged resistance ending in disastrous defeat. Consequentially, many in the coalfields and elsewhere condemned 'Traitor Thomas' and eulogised the integrity of the Miners' leader, A.J. Cook. Mosley had been prominent in his support for the Miners in the angry summer and sombre autumn of 1926. Unlike many Labour politicians he admired Cook; in contrast, Thomas had suggested to the TUC General Secretary, Walter Citrine, that Cook was insane.[4] Within the General Council, Cook was very much the outsider; Jimmy was one of the boys.

Mosley thoroughly rejected the puritanical ethos that was one of Labour's liberal legacies. Thomas similarly enjoyed the material benefits that came with his union salary. He personified conspicuous consumption and played the stock market; his children were expensively educated. Cartoonists presented him in evening dress, slightly dishevelled, glass in hand. His politics had never been radical. By the twenties his trade union strategy and his social mobility were generating a conservatism complemented by a Labour rhetoric that was essentially decorative. Inclination and circumstance combined to dilute his partisanship. As the pre-war Member for Derby, in a two-member constituency, he had inherited and endorsed an arrangement with the local Liberals. Once this Progressivism had been ruptured by war, Thomas topped the poll in every post-war Derby election. He built on Labour strength that owed much to the local prominence of his union and attracted the second votes of some Conservatives and Liberals. He ran consistently ahead of his Labour running mate. Such flexibility was evident in the Commons where Thomas was notable for his range of cross-party friendships, a flexibility facilitated by his fervent advocacy of Empire.

In June 1929 Thomas cut a distinctive and substantial figure both in the party and the TUC. His reputation rested on his negotiating skills. Flexibility in pursuit of stability and incremental benefits for NUR members, entertaining speeches at conferences and in the Commons to disarm critics through humour and sentimentality; such were valuable weapons in his armoury. Throughout his career Thomas had performed adroitly within rule-governed institutions to produce verbal formulae that could assuage differences. But his ministerial brief called for other talents. He had shown little interest in substantive ideas and no evidence of divergent thoughts.

George Lansbury could appear less conformist than Thomas. Perhaps such a reputation had led to his exclusion from the 1924 Government. His inclusion in the 1929 cabinet as First Commissioner of Works could be seen as MacDonald's token concession to the left, a symbolic compensation for the exclusion of John Wheatley. Lansbury's Christian Socialism and pacifist rectitude could fuel passionate denunciations of capitalist immorality accompanied by splendid anticipations of socialist salvation. His leadership of the Poplar councillors, gaoled in 1921 over a rates rebellion, had offered a municipal left politics that was critical of Labour respectability and caution. Through this mobilisation and his involvement with the radical *Daily Herald* he could seemingly offer an alternative Labour politics. But his criticisms were subject to a decisive limitation whose root lay in his pre-war political experience.

He had entered the Commons as Member for Bow and Bromley in December 1910. As a thorough supporter of women's suffrage he had denounced the forced feeding of suffragettes and had also been at odds with the PLP leadership on other issues. In 1912 he had resigned his seat to fight a by-election as an Independent Socialist, above all on the suffrage question. Defeat by his Conservative opponent took him out of the Commons for a decade. Thereafter, he was determined to avoid any separation from the Labour Party, whatever the disagreements he might have with its policies or distaste for some colleagues' lack of principle. He became accomplished in the employment of socialist emotion to secure pragmatic compromises. His chairmanship of the 1928 party conference and his benediction for *Labour and the Nation* demonstrated his value within the party leadership. June 1929 was his first experience of national office, but forty years in local government had shown him the inescapability of patience and pragmatism. 'Not only do the wheels of God grind slowly, but the wills of men are also hard to move.'[5]

Thomas and Lansbury belonged in contrasting styles to Labour's first generation. In contrast Thomas Johnston was seen widely as one of the coming men. He had been elected to the Parliamentary Committee in January 1927, just as Mosley was re-entering the Commons as Member for Smethwick. Like many Scots, Johnston had been heavily involved in the Independent Labour Party. When he entered the Commons in November 1922 he had already established a reputation as the accomplished editor of the Glasgow socialist weekly *Forward*. He and other contributors expressed a crusading zeal often tempered by a sense of practicality. Both elements owed much to the continuing influence of a broader Scottish Radical ethos. An observer depicted him as 'one of the old order with no flair for stunts, but with an inbred craving to be instructional... an excellent example of the didactic Scot who is always seeking to inform or to indoctrinate... a stranger to all the arts of sophistry'. The stylistic gulf between him and Mosley was immediately apparent. His attachment to the ILP had been reflected in his early Commons speeches where he showed a willingness to criticise Labour caution. However, his concern with practical proposals put him increasingly at odds with the leftward shift personified by Maxton and his close associates. His entry into the 1929 Government would mean a parting of the ways. Johnston, like Mosley, was an independent figure prepared to consider new ideas. He combined an interest in Hobson's under-consumptionist theory with a concern for imperial development. He increasingly felt that the challenge of unemployment necessitated a cross-party response. Such openness cohabited with a strong attachment to the Labour Party as was evidenced in his estrangement from the increasingly critical ILP. Unlike Mosley, the time that he could devote to unemployment was limited by his other ministerial responsibilities. As Under-Secretary at the Scottish Office he found that the Secretary of State, the Fife Miners' leader Willie Adamson, devolved much to his younger and more energetic colleague.[6]

The diversities of the quartet should be placed within Labour's broader political topography. Most notable and evidenced by Thomas was the continuing dominance of the founding fathers. MacDonald, Snowden and Henderson had established their eminence within the party before 1914. Divisions over the war might have left scars but by 1922 their old authority had been firmly restored. Whatever the personal and stylistic tensions, for example, between MacDonald and both Snowden and Henderson, they were politically secure. Criticisms over the character and downfall of the1924 Government became memories. Especially after the industrial defeats of 1926 the imperative across the labour movement was the election of a Labour Government. In June 1929 Snowden returned to the Treasury, Henderson went to the Foreign Office. Together with Thomas, Adamson, J.R. Clynes at the Home Office, Margaret Bondfield at the Ministry of Labour and Tom Shaw at the War Office, they expressed, at least in the opinion of the faithful, the potential of ordinary men and the occasional woman as holders of the highest offices. This collective personification of the arrival of democracy was at its most powerful in MacDonald's apotheosis as Labour leader. Any change in policy required that this group be persuaded. Except in the most exceptional circumstances they could not be removed.[7]

Such dominance was underpinned by the support of the trade unions. Within the PLP almost all union-sponsored Members saw themselves as party loyalists concerned to support their leaders against criticism from within and without. By and large they had little concern with the minutiae of most policy debates. They were concerned to protect and advance the interests of their particular industries and to defend the TUC position on broader economic issues. In the absence of effective policies to reduce unemployment, they focused on unemployment benefit, both the rates of benefit and the conditions on which payment should be given or withheld. These sectional priorities and common concerns indicated that trade union Members, their loyalism notwithstanding, did not constitute a blindly obedient monolith. They could be critical on sensitive issues, but their criticisms were characteristically expressed within the rubric of loyalism. Discontent rarely reached the floor of the Commons, whether in speeches or in the division lobby. Much depended on the relationships between trade union Members and specific ministers. Discussions were based on the assumption that all parties to the exchange shared common objectives; disagreement was limited to assessments of practicalities. Disenchantment could come only with accumulating evidence that such an assumption was misguided. Even then, any reassessment of strategy necessitated belief in a credible alternative.

Trade union Members not only faced towards their political leaders; they also had to be sensitive towards opinion within their own unions and on the General Council of the TUC. The former relationship generated few problems. Sponsored Members were typically allowed much discretion in their political work. The General Council's expectations posed a more complex challenge. Its relationship with the 1924 Government had proved disappointing. General Council members had hoped for access to and responsiveness from Labour ministers. The latter had generally felt compelled, whether out of principle or political necessity, to demonstrate that Labour was not a sectional party. General Council members hoped in June 1929 that there would be no repeat of 1924. Yet, the Government's dominant figures remained the same. Any deterioration in the economic situation could deepen the tensions within this complex relationship. General Council estrangement could percolate through into the trade union section of the PLP.

Critics of Labour's leadership could react impatiently against what they saw as the unthinking immobility of trade union Members. Such dismissiveness was insensitive to the complexities of relationships that were built on loyalty and trust, but which had to be constantly renegotiated. The issues at stake might appear modest, for example the precise words determining eligibility for unemployment benefit, but such disputes were seen by those involved as the very stuff of political bargaining. Outcomes could make an immediate difference to constituents' lives .This was why a Labour Party had been formed thirty years earlier. That this was defined as a basic purpose of the party carried a potentially radical conclusion. Accumulating disappointments could lead to pressures for the revision of the relationship, or in extreme circumstances to its fracturing.

Critics' stereotyping of loyalists was reciprocated. Many trade union Members dismissed critics as irresponsible intellectuals who were self-centred and self-advertising, preferring to parade their doctrinal purity rather than to support a Labour Government in the difficult art of governing. By 1929, such criticisms were targeted largely at the ILP left, only small in numbers but increasingly vigorous and unqualified in its criticisms of party leaders. In fact the ILP left, although not numerous, was diverse in its political interests and style. Parliamentary scenes were the preserve of the few; most articulated their criticisms through more nuanced contributions. The existence of the ILP left, and the plausibility of the Loyalist caricature, reduced the space for critical comment on the Labour Government, but this constriction was perhaps one manifestation of a broader shift. During the 1920s Labour had become a politically narrower party. Communists had eventually been rigorously excluded, feminists had been marginalised. This reduction in acceptable identities was in part initiated by, and subsequently controlled from, the top of the party. Labour in 1929 was increasingly a party that limited the space for dissent.[8]

Demands for loyalty were facilitated further by Labour's electoral position. The party had emerged from the 1929 election as the largest party in the Commons. 81 seats had been won for the first time. Yet Labour still trailed the Conservatives in the popular vote. The result vindicated those party strategists who had felt that Labour's prospects, despite 13 by-election gains in the 1924 Parliament, were uncertain. Labour's advance owed much to the revival in the number of Liberal candidacies compared with 1924, and consequentially to some erosion of Baldwin's appeal to Liberal voters. The party had benefited from a combination of Liberal revival, some Conservative unpopularity and the vagaries of the electoral system. The underlying sociology endorsed a cautious verdict. Electoral success remained restricted almost wholly to urban Britain plus the coalfields, and in particular to places dominated by well-unionised industries. Outside London and Bristol, Labour's southern presence was minimal and tentative. Mosley might have celebrated the Birmingham breakthrough, but Labour faced the challenge of whether this and other 1929 advances could be consolidated. The party had barely begun to escape from its electoral ghetto; concern that it might be driven back onto this narrow ground facilitated solidarity, not least against those who argued that the only acceptable strategy was to risk Commons defeat on a thoroughly socialist programme. Nevertheless, in June and July 1929 Labour was optimistic. Conservative disarray following an unexpected defeat, and deflation of Liberal ambitions, seemingly offered the Government its opportunity.[9]

The appointment of the quartet as an unemployment task force was at best a declaration of intent. Effectiveness necessitated appropriate institutional structures and resources. Thomas's brief was to co-ordinate and encouragement departmental initiatives. He was backed by a small team of civil servants headed by Sir Horace Wilson. Previously heavily involved in the Baldwin Government's response to the General Strike, he was an apostle of financial orthodoxy. Thomas chaired a monthly inter-departmental committee on unemployment; Johnston, Lansbury and Mosley were not included in its formal membership. This lack of integration marginalised any contribution that they might hope to make to any overall strategy. Rather, their role was limited to the consideration and development of specific policies. Thomas responded to his appointment with hyperactivity. He met businessmen, trade unionists, and members of local authorities. Good intentions and endeavour counted for little alongside the institutional power of the Treasury and the economic orthodoxy of its civil servants, Sir Horace Wilson and the Chancellor. Thomas's bonhomie and initial optimism offered no intellectual challenge to Snowden's remorseless logic. He was not alone. Lansbury ruefully acknowledged that 'whenever I hear Snowden, while I hate his conclusions, his logic seems unanswerable'.[10]

Such implacability shaped the King's Speech. It contained no traces of the more ambitious economic agenda that had been drawn up by senior Labour figures before the election. Thomas's prescriptions were based on making British industry more competitive with an eye to regaining lost overseas markets. He sanctioned a five-year programme of road construction, proposed guarantees for loans raised by public utilities and offered limited loans for colonial development. Such proposals offered minimal short-term alleviation of unemployment. Thomas was derisory about most public works. 'There is to be no consideration of schemes that merely mean spending money without regard either to consequences or benefit to the community. Anyone can spend money... there is no bottomless pit from which money can be drawn.' The ILP left were predictably dismissive; Maxton expressed his 'complete dissatisfaction', an assessment that was confirmed for him and his associates by Conservative approval of Thomas's prudence. In a subsequent debate Wheatley moved beyond dismay to a diagnosis of the Government's strategic choice. Ministers had a moment of opportunity, but they lacked courage. As yet, opponents would not risk the perils of an early election, but timidity would produce disaster. 'After the Government have disappointed their friends by 12 months of this halting, half-way legislation... and have been discredited in the country, then 12 months from now, there will be no party in the House poor enough to do them honour.'[11]

Whatever their disappointment, loyalist backbenchers were not prepared to criticise their newly elected government. Their ethos of solidarity could be seasoned with socialist rhetoric that dismissed rapid solutions. Lansbury provided a classic sedative to dispel criticism of Thomas's initial presentation. 'I know as a Socialist, that there is no real solution of this problem except a very drastic change in the social and industrial condition of our country... I pin my faith in an educated democracy and I believe that that democracy is coming into being.' Mosley's contribution to the debate struck a different note. Lloyd George, unlike the Conservatives, had been hostile to the Government's proposals. Mosley responded by suggesting the prospect of agreement between the Government and the Liberals. After all at the election, both parties had agreed on the need for 'a great united effort... by new measures and new enterprises.' His insistence on the need for a wartime spirit of 'unity and vigour' contrasted with Lansbury's reliance on the emergence of an educated democracy. Mosley, in defending Thomas, acknowledged the pervasiveness of economic orthodoxy. 'The raising of money by the State for the purposes of national development means merely taking that credit from existing industry and to that extent curtailing its resources.' This enunciation was clearly a testimony to his very recent experience. 'Any Ministers in charge of unemployment come up at once, of course, against the dilemma of the monetary experts.' Established wisdom seemed unanimous. As yet, Mosley was prepared to appear neutral. But despite his effort to play in the ministerial team, his relationship with Thomas emerged damaged from the debate.[12]

London's Liverpool Street station was notable for its intensive and wholly steam powered suburban services. The London and North Eastern was the most impoverished of the Big Four railway companies and lacked the resources to embark on a suburban electrification scheme. Mosley announced the possibility of government funding for such a project, and claimed that the consequential orders to industry would inject £75–100 million into the economy. The figure had been given to him by Thomas shortly before the debate. Opposition speakers insisted rightly that the figure was ludicrously high. Mosley insisted on its accuracy. Thomas subsequently was disarming and disingenuous. 'I cannot conceive that (he) said anything of the kind because I discussed the matter with him before he spoke.' He suggested that what Mosley must have said was that the Government would provide the facilities for the expenditure, not pay the bill. This explanation evaded the critics' point which concerned the amount, however borne. Thomas clearly had conjured up a figure that in subsequent exchanges was exposed as hopelessly inflated. Mosley's retrospective verdict was bleak. 'My relations with Thomas deteriorated.' Another upper-class recruit to Labour, Arthur Ponsonby, was pessimistic, not so much on policy grounds as on the minister's inadequacy for the task. 'Thomas with all his astuteness is going to be a trial.' The hyperbole of the consummate fixer, perhaps effective in achieving compromises in closed session, was irrelevant to the economic challenge. Some could be more scathing. Lord Arnold, the Paymaster General, complained in late July to Beatrice Webb. Thomas was organisationally incapable; he rarely met with Lansbury and Mosley; he was dominated by 'that arch reactionary', Sir Horace Wilson; failures in the Commons reflected his lack of command over detail; 'He gets "rattled" and when not under the influence of drink or flattery, is in an abject state of panic about his job.'[13]

Yet, in July 1929 Mosley articulated the initial optimism on the ministerial benches. He could talk at length on the necessity for any would-be statesman to constantly remain informed on subjects such as finance, and on the necessity for the Labour Government to improve the lot of the underdog. Impelled by such precepts he piloted the Colonial Development Bill through the Commons, winning ILP approval for his acceptance of an amendment that would protect working conditions for indigenous labour. However, in a debate on the provision of grants to local authorities for development works, he returned to the issue of whether fresh government demands on the money market would simply divert funds from private industry. Without offering a substantive response he returned to the thesis of 'Revolution by Reason' and the devastating impact of the return to the Gold Standard. 'It is that policy of severe and acute deflation which is responsible for very many of the industrial troubles which now confront us... that policy was chiefly responsible for the great struggle of 1926.' At the Durham Miners' Gala despite the return of a Labour Government, his audience lived with the legacy of that defeat. Mosley's rhetoric was uncompromising. 'I would rather see the Labour Government go down in defeat than shrink from great issues.' Even allowing for the emotion of the occasion the challenge was far removed from the speeches that summer, not just of MacDonald and Thomas, but also of Lansbury.[14]

Discontent over unemployment policy was largely limited to private pessimism and gossip about Thomas's flaws and foibles. More overt and focused dissent emerged on an issue that was a priority for the trade unions – unemployment benefit. On 11 July, the Minister of Labour, Margaret Bondfield, introduced what she called 'stop gap legislation'; this aimed at preventing a deficit on the unemployment insurance fund through an increased Treasury contribution. This limited initiative did not address the priorities of many within the party – the levels of bene-fit and the conditions of eligibility. The Minister's response on the latter was to set up the Morris Committee; on the former she offered nothing. Thorough hostility was limited as yet to the usual suspects of the ILP, but the meagre legislative offering disappointed many loyalists.[15]

The Labour Party Conference met in Brighton at the beginning of October. Delegates could enthuse about electoral success and specific ministerial performances, not least Henderson at the Foreign Office. His influence as party manager was evident in the tightly controlled agenda; progress was facilitated by Morrison's authoritative, or in the view of some, authoritarian, chairmanship. His opening address cel-ebrated MacDonald's talents as both party leader and Prime Minister. MacDonald was away in the United States; Henderson, Snowden and Thomas all made set piece speeches. Snowden was magisterial and patronising. 'Now I have no doubt that all that seems to you as clear as mud, but it is the simplest form in which I can express that very important fact.' His unapologetic orthodoxy provoked little criticism from delegates. As the party's acknowledged financial expert he could dominate his audience, aided by his reputation as a principled advocate of austere ethical socialism. A more detached observer, Walter Citrine characterised his sermon as 'a typical chancellor's speech'. In contrast, Thomas offered not analytical rigour, but manipulation and deception. Difficult questions were buried in abundant red herrings. His style verged on self- parody. A rhetorical flight on the demoralisation of the young unemployed was abruptly interrupted. 'I say to you as Lord Privy Seal – Lord knows what that means.' Delegates laughed. Citrine noted 'It was too typically Thomas.'[16]

Delegates beyond the ILP were doubtless uneasy about Snowden's inflexibility and Thomas's lack of substance, but there were as yet few overt criticisms. In contrast, the Government's response on unemploy-ment insurance came close to rejection by the conference. A relevant section in the Parliamentary Party's Report was almost referred back. The margin was only 77,000 votes, 1,100,000 against 1,027,000. Some major unions, including the Miners' Federation, voted with the critics. The ultra- loyalist General and Municipal Workers backed the Government, but only after one of its sponsored MPs, Arthur Hayday, had criticised the Government. Hayday was a senior and, on this subject, a highly respected backbencher. His intervention was the more telling since Bondfield was herself sponsored by the same union. Typically the reply from the platform was the responsibility of Lansbury. His conciliatory style combined with his radical reputation perhaps persuaded some delegates to give the new government the benefit of the doubt. For most critics such dissent was a bargaining ploy inspired by a hope that on a specific issue ministers might be persuaded to amend their position.[17]

Mosley, as a member of the National Executive, watched these exchanges from the platform. When the results of the NEC election were announced, he found that after two years' membership he had lost his seat in the Divisional Parties Section. As runner-up with 928,000 votes, he was just 6,000 votes behind the last of the successful candidates but well behind Morrison and Dalton. The defeat did not reflect political considerations, but rather the substantial reduction in the affiliation of the MFGB, in previous years a decisive component of his vote. Yet he might have expected some advantage from the retirement of two members of the Divisional Parties section. The setback perhaps suggested that even within the extra-parliamentary party his base was limited.[18]

The Party Conference came towards the end of the summer recess. Thomas had spent a month in Canada, ostentatiously but fruitlessly, trying to expand trade with the Dominion. Mosley, Lansbury and Johnston had attempted to give substance to a specific proposal in Labour's election manifesto. Enhanced pensions could be offered to the old, hopefully removing them from the labour market and allowing a reduction in unemployment amongst the young. The proposal did not address the basic problem of an under-employed workforce but offered some response to the plight of the young unemployed who over time risked becoming unemployable. Whatever its limitations, implementation of the proposal would indicate Labour's fidelity, in at least one instance, to its manifesto.

At the end of June, Thomas set up a sub-committee to assess the proposal. Its composition was anomalous. Johnston, Lansbury and Mosley were joined by civil servants and the government actuary. The latter were involved as members, not as normal to service the committee. The conventional distinction between politicians and administrators was blurred. Perhaps they were intended as a conservative counterweight to ministers who, with the possible exception of Johnston, were seen as potentially unsound. The committee's exploration of various possibilities resulted in a proposal favoured by the ministers. This would offer all insured workers, plus railwaymen, over the age of 60 a pension of £1 (double the current rate) for a single man, and £1 10s for a married one. The qualifying condition was that potential beneficiaries must retire within six months.

The civil servants on the committee were sceptical. They raised issues of cost, the accuracy of the predicted take up and the implications of the consequential vacancies for employment. Those likely to accept the proffered pension needed to be employed in sectors where the young unemployed could take their places. The perennial issue of equity surfaced. Enhanced pensions would be seen as unfair by those who had retired earlier on a lower rate. The ministers were determined to persevere with the scheme against multiple objections. Lansbury suggested that the civil servants be by-passed. The trio should produce a report recommending their preferred option. The civil servants should produce 'a colourless statement of the facts'.[19]

This strategy was agreed on 4 November. Mosley wrote the ministers' report. He argued that 390,000 out of a targeted 677,000 would take up the enhanced pension. This would mean the creation of 2000,000 vacancies. The cost of creating these through such enhanced retirements was only one fifth of what would be expended to secure the same result by public works. Mosley embellished his detailed and carefully presented proposal with typically dramatic rhetoric. 'The personal and collective honour of every Member of the Government is involved.' Here was a concrete proposal that could make an immediate impact. Failure to implement the measure would mean the definite failure of the Government on the home front. Mosley's rhetoric went beyond the merits of a specific policy to the fundamental question of Labour's effectiveness as a political instrument. The underlying challenge was 'the transition of Britain from a pre-war to a post-war basis'. The proposal tested Labour's competence. 'Labour can scarcely be trusted if they failed to carry out their immediate emergency measures to which the Party is so deeply committed. It would be trusted to more determined and competent hands.'[20]

The proposal was passed to a cabinet committee – A.V. Alexander, a co-operator and strong free trader, F.W. Pethick-Lawrence, a Treasury Minister, and a junior colleague W.R. Smith. Their thinking was shaped by the Treasury's fixation with annual budgeting, and they proceeded to compare the scheme's definite initial costs with the hypothetical longer term saving on unemployment benefit. Inevitably, issues of equity were raised. The negative response was a denial of what galvanised Mosley, and to some degree his colleagues. For them an emergency necessitated rapidly effective measures. Sensitivity towards relativities and fixation on short term costs prevented action.

The three ministers hoped against the evidence of recent months that Thomas would give strong support to the proposal in cabinet. His immediate response, however, was predictably hostile. Political calculation and economic orthodoxy combined. 'The country will think we are more concerned to give fresh "doles" than to improve employment.' The only credible employment policy remained the modernisation of industry and the lowering of the costs of production. The trio's scheme was inevitably at odds with this policy. This assessment was echoed by the committee's majority. 'If this scheme were adopted the cost per head of social services which is already considerably higher in Great Britain than in any other country would be materially increased, and this would have to be considered in relation to its possible effect on world competitive markets.' The cabinet considered the committee's verdict on 19 December. The sentiments expressed by Thomas, Alexander and Pethick-Lawrence were the accepted wisdom. The ministerial trio's proposal was rejected.[21] Arguably, its implementation would have been blocked by the parliamentary arithmetic, but beyond the merits of the proposal the episode revealed the incapacity of senior ministers when confronted by orthodox arguments. Some probably endorsed orthodox sentiments; others were uneasy but lacked the intellectual resources to justify any alternative position. Minority status offered a convenient alibi, both to the wider party and to themselves.

Such considerations similarly shaped ministerial responses to any proposal for the revival of the economy through an expanded work programme. Both Johnston and Mosley believed in the necessity of such a programme. The Government had inherited procedures guaranteed to engender procrastination. Public works were the preserve of local authorities; the Government's role was limited to financial support channelled through the Unemployment Grants Committee and the Ministry of Transport. This process was vulnerable to the orthodoxy already noted by Mosley that the practice simply diverted funds from private sector initiatives into projects that were irrelevant to economic modernisation. Early months were frustrating as Mosley and Johnston explored the complexities and sterility of current practice. In late September, they proposed that the Gordian knot be cut through the introduction of a national road-building programme. Labour had claimed that unemployment was a national issue; it needed a national response. The suggestion was dismissed by two of the younger ministers, Herbert Morrison and the Minister of Health Arthur Greenwood. Local government would be weakened; passive local authorities would wait for the national government to find all the funds.

Morrison had been a prominent critic of Mosley over the Smethwick nomination. Lacking Mosley's social, educational and financial advantages, he had made his way within the party as propagandist, opponent of the war, municipal politician and, above all, the increasingly dominant figure in the London Labour Party. His links with the unions were no more than cordial; his relationship with Bevin, at least as far as the latter was concerned, was appalling. But by the late twenties, despite the loss of his seat in 1924, he was seen widely as a coming man. Wertheimer stressed his 'self-sacrificing, simple, honest and retiring devotion'. He could be caricatured as the ultimate machine politician, loyal to the leadership and above all to MacDonald. He was, however, a serious thinker about the practicalities of policies, whilst seeking to inform legislative and administrative detail with a wider social vision. His diligent and decent persona offered a Labour identity attractive to many members and voters. Ponsonby found him 'business like, determined, unmoved by party bickerings and always friendly'. The clash with Mosley's flamboyance added an edge to departmental rivalries and policy differences. Morrison was under severe cross pressures. His own desire for a larger road construction programme was at odds with Snowden's austerity. Departmental advice was pessimistic about the need for new roads. Morrison was himself sceptical about the contribution that a national road programme could make to the unemployment problem. Sessions between Morrison and Mosley inflamed an already difficult relationship. Morrison felt himself the target of aristocratic hauteur; Mosley made little pretence of subscribing to Labour's democratic ethos. Beatrice Webb diagnosed a serious weakness. 'Mosley... is contemptuous of Thomas's incapacity, of the infirmity of manual working Cabinet Ministers generally and very complacent about his own qualification for the leadership of the Labour Party. That young man has too much aristocratic insolence in his make-up.'[22]

The drive for more public works proved fruitless. By December 1929 the extent and character of the unemployment challenge was changing. A problem to be solved – the intractable million – was becoming submerged beneath an escalating crisis as, month after month, the jobless total rose. Thomas's performances in the House became less and less convincing. He became the personification of an all-too-visible failure, not by one minister, but by the government. The familiar routines of bargaining with railway companies and disarming NUR critics through humour and sentimentality were a lost world. By early December, Henderson felt that Thomas 'is completely rattled and in such a state of panic, that he is bordering on lunacy'. Three weeks later came a ritualistic affirmation of the rapport between Labour and the centre of financial power. MacDonald and Snowden each received the freedom of the City of London at a Mansion House lunch. Thomas was the spectre at the feast. Beatrice Webb portrayed 'a pitiful contrast… his ugly and rather mean face and figure made meaner and uglier by an altogether exaggerated sense of personal failure'. The Lord Privy Seal was almost 'hysterical in his outbursts of self-pity… he panics when flattery turns into abuse'. MacDonald and Snowden basked in Establishment praise, but for Thomas 'the question is whether he will drink himself into helpless disablement'. Beatrice Webb noted that Thomas's relationships with Mosley and Lansbury had effectively ended.[23] This impasse, and the rising unemployment, encouraged Mosley to think through his discontent with the Government's policies in order to suggest what might prove an acceptable alternative.

Public Labour criticism of Thomas remained largely limited to the ILP left. When Thomas spoke in the Commons early in November, Maxton's response was scathing. The *New Leader* simply labelled Thomas a 'failure' and indicted him for a predictable lack of socialism.[24] Within days, criticism within the PLP became widespread, not over the level of unemployment, but over the treatment of the unemployed. Thomas's July statements had produced nothing new by November; in contrast Margaret Bondfield's difficult ministerial baptism had produced the Morris Report, and then in mid November a Bill that incorporated a response to its recommendations, the Unemployment Insurance (No 2) Bill.

The TUC's pressure for an increase in the standard rate of benefit achieved nothing against Snowden's opposition. Improvements for younger workers and dependents offered slight consolation. Trade union opinion was particularly outraged by the Bill's proposal on the key condition for benefit. The TUC and Labour Party position, often known as the Hayday Formula after a leading advocate, was unambiguous. A claimant would be denied benefit if he or she refused an offer of suitable work. However, the draft Bill, in line with the Morris recommendations, contained a lengthy stipulation whose ambiguity could suggest that really little had changed, and that benefits would still be denied on grounds that were unrealistic and punitive. In communities with high levels of unemployment the idea that claimants must be genuinely seeking work was a cruel absurdity. Bondfield vainly suggested that recent administrative changes would effectively satisfy much of the Hayday Formula.[25]

Criticism within the Labour Party was extensive. Forceful opposition from the ILP left was predictable and precipitated a conflict within the much larger ILP Parliamentary Group. The latter included many who had maintained ILP membership whilst becoming increasingly alienated by that party's shift to the left. The disagreement spread across the columns of the *New Leader*. One trenchant contribution came from Allan Young. In all probability Mosley would not have endorsed Young's presentation of the basic choice. 'As the gulf widens between the Labour Party, which has now become a "National" Party and the workers' organisations which form a "Class movement", the ILP will be forced to choose in which company it desires to travel.' Labour had become 'a Party committed to the impossible task of making Capitalism more acceptable to the workers'. But, presumably, by late November, Mosley had come to accept Young's assertion that 'the Party was being committed by speeches of some Ministers inside and outside the House to a purely Conservative view of unemployment'. Young was bemused. 'Still there was no revolt.'[26]

Yet, criticism over the Unemployment Insurance Bill went far beyond the persistent malcontents. Trade union Members concentrated, not on the rates of benefit, but on the conditions, and on a demand to cut the waiting time for benefits from six days to three. Benefit levels were vulnerable to arguments about affordability; at least in the short term, conditions for eligibility could be separated from broader economic issues. For these critics, loyalty was yoked with intense feeling. They were concerned to separate their position from the ILP critics. Will Thorne, a Labour Member since 1906, had once been a young, militant leader of the newly organised so-called unskilled. By 1930 he was a septuagenarian official in Bondfield's union, the ultra-cautious General and Municipal Workers. He distinguished between loyal and irresponsible critics; he presented the contrast to MacDonald in the hope that it would be persuasive. 'What we have seen and heard pains us all. We at any rate are anxious to support the Government in any way, but on the forgoing points we feel very strongly.' Eventually after chaotic scenes in the Commons the loyalist rebels secured a victory.[27] Some regretted that the ILP left would claim some credit. These fevered exchanges were early signs of a distancing between the TUC and the Government. The terrain would be in part procedural; many ministers were unwilling to consult with the General Council on sensitive issues. Such reluctance was testimony to ministerial understanding of the protocols of office and the limited status of trade unions within the party. In part, disputes were substantive, most notably and recurrently on unemployment insurance. Lobbying would involve appeals to hopefully common interests, a readiness not to stand on the dignity of principle, but to negotiate on particulars. Such a strategy avoided confronting the basic challenge of the Government's economic policy – precisely the question that Mosley in December 1929 wished to address.

The fracas over unemployment benefits had barely ended when Mosley met MacDonald in a brief revival of the access that he had enjoyed in opposition. He said that he had come to speak for the ministerial trio, but emphasised his own discontent. He had found it 'impossible to work with Thomas'; MacDonald claimed that Mosley threatened resignation. The experiment in creative tension had clearly failed. 'Probably impossible to work with them but I fear T has handled them badly. Both sides seem to hold each other in something like contempt.' Mosley also mentioned to MacDonald that he was preparing a memorandum on general questions relating to unemployment. In all probability MacDonald would have offered vague encouragement. Such a task would occupy an obviously discontented minister and his immediate colleagues. Henderson was dismissive of Thomas, and perhaps would have welcomed Mosley taking more responsibility on unemployment. Thomas seems to have been informed of the initiative. Mosley translated the preparation of a document critical of government policy, and specifically of Thomas, into emollient terms. An indictment and alternative policy became 'a number of new proposals… jotted down'. Challenge was represented as collegiality. 'Some of these ideas you will agree with and some you'll probably turn down; but in any case, Jim, I'd like you to see them.' Such diplomacy masked the objective and the underlying contempt. The initiative would appeal directly to the cabinet, by-passing Thomas. Mosley, having written his memorandum confided to Harold Nicolson, former diplomat and currently a Beaverbrook journalist, that he could not get on with Thomas at all. 'The foolish man simply does not understand what is happening.'[28]

Although the memorandum was properly coupled with Mosley, Johnston and Lansbury were supportive; Strachey and Allan Young were likely to have been involved in discussions. In mid January Mosley sent a copy to J.M. Keynes accompanied by a prediction – 'I am getting close to my "last word".' Keynes and his Cambridge colleague, Hubert Henderson, responded favourably. On 23 January Mosley forwarded the memorandum to MacDonald. He insisted that whilst his proposals were 'not any cast iron formula, it is impossible to continue as at present'. Simultaneously, Lansbury emphasised his 'substantial agreement' with the Memorandum. 'The limitations of present policy forbid success.' Johnston presented MacDonald with a shambolic picture. He claimed that the quartet had met only twice in the previous six months. 'The belief that such a Committee sits regularly with either deliberative or executive powers is likely to give rise to misunderstanding among members of the Government, the Party and the Public, and it is likely to place the three Ministers in undeserved difficulties in the future, as they may be held partly responsible for decisions which are not theirs and about which they were not formally consulted.' Johnston's belief in the possibility of consensus on critical issues led him to propose an all-Party committee to assess specific relief proposals.[29]

Whatever the differences of emphasis and expectation within the trio, the initiative was a clear rebuff to Thomas. Press reports emerged about a ministerial mutiny against him. MacDonald, alarmed at leakages, met Mosley and Strachey. On 19 February the Premier told the cabinet that the contents of the memorandum had been revealed to selective ministers and to some outside the Government. Thomas's response was predictably lachrymose. He could not remain in office. He had dedicated himself to a difficult task. All members of the Government needed to 'show a real team spirit', but 'certain forces were at work which make that help impossible'. He played for 'the side'. Mosley, by implication, played for himself. MacDonald soothed Thomas. The affair was 'most reprehensible', but 'none of us now are in a position to follow our own feelings'. Although Thomas's political credibility had withered, his emotional repertoire could portray Mosley as the discordant outsider who rejected the ethic of solidarity.[30]

The critical decision had already been taken. On 3 February the cabinet had referred the memorandum to a committee. Its membership hardly suggested a sympathetic response. Snowden was accompanied by Margaret Bondfield, a puritanical apostle of austerity, Tom Shaw, a cotton union official who headed the War Office and was hardly notable for divergent thinking, and Arthur Greenwood, who was establishing a credible reputation at the Ministry of Health. He had already clashed with Mosley over a national road-construction programme. The committee forwarded the memorandum to the Treasury for its comments. The deepening crisis was evident in the inexorable rise in unemployment. Politically it was evident in a sharp fall in the Labour vote at the Sheffield Brightside by-election.[31]

The document that arrived in the Treasury proclaimed the depth of crisis and the urgency of action. It combined economic and administrative diagnoses and proposals. The latter provided the starting point. Mosley argued that his brief experience in office demonstrated the need for a powerful executive. A committee should meet weekly under the Prime Minister; it would be underpinned by standing committees. This reformed structure would be backed by a secretariat of twelve civil servants under the Treasury. This reformed executive would be complemented by a research structure and a development bank. Such a blueprint reflected the frustrations of the trio. What mattered more were policies. Mosley insisted that a long-term strategy for economic modernisation must be liberated from the Government's unrealistic belief that the export trade could be significantly revived. Essential long-term rationalisation necessitated a thorough commitment to domestic development insulated from the shocks of world conditions. Such development should involve the formation of a development company in which the government had the major interest, thereby removing industry from the tutelage of the banks.

The memorandum drew a sharp distinction between long-term rationalisation and the urgent challenge of unemployment. Mosley emphasised the centrality of a national roads programme that would spend £100 million over three years. This expenditure should be accompanied by a further £100 million over three years, allocated to the Unemployment Grants Committee. Schemes in the depressed areas could be provided with 100 per cent government grants. Mosley calculated that together these proposals would employ over 300,000 men a year. More than 400,000 would be added through reviving the retirement pensions proposal and raising the school-leaving age. Such proposals posed the feasibility of appropriate loans. Encouraged by Keynes, he insisted that a major loan for employment projects in the context of his overall policy need not subvert the currency.[32]

Even before the cabinet had passed the memorandum to a committee, Morrison was sympathising with Thomas and demolishing Mosley's emphasis on a national road programme. He offered guilt by association. 'Mosley suffers somewhat from LG's complaint, the road complex.' More seriously, Morrison was blind to the broader economic consequences of public works. 'A road is a means of transport: road work can assist, but it cannot possibly be a principal cure of immediate unemployment.' As an enthusiast for established political institutions, Morrison dismissed Mosley's administrative proposals. The existing system worked well. 'Through the document there is manifested some distrust of the civil servants, apparently on the ground that they served under the last government... my own experience does not justify anything but respect for their loyalty, ability and sincerity.'[33] Snowden doubtless found these virtues in the draft report on the memorandum prepared by Sir Frederick Leith-Ross and presented to the cabinet committee on 14 March. This effectively rejected the memorandum. This verdict provoked no significant dissent from Snowden's colleagues. The trio were given one meeting to make their case, but made no impact. Against the backdrop of rising unemployment the committee only produced its report on 1 May. This last word was little more than Leith-Ross's verdict six weeks earlier.

Public works were characterised as 'shovelling out public money, merely for the purpose of taking what may inevitably be a comparatively small number of people off the unemployed register to do work which is no more remunerative and much more expensive even than unemployment'. Government schemes should be assessed not only for their employment opportunities, but also for their enhancement of productive efficiency. This erosion of Mosley's distinction between the long term and the short term was complemented by a robust justification of rationalisation. 'We must not be afraid to face these temporary consequences.' There was no alternative. 'Though the recovery may be slow we are convinced that the only hope is in the long-term programme, which will restore the competitive power of British industry.' Financial stability was essential. 'We must do all we can to combat the present feeling of insecurity in our financial prospects and we must therefore avoid all schemes involving heavy additions to Budget charges or grandiose loan expenditure.' Treasury orthodoxy was paralleled by political timidity. Any reversal of Government policy was presented in lurid terms – 'a campaign of unrestricted expenditure financed out of loans, with its inevitable concomitants of special powers to coerce labour, landowners etc and its attempt to force capital into un-remunerative channels or to attract it at the cost of subsequent increases in taxation'. The resulting shock to confidence would be 'a God-send to our opponents'. A shock would not require a change in policy, only the appearance of 'any serious element in the Government prepared to advocate such a policy'. Condemnation of the memorandum effectively extended beyond its content to its production.[34]

This bleak dismissal provoked a response from Lansbury. He did not address the economic riposte to the memorandum, but emphasised the political sensitivity.

> Our Party, and certainly not Mosley, Johnston or myself, do not cry for the moon nor expect our whole policy to be carried through in a year or even twenty years, but it is the apparently contemptuous rejection of policies adopted by the Party, and on which we obtained votes, which I object to… It makes me ask myself whether if the Cabinet does anything at all, we should not tell the nation without reservation that the statements in "Labour and the Nation" and in our Election Manifesto were ill-thought out and not worth the paper they were written on.[35]

Ministers faced increasing concern on the Labour backbenches. Three PLP meetings expressed demands for a discussion on the memorandum. Thomas spoke to the PLP on 12 March. Ponsonby found him 'again quite hopeless, wordy, confused and quite incapable of getting down to specific points'. But nevertheless Ponsonby felt that he had 'managed to get round the party meeting, more or less'. Following the third session on 9 April, Lansbury had written to MacDonald suggesting that he and Snowden attend a future meeting so that Members could 'open their hearts' and 'settle matters once and for all'. Lansbury's hope that 'the present uneasiness may be swept away' hardly suggested someone prepared to stand firm on an alternative economic policy. His subsequent hostility towards the committee's report was characteristically constrained by a visceral loyalty to the party. This response was widely shared; the committee's report posed a problem for party managers. The mood within the PLP suggested that a brutal rejection of the memorandum could lead to more 'turbulent and futile' meetings.[36]

The cabinet considered the committee's report on 8 May but avoided a decision. Instead the report was referred to a further committee to be chaired by MacDonald and including the ministers most involved with unemployment. Prolongation of discussion was a cosmetic compromise in the hope of curbing discontent within the PLP. The new committee met on 13 May and rehashed old arguments. Mosley insisted that delays at the Unemployment Grants Committee reflected deficiencies in basic principles. When he suggested that local authorities be short-circuited, Greenwood retorted that the consequences would be chaotic. These sterile exchanges fed Mosley's impatience. Before the next meeting on 19 May, he told MacDonald that he was going to resign. MacDonald persuaded him to come to the committee. MacDonald personalised the subsequent exchanges. 'Soon in difficulties. Mosley would get away from practical work into speculative experiments. Very bad impression. Thomas, light, inconsistent but pushful and resourceful; others overwhelmed and Mosley on the verge of being offensively vain in itself.' Mosley stressed the merits of Keynes's opinions as against Treasury orthodoxy. Thomas retorted that 'businessmen riddle Keynes' to which Mosley responded that 'Keynes wipes the floor with them'. Morrison offered detailed exposition of the unavoidable obstacles to any road-construction programme. He dismissed Lloyd George's, and by extension Mosley's, position as 'economic insanity'.

Mosley summarised his understanding of the problem. 'We must rationalise to hold our position at all. But it will lead to unemployment. This country, if it is to survive at present standard of life, has got to be isolated from other countries, not by tariff. The high purchasing power of home population is the only solution.' Morrison, having insisted on the multiple obstacles to road construction, hymned a rhetorical refrain. 'It is still open to us to remember that Socialism is the only solution.' MacDonald's assessment was puritanical. 'We are buying appearance not reality. Chinese tea instead of milk and oatmeal.' By chance, the Commons were debating unemployment. The reply for the Government at the end of the debate would be difficult. Johnston admitted that 'they'll ship us on Pensions and on Mosley's memorandum'. Predictably, Lansbury could offer an emollient perspective. The solution to unemployment was an international agreement. 'All else is patching up', to which MacDonald responded 'Who will query with that?' Mosley kept quiet.

Mosley resigned the following day, 20 May, but agreed to meet the committee that afternoon. Whilst awaiting his arrival, ministers revisited the recent past. The fracas over the leaking of the memorandum was raked over. Lansbury recalled a 'nice reasoning discussion' with Snowden that had had no follow up, only the bleak committee report. Johnston defended Mosley. He 'had nothing to do; he had been trampled on; his talents ignored... We, Lansbury and I, feel he should be used'. When he arrived, Mosley insisted that for him, the choice was acceptance of the memorandum or resignation. MacDonald maintained his procrastination; the committee report had not been accepted by the cabinet, but referred to this meeting. Mosley targeted the Chancellor. 'It was a case of Snowden v Mosley, and clearly Mosley must go.' Mosley's characterisation of his agenda became more dramatic. The crisis demanded 'a war footing... a revolution in administrative procedure'.

His conception of 'a machine for a vast programme' contrasted with the more restrained criticisms of Johnston and Lansbury. Resignation was, for him, inevitable. 'For ten months I have warned the Government and stood the racket for principles in which I fundamentally disbelieved.' He left his former colleagues with a profession of disillusion that pointed both to the past and the future. 'I perhaps misunderstood you when I came into the Labour Party.' Protestations of principle were complemented by expectation and calculation. He believed that rising unemployment and minority status would mean the ousting of the government and electoral defeat. Resignation would strengthen his position in the party as against 'the old Radical Free-Traders like Snowden and MacDonald'. He could benefit from the Government's economic and political failures.[37]

6
Critic

Mosley was the first minister to resign from a Labour Government. Beatrice Webb considered that he took few resources with him to the backbenches:

> He is entangled in the smart set and luxurious habits; he is reputed to be loose with women; he arouses suspicion, he knows little or nothing about trade unionism or co-operation, he cannot get on terms of intimacy with working-men or with the lower middle-class brainworker. He is in fact an intruder, a foreign substance in the labour movement, not easily assimilated. Mosley will be a great success at public meetings, but will he get round him the Arthur Hendersons, the Herbert Morrisons, the Alexanders, the Citrines and the Bevins, who are the natural leaders of the proletariat? Hitherto these men will have had little use for Mosley.[1]

Committed supporters amongst Labour MPs were likely to be few, as his derisory pre-1929 votes in Parliamentary Committee elections had shown. Yet the Government's record on unemployment had inevitably aroused anxiety amongst backbenchers, who returned at weekends to constituencies where the number without work rose remorselessly. Such concern cohabited with loyalty informed by a belief that public divisions within the party would prove disastrous. For many, this sentiment legitimised a draconian response to persistent critics. The PLP's Consultative Committee was intended as a channel between ministers and backbenchers. Its chairman, Harry Snell, combined mildness of manner with a readiness to impose sanctions against habitual rebels; he was vigorously backed by many colleagues.[2] Anxious loyalists were reactive; with the exception of a few, they had no alternative policy. Often they shared the economic preconceptions of ministers. Individual culpability offered convenient scapegoats. Criticism, therefore, concentrated on individuals, most notably Thomas and Bondfield. The controversy over unemployment insurance in December 1929 had demonstrated for many loyalists that careful lobbying aimed at revising specific elements of government policy could be effective. The Government's minority status and the bleak economic outlook necessitated that expectations be limited. Loyalists endured by defending the mediocre against the worse.

Despite economic difficulties and signs of a significant decline in electoral support, Labour's leadership remained firmly in control of the party. MacDonald might provoke unease on specific issues but his position was unquestioned. Few challenged Snowden's arguments despite the obvious damage inflicted by his revered free trade system and Treasury austerity. Intellectual dominance was complemented by widespread affection. For those who had served their political apprenticeships in the ILP Snowden still recalled stylistically a golden age of socialist evangelism. Arthur Henderson represented trade union interests at the highest level of party and government. He was not only the keeper of the cloth cap. He could shift from Foreign Office to party office in order to employ effectively the arts of the party organiser in order to defuse or defeat dissent. The ethos of loyalism was evident in George Lansbury's response to Mosley's resignation. Although he and Johnston had shared Mosley's dissatisfaction with Thomas, MacDonald knew how to ensure Lansbury's support in a crisis. 'It is not Mosley himself we now have to deal with, but a very serious situation, not only for the Government, but for the whole Party.' Lansbury's response was all that MacDonald could have hoped for. 'I hope that good will come out of apparent evil and that the movement we all love will speedily recover from its present discontents.' Lansbury and Johnston expressed anger at Mosley's resignation. They claimed inaccurately that 'they were beginning to win on essentials. The PM had played a good part in the three meetings they had had with them and Thomas.' They, too, sought a politics of compromise within the party, however limited the likely improvements.[3]

The small band of ILP critics stood unapologetically against such beleaguered pragmatism. They had antagonised trade union loyalists by their thorough opposition to Margaret Bondfield's unemployment insurance legislation. On the eve of Mosley's resignation they had abstained on an Opposition motion critical of Thomas. The growing estrangement of sections of the ILP from the Government was expressed in the emergence of a much smaller Parliamentary Group who were committed to the upholding of ILP policies, against both the Labour Government and the Labour Party. Increasingly, this small group sat together in the Commons and at PLP meetings. Some ostentatiously transgressed parliamentary conventions; they provoked and responded to the visceral antipathy of loyalists.[4]

Mosley, having resigned, faced a search for political space. Fenner Brockway, a thorough exponent of the ILP left's policies, was optimistic. He felt that Mosley's challenge to government failure would expand the ranks of critics. 'He will certainly voice considerable opinion which has not yet identified itself with the Left Wing group and his lead will decide many members in taking definite action.' Dalton, from a thoroughly unsympathetic standpoint, grasped Mosley's dilemma:

> He has a very difficult game to play. Rumour is that he will try to form and lead an inside Left ginger group, appealing especially to some of the younger members who are not associated with the present Left Wing group. All the resources of wealth, flattery, intrigue, proximity of his dwelling to the House and his wife's beauty to be brought into play... But it will be very difficult for him to steer quite clear of the Sore-headed Left, who are greatly hated by most of the rest of the Party. And many will say 'Why couldn't he play in the team?'[5]

John Wheatley had died a week before Mosley's resignation. He was one of the few people who might have effectively brought together Mosley and the ILP. But his influence had declined. His ministerial achievements were a distant memory; caricatured as embittered and recalcitrant he had been increasingly marginalised.

At 1 30pm on 21 May 1930 Mosley read his resignation letter to a PLP meeting; he gave notice of a motion critical of the Government's record on unemployment and demanding 'an alternative policy more in accordance with the programme and pledges of the Party at the last election'. Henderson successfully proposed that this debate be postponed to the following day. The vote in favour was narrow, 80–69. This suggested some disquiet, although Dalton felt that Mosley's reception was only moderate and not at all warm. This low-key overture was paralleled in the Commons, where Mosley read out his resignation letter. Within the PLP, the postponement produced speculation and plotting. Mosley's motion was portrayed by loyalists as a censure on the Government. In response they drafted an amendment. The ILP sought support for Mosley, thereby, Dalton thought, and doubtless hoped, 'ruining him'. John Strachey was 'visibly active' on Mosley's behalf. He was accompanied by another 1929 entrant, Aneurin Bevan, Member for Ebbw Vale. The Trade Union Group of MPs met and predictably decided to back the Government. Bevan, sponsored by the Miners' Federation, spoke with characteristic vigour on Mosley's behalf, only to be threatened with disciplinary action by the Northumberland Miners' leader Ebby Edwards. When a Durham Miners' Member welcomed the muzzling of Bevan, Dalton, an Etonian Durham colleague, celebrated the display of proletarian muscularity. Here was the 'Loyal Lump in action'.[6]

The PLP meeting was crowded, not just by the thoroughly engaged, but also by the habitually loyal, brought out of bars and tea room to defend their government against a well-heeled critic who had broken ranks. Mosley's opening speech made an impact. Even Dalton acknowledged that many were impressed. Mosley's presentation combined copious detail, professions of loyalty and a concluding call to arms. George Strauss, one of the youngest Labour Members, and one of the few within the PLP with experience in the City, was sceptical of Mosley's proposals. They were 'weak, remote and unconvincing. His figures were obviously fantastic'. But Strauss found the speech 'extremely eloquent,' with 'a very high note of emotion,' and a 'sustained dramatic fervour'. The performance played effectively on the widespread concern amongst backbenchers. Mosley's time as a minister and his magisterial style suggested that his criticisms were authoritative. Ministers and their supporters needed to respond.[7]

They began badly. MacDonald offered vague and unpersuasive phrases. Thomas appeared as a veteran performer whose act no longer won over the crowd. He was 'lachrymose… emotional… half-hysterical,' His appeal to 'we who built up the movement on the soap box' hardly reflected his lengthy experience as a full time union official. He had taken on the ministerial brief knowing that it would destroy his reputation. This was 'the greatest moment of humiliation in his life'. Strauss, perhaps reinforced with the scepticism of the young recruit, was left cold. 'Jimmy turns on this emotional tap, much too often nowadays, and at the back of the Committee room at any rate his appeal was received with smiles and sniggers.' Arthur Hayday was emerging as an influential backbench representative of trade union opinion. He employed the ethic of solidarity against Mosley. 'What would be thought in the Trade Union world of an Executive member who resigns and then tries to turn membership against Executive?' The critic was portrayed as an outsider who failed to understand the world that he had joined.[8] Yet General Council members were not monolithic in their antagonism to Mosley. John Bromley was General Secretary of the Locomotive Engineers. He was a volatile figure; his craft-based union often found itself at odds with the ecumenical ambitions of Thomas's NUR. Prior to 1926 he was sometimes identified with the trade union left. His response to the ending of the General Strike, and his subsequent criticism of the Miners' Federation, and especially of A.J. Cook, had made him a target of the left, not least at the 1926 TUC. He supported Mosley in what Dalton dismissed as 'a speech of garrulous egoism'. His intervention offered nothing significant to Mosley. Rather it typified the unpredictability that marked Bromley's political career; he would continue as a loyal supporter of the Government. In contrast to Bromley, the ILP left 'sat all night drilled and silent'. Dalton thought that Mosley 'has so safeguarded himself, after much preparation clearly from their direct embrace'. An amendment to Mosley's motion was moved by Ernest Thurtle, perhaps significantly Lansbury's son-in-law.[9] This referred not to 'dissatisfaction' but to 'growing anxiety'; it emphasised the impact of world -wide depression and asserted the inseparability of unemployment from capitalism. Having acknowledged the Government's achievements, it resolved 'to unite in supporting the Government in intensified endeavours on the lines of Labour Party policy to reduce unemployment'.

The discussion lasted for two and a half hours. When Henderson rose to wind up, Dalton felt that he faced a difficult atmosphere, not at all friendly to the Government. Henderson praised all contributors and in particular, Mosley, offering his sympathy through a recollection of his own resignation from the Lloyd George Coalition in August 1917. He moved to the critical issue. Any vote, with its inevitable divisiveness, would be a disaster; he appealed to Mosley and Thurtle to withdraw motion and amendment. If this procedure was followed, there could be a further PLP meeting to discuss unemployment. He ended with an appeal to solidarity; 'let us not give comfort to our enemies'. Thurtle predictably withdrew his amendment. Mosley exchanged acerbities with a hitherto silent Snowden. He addressed Henderson's suggestion. His first preference was for an immediate decision on the motion, but he was prepared to adjourn the discussion. Henderson's immediate response revealed that his objective was to end dissension. 'We must decide tonight.' Mosley was trapped by a tactician experienced in the manipulation of emotions and the construction of majorities, not least through the transformation of what was deemed at stake. The issue for many was no longer unemployment and ministerial failings but what qualified within party culture as reasonable behaviour. Henderson personified the organisation, a collective expressed through the style of an individual. His appeal contrasted with Thomas's sentimentality and self-pity, and with MacDonald's generalities, which barely camouflaged a frequently wounded sense of self. Mosley, with his refusal to follow Thurtle's lead, cast himself as the discordant and unreasonable voice.

Mosley went ahead with a vote; he was perhaps encouraged to do so by Strachey and Bevan. At least as important as any numerical assessment of the likely outcome, his experience as a minister had demonstrated that further discussion without a clear readiness to envisage a change in policy would be futile. The vote was 210 against 29, an overwhelming defeat but almost exactly the critics' support as predicted before the meeting. The minority was restricted to the ILP left, a few who were close to Mosley and a handful of others. Jim Simmons still retained his ILP card, although hostile to the left critics. He felt that the Government should be bolder but believed that, given the lack of a parliamentary majority, scope was limited. Socialism was the only solution.[10] In his case his association with Mosley in winning much of Birmingham for Labour remained influential and sufficient to align him with the critics. Those hostile to Mosley saw the decision to push for a vote as indicative of his failings as a politician. Dalton proclaimed that he was 'the worst tactician of the age! A head swollen to the size of an elephant.' Strauss was more judicious but in all probability exaggerated the hypothetical benefits of withdrawal. Mosley had made

> a grave misjudgement of the feeling of the meeting, and a tactical blunder. Had he agreed to do so, Mosley's position in the Party would have been exceedingly strong. Now as it is, he's looked upon with little sympathy by the ILP group even, who refer to him with disdain, and with complete lack of confidence with the Labour group as a whole. It will take a very long time for him to retrieve his blunder.

There seems little reason to believe that withdrawal of the motion would have strengthened Mosley's position in the party; the political topography remained the same.

Philip Noel-Baker was Henderson's Parliamentary Private Secretary. At the PLP meeting he had felt cross-pressured. In Dalton's scornful dismissal 'he ran away and did not vote'. Noel-Baker subsequently offered Mosley support on paper, plus optimism:

Your speech was superb; you made sense of all that 95 per cent of the party said on their platforms at the last election. The Govt. couldn't even make the semblance of an answer and in consequence you had them literally on their knees... I believe you can get the Govt. on the run and have them adopting your policy within months if you follow up your speech... at future party meetings and in the House.

Noel Baker suggested that Mosley did not lack for sympathy at the top of the party. 'I hope you will play for Uncle's active support.' The significance of this reference to Henderson is unclear. Perhaps it reflected the party secretary's desire to retain the services of a talented recruit. Yet some party loyalists trivialised the episode. Cuthbert Headlam was a Tory diarist travelling regularly between the North East and London. On one journey he discussed Mosley's resignation with two Labour Members, Ebby Edwards and the Member for Jarrow, Robert Wilson, a Co-operator and Nonconformist preacher. They were dismissive. 'The Mosley row had ended in smoke... it had done the party good.'[11]

Mosley appealed beyond the Parliamentary Labour Party when he spoke in the Commons on 28 May. This 70-minute speech has been viewed widely as the pinnacle of his political career. He fluently and rigorously elaborated his memorandum's analysis and proposals. His argument took him from the need for administrative reform to a dismissal of reliance on the export trade as essential to economic recovery. He confronted the susceptibilities of Labour and Liberal free traders by suggesting the necessity for an insulated economy; he emphasised his specific proposals on road construction, retirement pensions and the school-leaving age. He concluded with an appeal to Government and Parliament to give a lead in order to avert a calamitous decline. Although he referred often to 'crisis', he claimed that his greatest fear was 'a very long slow crumbling through the years until we sink to the level of a Spain, a gradual paralysis beneath which all the vigour and energy of this country will succumb'.[12]

His characteristic blend of facts, self-consciously robust analysis and emotional rhetoric produced an enthusiastic press across the political spectrum. The *Morning Post* noted his 'patrician ease', the *Daily Mail* asserted that he made the occupants of both front benches seem second rate. The *Daily Herald* was surprisingly magnanimous. 'Sir Oswald entered a brilliant defence of his own attitude, followed by a vigorous and sustained offensive. ... Rarely has a junior Minister, resigning under such circumstances received such a remarkable personal triumph.' J.L. Garvin, very sympathetic to Mosley, exaggerated his impact in *The Observer*. Mosley had 'left the majority of the Commons more than ever convinced that by one means or another national policy must be boldly changed'. Neville Chamberlain offered a critical but nuanced assessment. 'Mosley had a personal triumph. ... The matter of his speech showed a fantastic ignorance of realities, but the manner could hardly have been improved on.' Chamberlain, unlike many, was unimpressed by his sincerity. 'I thought he was clearly acting, though I must say he acted very well.'[13]

The most sympathetic response to Mosley's speech within the subsequent debate came from a member of the ILP Parliamentary Group. Frank Wise cut a very distinctive figure within that increasingly marginalised faction. He was the son of a Bury St Edmunds fishmonger, who had been educated at the local grammar school and then at Cambridge. A civil servant and vice-warden of Toynbee Hall, his outlook had been profoundly shaped by the war. His experience was not the Western Front but the War Office and the Ministry of Food. Very much one of Lloyd George's men of push and go, a close friend, Ted Lloyd, emphasised 'his animation and vigour... his whole being radiated energy'. His civil service career offered a continuous denial of stereotypes of caution and conformity. 'He was continually taking risks, doing unprecedented things, defying the precedents, incurring the disapproval of his colleagues... short circuiting the established routines, and stretching the authority given him to its extreme limits.' Post-war, he became a British representative on the Inter-Allied Supreme Economic Council, and an assistant secretary at the Board of Trade. His extensive work on food supply issues in post-war Europe brought a detailed knowledge of the Russian situation during the civil war and into the years of the New Economic Policy. Early in 1923 he resigned from the civil service and became an economic adviser on foreign trade to the Russian co-operative movement.

His civil service career had become increasingly a defence of the public welfare against private interests seeking to colonise the state. Initially a progressive social reformer, his wartime experience of state control led him to an explicitly socialist politics, and to post-war involvement in the Independent Labour Party. He became heavily involved in the attempt by Clifford Allen and his associates to transform the ILP into a socialist think tank for the labour movement. Wise brought his distinctive experience of state institutions and their relationship with the worlds of finance and industry to the ILP's discussions. He influenced the party's agricultural policy through the inclusion of proposals for the bulk purchase of agricultural imports. He extended their scope to embrace all basic commodities through his work on *The Living Wage* document. Elected to the Commons for Leicester East in 1929, his expertise informed his subsequent criticisms of the government. He attacked the irresponsible power of bankers, and argued for the public ownership of the Bank of England and the joint stock banks.[14]

Wise's vision of socialism had little sympathy for trade union radicalism. Facing the prospect of sympathetic action by the transport unions in support of the Miners' Federation in April 1921, he had found the prospect of victory for either side unattractive:

> If the Government wins trade unionism in this country has received an unprecedented setback, and I am sure that the bitterness that will be evoked will be extremely dangerous. If the men win then the seat of power has shifted from the Cabinet and Westminster to Robert Williams and his friends of the Triple Alliance. Either prospect is such as to cause alarm.

Such emphases on rationality and hard facts had affinities with Mosley. Wise could easily have presented his own views under the title 'Revolution by Reason'. When he responded to Mosley's resignation speech Wise largely supported his positions on the home market and public spending, adding robust criticism of MacDonald's woolly contribution to the debate and the government's overall strategy. Only on the export trade did Wise differ significantly from Mosley. Whilst acknowledging the difficulty, if not the impossibility, of regaining many lost markets, he felt that Mosley was too pessimistic about the consequences of rationalisation and technological change.[15]

Despite such affinity the two men never formed an effective partnership. Given the sparseness of Labour critics of their government's economic strategy, this is perhaps surprising. Wise remained a committed member of the ILP left. He participated in its lobby rebellions and made critical speeches whilst not endorsing some of its members' individual crusades and eccentricities. Such organisational loyalty could be a barrier. Possibly there was a stylistic clash; Wise's detailed presentations were far removed from Mosley's high drama. Jennie Lee was a committed supporter of the ILP left; she and Wise became close companions during the 1929 parliament. He perhaps endorsed her verdict. 'The Mosley–Bevan group is young, vigorous, unscrupulous. They are to be reckoned with, but I cannot conceive of myself working with them. There is something unsound mentally and spiritually.' Arthur Ponsonby reflected such criticisms in characteristically less dismissive terms. He admired Mosley's vitality and drive but 'there is something a little flashy and vulgar about his personality'.[16]

Whatever the negative sentiments within the PLP, Mosley's resignation and Commons speech produced some supportive responses within the wider party. He rapidly confirmed the backing of his Smethwick base; his detailed explanation to the Trades and Labour Council reasserted the themes of his PLP motion. He emphasised that his position remained that of the party at the 1929 election. He would seek to change policy through the PLP and at the party conference. The Doncaster Labour Party met four days after his Commons speech to consider its resolutions for the party conference. Mosley's case had made an impact. One of the Doncaster Party's chosen resolutions urged the government to adopt the policy of the memorandum as presented to the Commons. The political character of the Doncaster Party was loyalist. The ILP presence was small; there was no record of sympathy for left-wing causes. More than half of its affiliation income came from the railway unions, almost all from branches of the National Union of Railwaymen. Much of the remainder came from three branches of the Yorkshire Miners' Association, a byword for Labour loyalism. Jimmy Thomas was widely seen as the principal target of Mosley's criticism, yet a divisional party in which his union had a major stake responded sympathetically to the case put by Mosley, in part perhaps because he was seen as free from association with a left that many saw as needlessly divisive. In contrast, the Birmingham Borough Party decided not to debate a motion congratulating Mosley on his resignation.[17]

Such sympathy within some local parties barely percolated into the PLP. John Strachey's support was predictable given their personal and intellectual comradeship. Cynthia Mosley's backing could be readily characterised as the adherence of a privileged socialite who had entered politics at the behest of her husband. Yet she could not be dismissed as a decorative spectator admiring his prowess and endorsing and discarding political nostrums as he required. Party members responded warmly to her spontaneity. Her first Commons speech in October 1929 on pensions had made an impact. She had responded to Conservative complaints that recipients were 'demoralised' because they received 'something for nothing'. 'All my life I have had something for nothing. Why? Have I deserved it? Not a bit. I have just got it through luck... I stoutly deny that I am demoralised.' In those early months of the Government optimism had still been possible.[18]

They were joined by a few others; two were particularly significant. W.J. Brown, General Secretary of the Civil Servants' Assistant
Clerks' Association, had established a reputation as a formidable trade
union negotiator. He had entered the Commons as Member for West
Wolverhampton in 1929, and had reacted rapidly against what he saw
as the government's disastrous passivity. Either a socialist agenda or a
reforming progressive alliance would be preferable. Mosley seemingly
offered a way forward. Brown, like Strachey, straddled the Mosleyite section and the ILP left for whom he acted as secretary. An ILP colleague
remembered his stimulating company; 'he held court in the smoking
room with those of us who were off duty, outlining and eulogising whatever scheme he thought of while he talked'. In contrast Aneurin Bevan
had no affinity with the ILP, whom he dismissed as impractical purists.
He had known both the last pre-war years of boom in the south Wales
coalfield and the destruction of the twenties, as the coal trade collapsed
and communities began to disintegrate. Formed by the coalfield and
its ecumenical radicalism, he had lived the vulnerability of an industry
that depended on the vicissitudes of international markets. The defeats
of the Miners' Federation in 1921 and 1926 had shredded any hope
of radical transformation through industrial strength. The search for
political power remained as the only solution to the coalfield's travails.
He had entered the Commons in 1929 aged 31, the beneficiary of the
sitting Member's de-selection; this contrasted with the experience of
the typical Miners' Member who arrived at Westminster after lengthy
service as a district or lodge official. Bevan was also distinctive within
the Miners' phalanx in his thoughtful and passionate speeches and
his liking for metropolitan society. Not a habitué of the Commons Tea
Room, he formed a close friendship with John Strachey. 'You are very
good to me John. It hurts me a little that you give so much and I can
give nothing in return. So few people have given me anything that I feel
a little strange and bewildered. I count our friendship as the one thing
of value that parliament has given me.' Other sympathisers with Mosley
came from the same generation. Robert Forgan was a Scottish medical
man who had served on the Western Front; Oliver Baldwin was the son
of the Tory leader and at odds with the culture of the Commons. Brown
depicted him wandering its corridors 'a desolate and lonely figure'.[19]

The aftermath of Mosley's resignation showed no significant shift in
government responses to rising unemployment. Thomas served as the
symbolic sacrifice; he moved to the more congenial Dominions Office;
a reshuffled ministerial team rapidly concluded that little more could
be done. Bevan's attempt to open a discussion within the PLP on an

alternative policy produced lengthy and inconsequential meetings. Mosley's publicly expressed views were beginning to take him beyond the limits of Labour sentiments. His desire to insulate the British economy against global instability was vulnerable to the objection that British dependency on international trade made this policy impracticable. By early July his suggested insulation was no longer of Britain, but of the empire. In a parliamentary debate he stressed the need to protect the living standards of 'white labour' against the competition offered by 'cheap Oriental labour' increasingly equipped with the benefits of modern technology. His solution had similarities with the 'White Australia' policy which had been zealously championed by the Australian Labor Party. The strategy must be 'to insulate these islands and this commonwealth from the shock of world conditions, and in the area under our own control, to build, while there is still time, a high standard of civilisation which may absorb the production of our industrial machine.'[20]

Mosley's agenda was already suggesting some divergence from that of his close associate Allan Young. He, too, expressed a self-conscious pragmatism. If socialists rejected a revolutionary strategy the only option was to rally together energetic minds capable of grasping the present situation and pursuing a policy which would make capitalism work. But for Young such a response must not only avert immediate dangers, it must prepare the way for ultimate socialist victory.[21] Leo Amery, a zealot for Protection and Empire, had successfully defended his Sparkbrook seat against Allan Young's candidacy and Mosley's money in 1929. Mosley's argument for 'protection and Empire economic unity' aroused Amery's enthusiasm. In his view, Mosley's suggestions had been well received amongst Labour Members. 'The Socialists who had not at all liked Snowden's speech listened with keen attention and mostly with approval.' Mosley was supported in the debate by Frank Wise; other Labour backbench contributions were insubstantial. On his own admission MacDonald's winding-up speech was a disaster. 'Last night one of the worst speeches in House I ever made. Said what I did not want to say and did not say what I wanted.' Ministers might despair of any improvement, but Labour's few critics remained divided. Brockway welcomed Mosley and Wise's presentation of the case for Import Boards, but felt that the former's speech had been 'marred by a dangerous leaning towards a Labour Economic Imperialism'.[22]

Mosley had achieved virtually no progress within the Parliamentary Party. He had failed in his attempt to win election to the PLP Consultative Committee; the attempt by Bevan to initiate a discussion on new proposals to reduce unemployment had proved abortive.[23] Early in October the party conference met in Llandudno. Arthur Henderson had successfully proposed that proceedings be organised around presentations by three ministers who could offer credible claims of achievement. This should reduce pessimism and would limit the time for critical debates. Agenda politics was supplemented by MacDonald's performance. The party leader spoke early in the proceedings. The R101 airship had crashed on the eve of the conference. He began with an emotional reference to the disaster, before painting an evolutionary vision of socialism which blamed unemployment on capitalist break-down. Dalton offered a judicious assessment, 'a good conference speech which really said nothing'.[24]

The unemployment debate demonstrated the established topography that hampered Mosley's presentation of his case. The core resolution was moved and seconded by two ultra-loyalist unions, the General and Municipal Workers and the Cotton Workers. Even in these redoubts of loyalism there were concerns about ministerial shortcomings, albeit expressed within a supportive framework. Maxton's demand on behalf of the ILP for the rapid introduction of a socialist programme simplified the options. No major union would support this agenda in opposition to the government. The ILP amendment was rejected by a majority of almost six to one, and the essentially loyalist resolution was carried.[25]

This easy victory for the leadership was followed by a debate offer-ing a very different choice. The resolution submitted four months previously by the Doncaster Divisional Party emerged onto the confer-ence floor in a modified form. The initial submission had demanded that the Government should adopt the Mosley Memorandum. The revised version asked that the document be considered seriously by the Parliamentary Party, and that the National Executive should examine its proposals and prepare a report. It was moved by the Doncaster delegate, Councillor Herbert Heaviside JP. He was no fire-eating radical, but the local party's Secretary-Agent, a pillar of the local Labour establishment. The resolution could not be dismissed as yet another challenge from the left; rather it suggested a practical response to an immediate crisis.

Mosley's dramatic contribution offered macho-rhetoric and a plea for national reconstruction. He enunciated the issues that had led to his resignation and attacked the illusory salvation of a revived export trade. He insisted on the need to insulate the home and possibly the imperial market. The economy had to be planned, a 'scientific' response to the blind and destructive forces of capitalism. He introduced a new element in his agenda for a 'modern' solution. Parliament must be streamlined. It must cease to be 'a talking shop' and become 'a business assembly'.

His language was not that of class but of nation. The crisis was national; the objective was to build 'a great national civilisation'. Dalton might deprecate the speech as 'a dramatic piece of tub-thumping', but for the first time at the conference the leadership were under pressure.

The NEC's response was given, perhaps predictably, by Lansbury. He chose not to discuss the merits of Mosley's case. Instead he began with a procedural objection. Why should the Memorandum be sent to the NEC but no other cabinet document? For Lansbury such details were overshadowed by the grand vision. The only way forward lay through an educated socialist majority. 'Therefore let them educate, agitate and organise… until they had got the teeming millions of their people imbued with Socialist ideas, and when they had got that, they would not want anybody's Memorandum to bring about Socialism.' Lansbury's rhetoric probably had minimal impact on the subsequent vote. The Doncaster resolution was lost by 1,251,000 to 1,046,000. Some major unions were attracted by a call for immediate action. This could send an essentially loyalist message to ministers; for some trade unionists this could be accommodated within their culture of pragmatic bargaining with government.[26]

A contemporary portrait emphasised the power of Mosley's oratory. 'Like all his set speeches beautifully delivered and with that touch of demagogy which he adds to the effectiveness of his more popular orations.' So much had been acknowledged for several years-but the observer made a further comment fuelled probably by the recent Reichstag election that had seen a dramatic increase in the Nazi vote:

> We cannot resist transcribing the comment of an acute Continental observer at the conference that in Sir Oswald Mosley, British Labour may yet find its Hitler. The parallel is not as absurd as it sounds, for in some respects at least, resemblance might be found between the cruder aspirations of the Nazis and the new Socialist Imperialism subordinating Parliamentary institutions to its own imperative needs to which Sir Oswald Mosley is drifting.[27]

A Treasury official was sceptical about the impact of the Llandudno performance. 'I don't think the country will really follow Sir Oswald Hitler.'[28]

Whatever the character of Mosley's politics in October 1930, delegates elected him back onto the National Executive after a year's absence. How far this success indicated sympathy for his criticisms of the government is unclear. Perhaps some unions favoured his election on the ground that collective responsibility for NEC decisions would limit his criticism of the government. Policy issues were not absent from these NEC elections. This was evident in its most sensational result. Jimmy Thomas was comprehensively defeated in the vote for the Trade Union Section. His union had been central to the founding of the party; for the first time it would be unrepresented on its governing body. Dismay at government failures on unemployment was expressed in a personalised form. Once again, Thomas was the sacrificial victim. Other cabinet ministers, whatever their culpability, were comfortably re-elected.

The NEC offered an even less hospitable environment for critics than the Parliamentary Party. Apart from Mosley, the only dissenting voice would be Fred Jowett, a mild and gentle ILP veteran. In contrast the Trade Union Section included hard-line disciplinarians, the Women's Section was a loyalist phalanx; Mosley's old adversaries, Dalton and Morrison, had strengthened their positions. Any would-be critic faced a discouraging prospect.[29]

The problem soon became evident when the National Executive considered the increasingly tortuous constitutional position of the ILP. A by-election was called in East Renfrewshire. The constituency had been a Labour seat in 1922 and 1923, but Glaswegian suburbanisation was transforming its character. In the economic circumstances of November 1930 there was no hope of a Labour gain. The local party selected Thomas Irwin, a conventional Labour figure, whose ILP membership signified not so much his radicalism as that party's centrality to Scottish Labour politics. The prospect of an ILP-sponsored candidate nevertheless alarmed Labour's disciplinarians. When asked whether he would sign the new ILP commitment to the decisions of the increasingly critical Parliamentary Group, Irwin initially expressed his loyalty to Labour, but later said he would be prepared to sign the ILP pledge. A special meeting of the NEC adopted Morrison's proposal that endorsement be withheld from Irwin, by a vote of eleven to three. Jowett and Mosley were joined on prudential grounds by Dalton. 'Minority (Jowett, Lord O and I) wanted to send him a letter which would give him a chance to climb down, but the majority was for rigid discipline. The ILP have brought this on themselves by twisting and delaying tactics. But we can't, in my opinion, afford a serious breach at this stage.' The ILP left MPs responded by making the by-election their distinctive campaign. They were joined by Mosley. After Irwin had been heavily defeated, Mosley was challenged at the NEC on his participation. He expressed his contempt for the Government and insisted that he reserved the right to criticise them in his speeches.[30]

Such exchanges were peripheral to Mosley's concerns. At best the ILP offered a recruiting ground for individual supporters of his programme; at worst the escalating conflict over constitutionality and socialist rectitude was a distracting irrelevance. Initially, Mosley attempted an alliance on the NEC with the beleaguered Jowett. At the November NEC meeting they proposed a resolution on the Government's economic failure, and suggesting a NEC deputation to the Government expressing 'grave concern and dissatisfaction'. Henderson typically deflected the criticism. As Party Secretary he had already assessed the reasons for the party's recent poor performance in the municipal elections. A report would be sent to MacDonald emphasising the electoral damage resulting from unemployment. Mosley withdrew the resolution.[31]

Such stonewalling was endorsed by loyalists, but November was a febrile month. A by-election defeat at Shipley meant 'everyone is in a temper and a panic'. Brown claimed to have written to Henderson saying that he and Mosley wanted a meeting with him away from the Commons. Demands for Snowden's resignation were allegedly growing amongst Labour backbenchers. A clash erupted at a PLP meeting between the Chief Whip Tom Kennedy and Mosley. The flashpoint was a supposed offence by W.J. Brown. Mosley denounced the Government and insisted 'if there is to be a scrap he'll be in it'. The style of his intervention jarred with the party's ethos. Clement Attlee, another public-school educated Member with military service demanded, 'Why does Mosley always speak to us as though he were a feudal landlord abusing tenants who are in arrears with their rent?'[32]

The Government's predicament made loyalist MPs increasingly intolerant of any criticism. Mosley, like the ILP left, became a target. Marion Phillips was the Labour Party's first Chief Woman's Officer. She had worked tirelessly encouraging the growth of local organisation. Her election at Sunderland in 1929 could seem the finale to a decade of commitment. Understandably, she saw Mosley as a disruptive influence. She wrote to one of her local party members in Sunderland about claims that Mosley was circularising local parties with copies of a Protectionist speech and an offer of a visit. Phillips condemned his recent behaviour as 'very difficult indeed'. His policy was 'entirely different' from that agreed by the party conference. At a recent PLP meeting he was seen as making 'a definite bid for leadership of a Party in opposition to the present Party'. Phillips hoped that such a proposal would be viewed critically in Sunderland. 'If the Party are inclined to accept the offer, I hope they will not do so until they have an opportunity of discussing it with me.'[33] For loyalists Mosley was increasingly outside the pale.

Mosley's oratorical performances in the Commons and at the party conference had been widely acclaimed. In Labour Party terms they had proved politically barren. In late 1930 he was a highly visible, but in policy terms, un-influential, member of the Parliamentary Party. His re-election to the National Executive had only served to place him in a small minority on contentious issues. Significant unions had supported the Doncaster resolution and had ensured his election to the NEC. At most, these votes were statements of concern about government policy and the increasingly difficult relationship between ministers and the Trades Union Congress. They did not indicate support for the distinctive policies presented by Mosley. Major unions remained unsure about any alternative policy; they were divided on the merits of Protection. As yet the TUC was not prepared to openly criticise Labour ministers.

Despite rising unemployment and disappointments on specific issues, in late 1930 the Labour Party and the wider labour movement remained largely united. The challenges and traumas of office had generated dogged solidarity rather than fragmentation. This resilience contrasted with the state of the opposition parties. Conservatives and Liberals had been disappointed by the outcome of the 1929 election. Post-mortems and the strategic choices of opposition had meant divisions in both parties. Mosley, with his social networks and distinctive political biography, had connections across the political spectrum. As first the Labour Government, and then the Labour Party, proved unreceptive to his agenda, he began increasingly to explore the prospects for party realignment.

7
Explorer

The 1929 election defeat weakened Stanley Baldwin's position. He had miscalculated with his Protectionist appeal in 1923; the achievement of a massive majority in October 1924 had seemingly established his dominance over the party. Unexpected defeat in May 1929 diminished his credibility as leader. Many criticised what they viewed as a woolly and personalised appeal epitomised in the slogan 'Safety First'. Orthodox partisans and campaigners for Protection felt that Baldwin was too accommodating to diverse views. Yet, his consensual style was complemented by a willingness to benefit from, and on occasions participate in, the labelling of Labour as unpatriotic and dangerous. His 1924 landslide had owed much to a campaign that emphasised that Labour was unfit to govern, a claim confirmed for impressionable electors by the *Daily Mail's* parading of the Zinovieff letter. An experienced journalist on first meeting him was struck by the contrast between image and reality. 'In his photographs his face had always seemed to be chiefly amiable and a little whimsical, just as his speeches sound simple, honest and ingenuous… But the characteristic of his face is its determination and shrewdness… in a rather hard and grim way.' Many within and beyond his own party failed to grasp the complexity of what one contemporary presented as the 'Methody Machiavelli'.[1]

Critics bemoaned his lack of vigour in opposition; the indictment strengthened as the government's position deteriorated. The press lords, Beaverbrook, once a confidante of Bonar Law, and Rothermere, younger brother of Lord Northcliffe, campaigned vociferously for Empire Free Trade. Rothermere seemed implacable; Beaverbrook's relationship with Baldwin fluctuated between hostility and accommodation. The Conservatives shifted discreetly towards Protection not because of the press lords' campaign, but because of the assiduous efforts of

Neville Chamberlain. As a senior member of a collective leadership he avoided any association with Beaverbrook and Rothermere, who could be portrayed as populist, demagogic and irresponsible. Modification of the Conservative position on Protection could not end the disaffection within the party. When Baldwin responded favourably to the Irwin Declaration in favour of progress towards Indian self-government, he exposed a sensitive nerve amongst Tory activists. Winston Churchill's response was hostile. He was already becoming separated from the party leadership. His attachment to free trade had left him increasingly isolated as sentiment and the need for party unity shifted the Conservatives towards Protection. For Churchill, India and broader issues of imperial defence suggested an alternative basis for Tory unity which might attract some Liberal support. The result could be an anti-Labour arrangement reminiscent of the post 1918 Lloyd George Coalition.[2]

Any such expectation depended heavily on the Liberal Party. The electoral outcome had left the party with the arithmetical ability to make and unmake governments, but this position of apparent strength posed basic strategic problems. Lloyd George had briefly considered the prospects for an alliance with the Conservatives in pursuit of electoral reform. Baldwin's antipathy was an insuperable obstacle. Instead he sought an accommodation with Labour. This quest for a Progressive Alliance in part reflected a Liberal response to the Conservative move towards Protection; it also indicated a hope that Labour might prove sympathetic to electoral reform, and an expectation that scope existed for collaboration on economic and social policy. Bargaining was inevitably protracted, deepening the divisions within a party already marked by personalised factionalism. The private character of inter-party bargaining fed rumours and speculation, and necessitated public inconsistency. A small group of Liberal MPs sympathised with the partially revealed project of sustaining the government. Those whose political identity could be summarised as free trade, retrenchment and antipathy to anything associated with Lloyd George endured as a political monument. The aftermath of the election inevitably meant the resumption of hostilities between Lloyd George and these heirs to Asquithian rectitude. Most crucial were those increasingly identified with Sir John Simon, once widely viewed as the personification of Liberal high-mindedness, who believed that the Labour Government was a disastrous failure and that a Progressive Alliance would terminally damage the Liberal Party. The party's electoral performance seemed to confirm this diagnosis. The Liberal hold on the balance of power, as in 1924, was proving to be a poisoned chalice. The Liberal dilemma strengthened the sense of political plasticity. Lloyd George, like Churchill, threatened to become a 'big beast' looking for a new home.[3]

The prospect of fragmentation predictably interested Mosley as he increasingly experienced the recalcitrance of Labour Party loyalties. His political formation had been in a post-war world of shifting and unstable identities where the apparent settlement of 1922–4 was only one outcome amongst several possibilities. He envisaged similar uncertainties in the political and economic vortex of 1930 where no established party leadership appeared to have credible answers to economic crisis; party identities and alignments seemed increasingly irrelevant and therefore damaging. Scepticism about traditional loyalties was accompanied by increasing criticism of political institutions. Parliament and executive seemed ineffective in the face of economic crisis, and in need of thorough reform. Beaverbrook's Empire Crusade oscillated between attempting to influence the Conservative Party and setting up a new organisation. Either way he could seem a stimulating challenge to the established order. Beaverbrook's view of Mosley was already favourable and he responded rapidly to Mosley's advocacy of imperial insulation in July 1930. 'I am ready at any moment to make overtures in your direction in public if you wish me to do so. On the other hand I will be glad to organise a Committee to work with you and your colleagues in the hope of hammering out an agreed policy.' Rumours circulated of Mosley spending weekends with Beaverbrook. The relationship remained positive, but the longevity of Beaverbrook's enthusiasms was unpredictable.[4]

One option for Mosley was to explore the prospects for co-operation with younger Conservatives who were disenchanted with Baldwin's leadership, and unhappy about the lack of serious thinking on contemporary issues that characterised much of the Tory Party. Such disenchantment was expressed in high-mindedness, intensity and intellectual flirtatiousness. *Industry and the State: A Conservative View*, published in 1927, had presented their vision for the party. This collection of essays emphasised the necessity for state intervention backed by an Economic General Staff. Proposals included an enquiry into the financial credit system, an international conference to develop continuous co-operation between banks, an imperial wheat insurance scheme, an import board, labour co-partnership with all employees and a national wage board in each industry. The populist face of the Tory press was vitriolic. The *Daily Mail* dismissed the authors as 'Socialists in Conservative disguise'; the *Sunday Pictorial* exhumed the passions of the Zinovieff Letter and the spectre of Bolshevism: 'The Party must be purged of its woolly-minded, semi-Socialists. These Kerenskys will, unless they are hauled up, only prepare the way for Lenin.' Three of these harbingers of revolution would explore political prospects with Mosley. All had entered the Commons in the Conservative advance of 1924.[5]

Robert Boothby, a close friend of John Strachey since their time at Eton and Magdalen, had socialised with the Mosleys since the mid-twenties. He celebrated a Venetian holiday. 'Never in my life have I experienced such sustained enjoyment at such a high pitch... a glorious and quite incredible dream.... when sunburn and mosquitoes were all that troubled.' Over fifty years later he recalled the Piazza San Marco and 'a society that no longer exists. The band was playing Wagner, and Sir Thomas Beecham strolled by humming the tunes. In those days Tom saw himself as Byron and swam long distances in the lagoon'. Holidays at Antibes included lunches at a mountain inn with Mosley, John Strachey and George Bernard Shaw.[6]

He eulogised Mosley as a future prime minister. 'He has the Divine Spark which is almost lost nowadays.' Conservative press tactics at the Smethwick by-election provoked him into a letter under the pseudonym, 'Unionist MP'. This condemned 'the campaign of vilification and cheap personal abuse of the Socialist candidate and his wife conducted without regard for the truth, and with a vulgarity unsurpassed, even in the present age'. The letter remained unpublished. In a flight of fancy he could imagine a transformed Labour Party where he would feel at home. 'I shall join the Socialist movement as soon as they turn out Snowden, Graham and the mugwumps and substitute Wheatley and Johnston. I agree with everything *they* say.' Perhaps such sentiments had their root in regret about the fall of the Lloyd George Coalition and the former premier's marginalisation. Many years later he would contrast Lloyd George's 'fantastic energy and insight' with 'Baldwin's stagnant lethargy and Neville Chamberlain's petty small-mindedness'.

As Mosley contemplated resignation from the government in May 1930, Boothby sought to dissuade him. Whatever the merits of the case he would be isolated. Rather, he should consolidate his position within the Labour Party in the expectation of a new Progressive alliance. 'Why should you not work with, and ultimately direct, a moderate Government of the left?' Boothby nevertheless was bowled over by Mosley's resignation speech. 'Your speech exceeded my wildest expectations and hopes. It was, I suppose, the most tremendous "tour de force" that this generation will know.'[7]

Boothby and Harold Macmillan shared a commitment to state intervention, economic expansion and a consensual social Toryism. A scholarly son in law of the Cavendishes, Macmillan, after Eton and two years at Balliol had served on the Western Front with the Grenadier Guards. For the rest of his life he would be marked by the scars, both emotional and physical, of the Somme. The shared hardships of the trenches combined with experience of economic depression in his industrial Stockton seat to strengthen his intellectual convictions. He lost his constituency to Labour in 1929; he soon effectively lost his wife to Boothby. Both men, whatever their painful personal differences, were marginal figures within the party. In contrast, Oliver Stanley was by any measure an insider. The younger son of Lord Derby, Lancashire's 'uncrowned king', he too had been educated at Eton and Oxford. He had won a Military Cross and the Croix de Guerre. He had arrived at Westminster with a commitment to social Toryism and with every expectation of a significant ministerial career.[8]

Walter Elliot had not been involved in this collaboration, but his political career already suggested a pre-disposition to cross-party solutions and a commitment to state intervention, not least in the application of science. The son of a Scottish livestock auctioneer, he had taken a medical degree at Glasgow before military service with the Royal Army Medical Corps. He returned with two Military Crosses, and entered the Commons with Mosley in 1918. His support for a Centre Party was demonstrated in his membership of Colin Coote's New Members' Parliamentary Committee; his continuing commitment to this project had placed him in the minority at the fateful Carlton Club meeting in October 1922. His experiences and values made him a natural participant in the discussions of 1930. The deteriorating situation and the lack of response from party leaderships could engender dramatic projections. Ambience and alcohol could stimulate exaggeration. In February 1930, when Mosley was still a minister, he and Cynthia spent an evening with, amongst others, Boothby, Stanley and Elliot. They talked of 'the decay of democracy and parliamentarianism'. They discussed the merits of 'a fascist coup'. Five months later Macmillan presented a diagnosis and a putative future. 'The old party machines are worn out … the economic situation is so serious that it will lead to a breakdown of the whole party system. …the Tories may return with a majority of 20 and then be swept away on a snap vote. No single party will form a Government and then there will be a Cabinet of young men. Mosley as PM and others including himself and Wise.'[9]

Macmillan's sympathy with Mosley became evident following the latter's resignation from the government. A letter from Macmillan appeared in *The Times* on the day before Mosley's acclaimed speech in the Commons. Macmillan suggested that Mosley's insistence that election pledges should be honoured posed a challenge to a comfortable but sterile party system in which a party of the left sought office through extravagant promises whilst the response from the right was a programme that was either self-contradictory or obscure. 'If these rules are to be permanently enforced, perhaps a good many of us will feel that it is hardly worth while bothering to play at all. Sir Oswald Mosley thinks the rules should be altered. I hope some of my friends will have the courage to applaud and support his protest.' Four Tory backbenchers were perfunctory and dismissive. 'When a player starts complaining "that it is hardly worth while bothering to play the game at all", it is usually the player, and not the game, who is at fault. It is then usually advisable for the player to seek a new field for his recreation and a pastime more suitable to his talents.' One of the signatories was R.A. Butler; eventually Macmillan would demonstrate himself the superior player. Macmillan continued in his critical vein through the summer of 1930. He acknowledged that the established party system might produce reasonably good government in normal times, despite its uninspiring character.

> In times of crisis such as war or economic dislocation, it is a real danger to the country. It is pretty clear that the condition of Trade and Industry and the rising tide of Unemployment constitute such a situation. The Socialist Government is already cracking under the strain. It will probably very soon collapse altogether... . The question is – can something really be done and who is going to do it?[10]

Mosley had posed this question; he believed he had an answer.

In late September, Mosley visited Oliver Stanley in Westmoreland. Cuthbert Headlam, a past and future Tory Member and another guest, was typically sardonic. Defeated in 1929 in County Durham, his response remained within party orthodoxy. He noted a document 'which is to unite Boothby, Macmillan, Oliver etc with Tom Mosley in his scheme to save England... a terrible lot of boards and public utility companies... it really is tripe'. Headlam drew a sharp distinction between the two potential collaborators. Stanley had an insider's track; for him loyalty must pay. 'He is now in an assured position... politically: he has only to carry on as he is doing to reach a high, possibly a very high, position in the party.' In contrast Mosley saw parties and individuals as instruments for his ego. Dismissive of Mosley's supposed socialism, Headlam presented him as

> first and always an Oswald Mosleyite, he professes a policy which he thinks would enable him to become an English Mussolini, governing by Orders in Council rather than in Parliament. The idea is picturesque-and to carry it through all that is required is that Oswald Mosley shall have a party – what the politics of that party might be is quite immaterial – so long as he is the big noise.

The indictment, whatever its validity, drew out the contrast between the rule-bound party figure and the iconoclastic transgressor of partisan boundaries. Boothby, sceptical of such boundaries emphasised to Mosley the purely verbal iconoclasm of his colleagues

> I know to my own cost the limitations of the existing young Conservatives. They are charming and sympathetic and intelligent at dinner. But there is not one of them with either the character or the courage to do anything big. Walter Elliot is the best, and his mind is the most interesting-and he will never take a step that might even remotely prejudice his political or parliamentary position.[11]

Late in October, the weekend before Parliament reassembled, Tory critics discussed strategy at Cliveden, encouraged by their hostess, Lady Astor. Terence O'Connor, a recent by-election victor, had drafted an amendment for the Debate on the King's Speech that was antipathetic to all three parties. Attempts were made to persuade Elliot to move this. Optimists reckoned that it could secure the support of 30 Tories, six Liberals and hyperbolically 20 Mosleyites. The shadows of Mosley and Lloyd George hung over the exchanges. Tom Jones, an informed spectator and confidante to successive prime ministers, noted that the young Tories admired Mosley's courage, but loathed his personality. They also found Lloyd George's 'incomparable executive power' attractive. Supporters of Mosley within the Labour Party became caught up in this speculation. In the interlude between the Labour Conference and the meeting of Parliament John Strachey wrote from London to Aneurin Bevan in Tredegar about metropolitan rumours. 'Things are moving so quickly... Not that anything very special is happening objectively, but there does seem to be a tremendous mass of opinion on the OM lines, and I am pretty anxious to have a hand in shaping what these lines shall be, and in that way it is the early stage that counts.' Strachey's endorsement of Mosley's position was evident in his contribution to a tri-partite symposium in the *Weekend Review*. Parliament was dominated by 'elderly gentlemen whose whole way of life and habits of thought were formed before the war'. Above all, Snowden seemed 'as determined as ever to prove that a Socialist Chancellor of the Exchequer can be the Casabianca of *laissez-faire*'. A fellow-contributor, Strachey's close friend Boothby, rejected both *laissez-faire* and nationalisation; instead the necessity was for 'scientific organisation and co-operation'. Many Conservatives would play a vital part in such a policy, but 'a situation may well arise which will transcend party politics'.[12]

Whatever the differences and the wishful thinking amongst the critics, the resumption of parliament demonstrated the partisan diversity of Mosley's connections. His own contribution to the Debate on the Address reiterated the economic arguments he had developed over the summer. He emphasised the incompatibility of free trade and trade unionism. 'Directly trade unionism intervened in our national affairs... to maintain the price of labour, sooner or later some regulation of the price of the article became inevitable. How can you maintain the price of labour unless you also maintain in some degree the price of the article which labour produces?' A search for international solutions was a delusion.

> It is no use saying that we must wait for the organisation of our trade until all the backward people in the world have come up to our standard of socialism. If we wait until the sweet small voice of the President of the Board of Trade at Geneva has drowned the strains of 'Giovinezza' in every Fascist capital we shall have to wait for a very long time.

He insisted on the need 'to face modern problems with modern minds. We should then be able to lift this great economic problem and national emergency far above the turmoil of party clamour and with national unity could achieve a solution adequate to the problem and worthy of the modern mind.' Here was a vision that sectional interests and partisanships could be transcended. Mosley's commendation of the 'modern' would become increasingly evident. One commentator characterised Mosley's performance as 'brilliant and biting'; the 'Protectionist substance almost made one wonder if in him the Conservative Party may one day find a leader'.[13]

Conservative critics emphasised that the dead hand of the parties must be removed. Elliot insisted that 'the danger... is that not merely one party but all parties are discredited as long as the present deadlock in the House persists'. Stanley wished to exorcise anachronistic mentalities. 'Socialism, Individualism, Cobdenism, Protectionism – let us cut out the isms. It is only by doing this that we can avert the catastrophe that is looming over our heads.' Terence O' Connor offered the prospect of consensus. 'Half-a-dozen men of common sense and prudence... selected from all parties, could draw up between them, on a couple of sheets of note paper, an emergency programme on which there would not be room for very much difference of opinion.' He urged a much stronger Executive and an accelerated legislative process. But his expectation of an agreed policy was hardly radical. 'We need at once, strict, scrupulous and almost Gladstonian finance.' Boothby insisted that the machinery of government was obsolete. He noted how some backbenchers on both sides acknowledged that the British trade position had changed radically compared with pre-war. By implication the party leaderships had failed to grasp this essential fact.[14]

Labour supporters of Mosley's case emphasised the centrality of crisis. W.J. Brown attacked free trade. 'While this drive of rationalisation continues in the hope of enabling the British capitalist system to compete with other capitalist systems, we are going to see the drive downwards to coolie conditions in our own country.' The consequence was a narrowing of political options. 'The line of social reform by the slow, easy, and comfortable method... is precluded unless we can insulate this country.' Already there was developing 'a profound distrust... not merely with the various parties, but with the institution of Parliament, and with democratic institutions themselves'. Labour's failure had intensified this distrust. There was a risk either of an attempt from outside Parliament to seize power, or alternatively a slow decay in which Parliament would become irrelevant.

Strachey foresaw a serious attack on wage standards. In this desperate situation the option offered by Mosley and others should be considered seriously. He acknowledged that the policy might appear 'novel, unorthodox and even fantastic'. Its policies 'may outrage some of our oldest and deepest prejudices'. But 'in a period in which the world is growing into an economic madhouse may not economic nationalism be no more than a measure of self-preservation?' Bevan commended Import Boards and highlighted the cynical indifference to the Commons brought about by the fact of two million unemployed. He emphasised the need to ignore 'outworn shibboleths', but his strategy did not focus exclusively on a combination of the young of all parties. Rather, he thought the Government should take seriously an offer of support made by Lloyd George. If this proposal was sincere there existed a Commons majority for the unemployment policy presented in *Labour and the Nation*. A Progressive Alliance could address the economic challenge. Other Labour backbenchers who were not close to Mosley endorsed element in the cross-party critique of Front Bench sterility. Phillips Price claimed the increasing irrelevance of established party divisions; Seymour Cocks felt that the crisis required the parties 'to rally together in order to make this Assembly something of a council of State'. Notable speeches had come not from those who represented their party orthodoxies, but rather 'the younger generation of this country and who are rather tired of affairs being ruled by a pre-War generation in every party in this House'.[15] Such speeches might have coloured much of the lengthy debate, but their diagnoses and prescriptions had little impact on dutiful loyalists of all parties.

The ILP Group moved their own socialist amendment; Jennie Lee drew a firm demarcation between Labour Mosleyites and the paragons of socialist virtue. She rejected 'the idea that we on these back benches can clutch the hands of the people on the other side who have really nice dispositions and who are earnestly wanting to help – that we can make a sort of political cocktail containing elements from all sides of the House and apply it to our national needs'. Ultimately, the question remained 'the need for reorganising our industry on Socialist lines'.[16]

The most uninhibited Labour attack on Mosley came from the Southampton schoolteacher Ralph Morley. He defended internationalism against 'economic nationalism', a phrase 'totally alien to the working class movement'. His indictment extended beyond an orthodox Labour defence of free trade that seemed impervious to its economic consequences to the making of contemporary political comparisons. 'The term "economic nationalism" may seem very acceptable in the mellifluous accents of the Italian language or the more guttural accents of Bavaria', but it would not be endorsed by the British working class. The progressive Liberal, Frank Owen, later a co-author of *Guilty Men*, recalled how Mosley had once extolled the doctrine of the League of Nations. 'In those days these instruments were to be the levers of a new, social, economic and political reconstruction of our broken world... We used to hear that wars and revolutions sprang out of the greeds and fears of economic nationalism. Now we.... hear from the same fount of truth that peace and plenty are the fruits of economic nationalism.' Mosley 'takes us right away from the responsibilities of civilisation and hides behind the barbarity of economic isolation'. The Reichstag election offered a precedent. Mosley was 'three months after Hitler with his National Socialism'.[17]

Attempts to associate Mosley with fascism contrasted with assertions that his ideas were very old ones. Baldwin recalled his own Protectionist roots. 'He is now producing ideas which I remember giving voice to in the year 1903.'Scepticism about the efficiency of the parliamentary system was beside the point. 'We must make the best of it.' Baldwin emphasised the post war challenge, not least for the Conservative Party. 'We have come into a fully-fledged democracy before we are ready for it. Rejection of parliament would mean either 'anarchy which you will not get in this country, or some form of dictatorship which... is still a long way off'.[18]

Baldwin's pragmatism and self-consciously British empiricism were seen by some as wise and by others as dangerously blinkered. One Conservative elder statesman, who was strongly supportive of Baldwin, had been disturbed by what he felt was Mosley's growing influence. 'Mosley's advance is rather disquieting and I think he will impose on young men of all parties and no party. Harold Macmillan will probably join him ere long.' Autumn 1930 resounded with the rhetoric of crisis and prognoses for 'national' government. Typically, such expectations offered a sharp contrast with Mosley's exploration of renaissance through a combination of young modernising nationalists. Rather, the scenario canvassed in some sections of the press, not least by J.L. Garvin in *The Observer*, and discussed at politicians' dinner parties, was for an elite pact between established politicians drawn from a variety of partisan positions. Mosley typically had a supportive role in such scenarios. An obvious focus for such initiatives was seemingly available in Lloyd George, a former Coalition Premier who carried little partisan baggage. Neville Chamberlain, perhaps influenced by bruising encounters with both men, envisaged one possible and bleak future. If a financial crisis precipitated the collapse of the Labour Government, Lloyd George and Mosley could become 'an unholy combination and a dangerous one'. But Chamberlain believed that this threat could be averted; its realisation would require a political failure by the Conservatives. In late 1930 despite the rhetoric of crisis there was little expectation of immediate cataclysm that could engulf established partisan loyalties.[19]

In this context Mosley continued to seek support within the Parliamentary Labour Party. The publication of the so-called Mosley Manifesto in December offered a left-leaning version of the policy presented in the Commons six weeks earlier. The text echoed Strachey's recognition that socialist measures must be placed on hold in order to address the contemporary crisis. The immediate issue was not the ownership of British industry but its survival. Once this had been achieved then there could be debate on fundamental principles. The emergency strategy necessitated the removal of the outdated parliamentary machine in favour of a cabinet of five. Parliament's role would be limited to 'general control'. The national survival plan focused on the home market, with an Import Control Board for agricultural products and a Commodity Board able to grant tariffs to industries that met criteria of efficiency, prices and wage levels. This suggested the possibility of a coalition of the useful people, the producers, against the financiers; the agenda had a lengthy radical pedigree. This long-term reorganisation required the complement of short-term constructive works financed by loans. Previously, Mosley had emphasised road construction; now the focus shifted to housing. The slums must be replaced. A war-time parallel was apposite. 'The State should contribute a public utility organisation to turn out houses and building materials as we turned out munitions during the war.'[20]

Seventeen Labour Members signed the Manifesto. Seven – Sir Oswald and Lady Cynthia Mosley, Bevan, Brown, Forgan, Strachey, and, to a lesser degree, Oliver Baldwin, constituted the Mosley group. Three of them – Brown, Forgan and Strachey – were also members of the ILP Group, as were two more signatories, James Horrabin and John McGovern. Three others – John McShane, H.T. Muggeridge and Phillips Price – had made Commons speeches that suggested some sympathy with Mosley's ideas. Jim Simmons still carried an ILP card but had no sympathy with that party's shift to the left. The other four signatories were Joe Batey, a Durham Miners' Member, Will Cove, a spokesperson for the teachers, and two who would soon be attracted by coalition politics of an as yet inconceivable variety: James Lovat Fraser and Sydney Markham would become supporters of the National Government. The signatories were mostly young. Only Batey, Cove and Oswald Mosley had sat in the Commons before 1929. Few had working-class backgrounds. Batey and Bevan were the only ones to have trade union sponsorship. McShane, formerly a headmaster, was the son of a miner. Seven represented Birmingham or Black Country constituencies. Perhaps this indicated Mosley's regional influence, or possibly a West Midlands readiness to respond to depression by embracing Protection.[21]

Phillips Price was a Harrow-educated ex-Liberal and cousin of another Harrovian ex-Liberal, C.P. Trevelyan. He had been radicalised through his time as a correspondent covering the Russian Revolution for the *Manchester Guardian*. He recalled how in the 1929 parliament intellectually curious and dissatisfied backbenchers came together. 'With certain Labour MPs with long outlooks like Frank Wise, I began… to think in terms of regulating imports by publicly controlled banks, and not of leaving everything to the crude law of supply and demand.' The Mosley Manifesto offered a credible agenda –'the only sensible and practical proposal to come from the rank and file of the Parliamentary Labour Party'.[22]

Simmons rejected the dominant interpretation of the Manifesto's trade policy. He insisted that tariffs as such were not advocated. He seemed untroubled by the proposed institutional reforms. Like several other Labour Members he had responded critically to his introduction to parliamentary procedures. He had felt that Birmingham City Council could achieve more in six days than parliament could in six months. Simmons's endorsement of the Manifesto was underpinned by loyalty to the Government. The only solution lay in a parliamentary majority that could secure effective control of industry. Within that context, the Manifesto offered proposals that were worth discussion.[23]

Characterisation of the Manifesto as a practical response by socialists to a crisis would be endorsed by its eighteenth signatory. By late 1930 A.J. Cook, once the personification of the miners' battle against wage cuts and longer hours, had been politically marginalised. Still viewed unsympathetically by those within the labour movement who had caricatured and condemned his strategy in 1926, he was at odds with the Communists as, with varying zeal, they pursued their sectarian 'Class against Class' strategy. In the 1929 election Cook had argued passionately for the return of a Labour Government as the best way forward for a weakened and beleaguered Miners' Federation. The Government's subsequent legislation for the industry had been hampered by its minority status, the state of the industry and employers' opposition. The result had disappointed this most solid of Labour constituencies. Cook, ever the pragmatist, sought alternative ways forward. The Manifesto proposed action informed by divergent thinking and energised by Mosley's advocacy. Pragmatism combined with a bond forged in the summer of 1926. The thinking behind Cook's support was evident in his criticism of the ILP left. 'While many of our critics are dreaming and preaching about Socialism, the working class, section by section, are faced with attacks on their standards and conditions.' He acknowledged that there could be no definitive solution under capitalism. 'I want International Socialism, but the miners alone cannot secure that.' The politics proclaimed by the *New Leader* were effectively the same as those of the

Communists. It 'will not bring Socialism nearer but destroy all hope of it, by creating mistrust, differences and divisions among Trade Union members'.[24]

Labour leaders were scathing about the Manifesto. MacDonald dismissed the signatories, who included two future cabinet ministers, as tenth rate; Morrison hit out at 'swell-heads not of working class origins,' with 'Tory blue blood running in their veins'; Dalton saw its contents as 'a move towards Toryism'. The ILP's official response was hostile. Admittedly some specific proposals had been 'borrowed' from the ILP programme, but 'in their new relationship in the general Mosley plan they were being directed to objectives which destroyed their value in any Socialist sense'. Particular hostility was directed to the focus on Empire trade. 'Conceptions of economic Imperialism' have no place in Socialist thought. The proposals for institutional reform were dismissed as a conservative revolution from above- 'the Executive control of a social revolution-but operating for Capitalist purposes in a Capitalist State'.[25]

W.J. Brown had a foot in both camps. He acknowledged that both the ILP and Mosley had failed to change government policy. 'The urgent need is to break through the present stalemate. That is the condition of saving the political Labour Movement... it is necessary to mobilise a stronger force than the ILP Group and the Mosley Group can separately be.' Socialists believed in the domestic regulation of hours and wages, so why not the modification of fiscal arrangements? Pat Dollan, Glaswegian ILP leader and critic of the ILP left, ignored such arguments. His case was tribal. 'The terms of the manifesto are not in harmony with Socialist principle and policy, and have been more favourably received in Tory protection circles than in ILP halls.'[26]

The Manifesto's limited appeal within the Labour Party was to some extent a consequence of its transgressing of familiar alignments. In contrast, Keynes welcomed its emphasis on planning and insisted on its relevance for socialists. 'I do not see what practical socialism can mean for our generation in England to-day, unless it makes much of the manifesto its own.' He emphasised that the existing political parties did not reflect the significant divisions over economic policy. 'So long as party organisation and personal loyalties cut across the fundamental differences of opinion, the public life of this country will continue to suffer from a creeping paralysis. We should be grateful to Sir Oswald Mosley for an effort to clear the air.' Keynes, however, commanded no legions.[27]

The impact of the Manifesto was slight amongst those Conservatives with whom Mosley had been speculating on imaginary futures. Leo Amery was always keen to mobilise support for Protection; shortly after the Manifesto's publication he dined with Mosley and what he called 'a mixed crowd'. W.E.D. Allen, the Ulster Unionist Member for West Belfast, would prove to be a durable Mosleyite. Arnold Wilson from the orthodox Tory right contrasted with Strachey and Allan Young. Amery responded to Young's qualities, 'keen intellectually', and perhaps more so to his politics. 'He has come round entirely to protection and realizes that nothing progressive can be done in his party until the old gang have been got rid of.' Amery's advice to Mosley was to concentrate on shifting Labour. 'I told... him that I did not think he would do much good by association with members of our party, but that his business was within his own party to destroy the present Government as quickly as possible in order to give a chance to his constructive minds to get to the front while in opposition.'[28]

Amery's assessment of the meagre prospects for Mosley within the Conservative Party was borne out in the tepid and limited Tory response to the Manifesto. A handful of letters to the press offered little. Walter Elliot's letter to *The Times* praised the signatories' courage and welcomed proposals for tariffs and imperial planning as in line with Tory policy. Cabinet reform was endorsed as a necessary condition for vigorous executive action. More broadly, Elliot welcomed what he saw as the Manifesto's realism – the dire state of the national finances, the awareness that the survival of industry was at stake, and that industrial decline, if not addressed, would precipitate a series of wage struggles. 'The opposing pulls in the country have halted the nation at a dead centre and we are drifting down stream'.[29] This modest commendation provoked an irate response from Baldwin. Probably he saw Elliot, unlike Boothby and Macmillan, as amenable to the prospect of office and influence. His reproof produced apology and conformity; Boothby's assessment of the limits to Elliot's radicalism had proved accurate.

Within days of his *Times* letter, Elliot published a second letter in its columns. Co-signed by Oliver Stanley, a former Chancellor of the Exchequer, Sir Robert Horne, and the novelist-cum-politician, John Buchan, this struck a very different note. Absent were the emphases on high wages, central planning and industrial reorganisation. Instead, the motifs were of retrenchment – government economies, revision of the national insurance system and a drive for lower wages in the sheltered industries.[30] Elliot and Stanley's criticisms of the Old Guard were smothered by the prospect of office in a future government. Their quest for new policies was trumped by economic orthodoxy and the principle that state involvement in the economy should be limited to the removal of distortions. Capitalism should be largely left to reorganise itself.

The distance between Mosley and some of his young Conservative associates was greater than the content of the Manifesto and their responses suggested. A document previously circulated to at least some of his non-Labour collaborators suggested the possibility of a more radical shift. Its language resonated with a sense of immediate crisis and the redundancy of established methods. The emphasis was on an emergency equivalent to a major war.[31] This necessitated 'intensive organisation' and active and comprehensive State intervention and control. The specific political reforms and the economic analysis were familiar. The latter now justified the placing of the Unemployment Insurance Fund on an actuarial basis. Such drastic steps required political innovation. Institutional reform was not enough. 'We contemplate for the first time a movement strong and courageous enough to withstand the pressure and the clamour of affected interests.'

Indian nationalism necessitated a robust response. Both major parties were deemed the captives of prejudice. 'The Tory sees a brown face and wants to hit it; the Socialist sees a brown face and wants to kiss it.' Instead the preferred approach was 'Caesarism'. A reasonable constitutional settlement would be available to anyone reasonable enough to accept it. The other face of 'Caesarism' was 'a very thick stick which it is known will, if necessary, be effectively and ruthlessly used'. Any attempt by Indian politicians to raise the stakes would precipitate 'the maintenance of law and order with ruthless severity... the methods of discipline and civilisation'.

The specific agenda had shifted to the right; the rhetorical setting, compared with earlier presentations, showed a much more thorough change. The contemplated movement was 'in essence authoritarian and realistic in character'. It 'must evoke a new ideology and create a new psychology'. A morality based on 'mental and physical efficiency' would replace 'irrational taboos and repression'. Mosley's invocation of the 'modern', hinted at in his Commons speech in October 1930, was specified as a movement of national regeneration. Its pedigree was ideologically mixed. 'The movement which has thrown up the follies and the excesses of Bolshevism, Fascism, the Young Turk Movement and Kuomintang should evoke in these islands a face typical in its English character, and in its toleration, sanity and executive ability far superior to its Continental prototype.' Yet the emphasis on the singularity of the English was yoked with an expectation derived from very different contexts. 'Everywhere they have gone through old men and old systems like steel through butter.'

The extent of collaboration on this document is unclear. It seems that the proposals were the focus of serious discussion between some Conservatives and Mosley, but that he supplied the radical passages. The document noted by Headlam during his visit to Oliver Stanley in Westmoreland is likely to have been a draft. Macmillan seems to have been significantly involved. He sent a copy to Lord Lloyd, widely seen as a rallying point for Conservative critics, in mid-November. Macmillan emphasised its confidential status and suggested that it was the result of serious work. 'Unfortunately I have not yet received it in the modi-fied form, after the long discussions which we have had about it.' The proposed changes principally concerned the section on unemployment insurance with slight amendments on finance. On these Macmillan was reassuring – 'all of a more conservative tendency than the original document'.[32]

Certainly, in December 1930 Macmillan seemed prepared to envisage a new political organisation, but remained agnostic as to any outcome. 'How the matter is going to develop I do not know.' He was distinc-tive amongst Conservatives in his positive response to the Mosley Manifesto. It 'may ultimately lead to a complete reorientation of the Labour movement. The signatories demand the protection of the Home Market and the development of the Imperial Market. They ask for centralised and efficient government. They call for a policy of national planning rather than a policy of national drift.' His assessment was naive about the internal politics of the Labour Party. Equally unreal-istic was Macmillan's hope for a supportive Conservative response. He claimed not to understand 'any Conservative who does not welcome such doctrine; unless indeed he cares more about party machinery and the survival of old party conflicts than about national unity and national effort'.[33] Macmillan's relationship with Mosley remained close; in December 1930, he commended Mosley, 'a gentleman who... is, I think at the present time worth knowing', to Captain Edward S. Morris of the National Farmers' Union. He could be seen as the most independent of the Conservative critics. Prepared to develop his own ideas, and since May 1929, outside the Commons, he had also shown interest in Beaverbrook's Empire Crusade. 'Oh! Dear Harold, What does it all mean? Has Lord Beaverbrook bewitched you?' had been his father in law's response from Chatsworth. Ultimately, neither Beaverbrook nor Mosley cast a decisive spell. Already, Macmillan was exhibiting the style that would provide the sub-title for a biographer. He was 'a study in ambiguity'. As he commented to a subsequent biographer, 'I think gardens should be divided, so you can't see everything at once'.[34] The student of ideas and collaborator across party boundaries could also present himself as a robust partisan who understood the indispensability of a political base.

The December Manifesto could be interpreted not as an attempt to increase influence within the Labour Party, but as a gambit to recruit putative participants to an independent initiative. Rumours circulated that Mosley was on the verge of organising a party of young nationalists. Boothby, alarmed by such a prospect, warned Mosley that the consequences would be disastrous. He was thoroughly and rightly sceptical as to the possibility of Conservative recruits. 'Our chaps won't play and it's no use deluding yourself that they will.' Elliot had borne out his earlier assessment. He insisted that Macmillan would be a liability. 'Even on the assumption that he decided to play (a large one) how many votes can he swing? Not two.' He thought the prospects for Labour recruits no more promising. The trade unions would not be sympathetic; 'the intelligentsia of the Dalton–(Noel) Baker school will be ultimately and venomously hostile'. Those few committed to Mosley would lack credibility as a potential government. 'Do you really think that you can send Aneurin Bevan to the Admiralty to lay down more cruisers, and John Strachey to spank the blacks?' He dismissed the value of support from the press lords. Rothermere was unpalatable, Beaverbrook was unreliable. Lloyd George might be seen by some as a potential political saviour. Boothby felt that his record led him to be dismissed 'rightly or wrongly... in many quarters as a shit'. The prospect of a coalition of outsiders – 'a Beaverbrook–Mosley-Rothermere–L. G. –Macmillan–Stanley–Boothby combination' would provoke a dismissive verdict. 'By God now all the shits have climbed into the same basket.' Boothby insisted that only two political machines would compete for power in future. 'The only game worth playing is to try and collar one or other of the machines, and not ruin yourself by beating against them with a tool which will almost certainly break in your hand.' He suggested that Mosley's position was powerful; he was able to act within either machine.[35]

Boothby's diagnosis appeared to be supported by broader political developments in the early weeks of 1931. Economic deterioration and mounting budgetary difficulties did not intensify the rhetoric of crisis, nor heighten demands for a national administration. Rather, the Labour Government temporarily shelved one problem through the appointment of a Royal Commission on Unemployment Insurance.

All politicians anticipated that its recommendations would involve retrenchments, but the initiative relieved immediate pressure on the Government from other parties and the inevitable arguments between ministers and the TUC were at least postponed. The complex bargaining between ministers and Lloyd George was gradually forging a more stable parliamentary majority, albeit at the cost of some Liberal fragmentation. The consequences became evident on 11–12 February. During a debate on the need for expenditure cuts the Government accepted a Liberal motion for an economy committee. The next day a debate paraded Labour–Liberal agreement on employment policy. The Conservative counterpart was a growing solidarity around economy and Protection. Baldwin's position still seemed fragile; the press lords tested their strength with by-election candidates. More significantly, strong Conservative performances in Labour-held seats suggested that the next general election would result in a Conservative majority. In the early months of 1931 the parliamentary configuration and perhaps the broader political argument was polarising around the poles of Progressive and Conservative. How far Liberal voters would endorse this development might be questionable. The forthcoming recommendations of the Royal Commission and of the economy committee under Sir George May would test any Progressive understanding's durability. Whatever the long-term difficulties may be, there seemed, as yet, little space for a new political initiative.

Mosley and his few sympathisers were even more beleaguered within the Labour Party in the aftermath of the Manifesto. Mosley spoke to the Smethwick Trades and Labour Council on its contents and met with some sharp questioning before securing delegates' support. Before such an audience he still insisted that socialism was the only solution but that urgent responses were needed. Sympathy in his former Birmingham base had withered. The Borough Party rejected a proposal that Mosley be invited to speak on the Manifesto. A unanimously supported resolution claimed that 'no good purpose would be served'. Demands for an emergency party conference on unemployment met with little support on successive days within the PLP and on the NEC where Mosley was backed only by Jowett. Dalton was predictably scathing. 'The fellow always forces these points to a division, I suppose in order to exhibit himself afterwards to the crowds as the only righteous man.' Mosley and Jowett might vote together in isolation on the NEC, but the ILP left strengthened its defences against Mosley's policy. The party's South Wales Divisional Conference deplored the action of those ILP Members who had signed the Manifesto. Cove and

McGovern withdrew their signatures. Brown quit as secretary of the ILP Parliamentary Group. Early in February, Allan Young spoke at the ILP's London Divisional Conference. He argued cogently for the 'short-term policy of setting capitalism on its feet, at the same time securing control over wages, prices and general economic conditions'. Whatever Young's intellectual rigour, this audience did not want to hear about the stabilisation of capitalism. Young's position was heavily defeated.[36]

Mosley contributed to the Commons debate on unemployment that demonstrated the Labour–Liberal concordat. His criticism was scathing. MacDonald was complacent; Snowden was the exponent of Treasury orthodoxy and the prime mover behind Labour's fatal acquiescence in the return to the Gold Standard. The appropriate policy was one of planning for producers against the interests of rentiers. This plea on behalf of the useful people was decorated with gendered rhetoric. The Government's policy was 'to put the nation in bed on a starvation diet... the suggestions of an old woman in a fright'. Rather, there must be 'a policy of manhood which takes the nation out onto the field and builds up its muscles and constitution in effort'. The ministerial riposte came from Thomas. He deplored Mosley's personal attack on MacDonald and typically responded in kind. MacDonald had brought Mosley 'from obscurity into notoriety'. Thomas identified himself with the ethos of the labour movement against the back-stabbing of political parvenus.[37] Such personalised appeals to solidarity against irresponsible critics intensified as Labour's electoral predicament worsened.

Four Mosleyites produced an extended version of the Manifesto, *A National Policy*. Allan Young, Bevan, Brown and Strachey wrote as socialists concerned to address an immediate crisis through 'a programme of disciplined national effort'. The emphasis on the nation entailed co-operation between capital and labour in order to address the challenge. 'As far as is humanly possible employers and workers should meet the emergency by a common effort.' Beatrice Webb welcomed the emphasis on planning, 'it was an able document', but she dismissed it as politically inept. The emphasis on Empire Trade would offend Labour, Import and Investment Boards would upset capitalists, the proposals for institutional reform would not persuade experienced politicians and administrators. The programme appeared a collection of disparate items that fitted poorly alongside established political identities. 'The curious assortment of reforms do not hang together; they are based on no political philosophy; they have no emotional appeal-they excite neither love nor hate.'[38]

The preparation of the programme was a prelude to the formation of the New Party. At the end of January Boothby responded to
evidence that Mosley was raising funds in the City rather than seeking
to strengthen his position in the Labour Party. He dismissed such an
initiative as 'madness... I don't believe money even in large quanti-
ties, can ever start a new political movement in this country.' Mosley's
response expressed his growing distance from 'normal' politics and
the practice of muddling through. If this familiar politics remained
feasible, he and his proposed movement would have no purpose. He
would wager on a different future but acknowledged the risk of failure.
'If I cannot do things, I will have no interest in politics.'[39] November's
rumours were becoming February's facts or, in crucial respects, its wishful thinking. At the beginning of the month Mosley met Gerald Barry
of the *Weekend Review*. Barry, a keen advocate of a planned economy,
found Mosley impressive, but admitted to feeling vaguely distrustful.
Mosley presented his expectations for a new party in the hope that
Barry would give his support. Whether his claims about likely political
backing demonstrated misjudgement or a desire to impress a potential
backer is unclear. He claimed Elliot, Boothby and Macmillan as prob-
able Conservative recruits.[40] More significantly, Mosley could point to
the financial support of the motor manufacturer William Morris. His
£50,000 was perhaps a decisive factor in precipitating the formation of
the New Party.

The party's launch coincided with the last serious challenge to Baldwin's
leadership. Criticism from the Beaverbrook and Rothermere newspa-
pers and hostility within sections of the party to his India policy fed a
growing belief on the part of some senior figures, most notably Neville
Chamberlain, that Baldwin's departure would be beneficial. The focal
point became a by-election in a Conservative stronghold, Westminster
St George's. The intervention of a Beaverbrook–Rothermere candidate provoked a fighting response from Baldwin. His decision to attack his critics
over India and to indict the power and irresponsibility of the press lords
culminated in a decisive victory for the official candidate. The leadership
question was resolved, contributing to the stabilisation of the party system.
Ambition, electoral optimism and the pacification of the Conservative
Party all argued against a leap in the dark. No Conservative Member joined
the New Party.

The only Opposition Member to join the New Party at its incep-
tion was the Etonian Ulster Unionist, W.E. Allen. Elected for West
Belfast in 1929 his thorough Unionism was coupled with a powerful
advocacy of Empire and a strong attachment to Protection as vital for

the Six Counties' battered industries. These sentiments fitted within an Ulster Unionism that often found British Conservatism too cautious in their advocacy. Allen's priorities and his scepticism about the effectiveness of existing parties had brought him into the conclaves of younger Conservatives who were courted by Mosley. Unlike them, Allen's links with official Conservatism were indirect. By early 1931 whilst the Conservatives who had flirted with radical initiatives were accommodating themselves to their party, Allen was emphasising the Mosleyite themes of crisis, action, planning and the reform of political institutions.[41]

Failure to recruit from the Conservative benches was matched by a disappointing Labour response. Two of the collaborators on *A National Policy* withdrew from the venture. Bevan stayed with the Labour Party. He was a sponsored Miners' MP and believed that, with all its limitations and flaws, the Labour Party was in British conditions the only viable instrument for working-class advance. The New Party project was as untenable as the ILP left. Allan Young's hope that Bevan would join at a later date demonstrated a basic misunderstanding. Bevan would acknowledge his responsibility for *A National Policy*; that he might break with organised labour was wishful thinking. W.J. Brown's response was more complex. He resigned from the Parliamentary Party but refused to join the New Party. Subsequently he suggested that his refusal resulted from a perception of Mosley's incipient fascism. More likely, Brown felt that membership of the New Party would pose problems for his position as a trade union official. His espousal of independence might also have demonstrated the individualism that would increasingly mark his political gyrations. Oliver Baldwin's concurrent decision to quit the PLP, but not to join the New Party, meant that the launch involved just five MPs – Sir Oswald and Lady Cynthia Mosley, Allen, Forgan and Strachey. George Strauss knew Strachey and Bevan ; he contrasted their responses. 'Aneurin Bevan who was much more politically wise saw that this movement must end in moving to the right, and break up, if successful, the Labour Party... That's why... Bevan would have nothing to do with it from the very beginning although accepting many of the proposals... But... Strachey was really fascinated, excited and intrigued by the ideas and the new message and idealism which Mosley expanded at that time.'[42]

One member of the ILP Group perhaps was a possible recruit. John Beckett, a former soldier, had always been uncomfortable with the ILP's pacifistic ethos. He had been active in the National League of ex-Servicemen and had worked for Attlee in his successful Limehouse campaign in 1922. Elected to the Commons in 1924, Beckett had become an increasingly outspoken critic of the Labour leadership. In the 1929 parliament he became notorious for his seizure of the Commons mace as a gesture of opposition to Fenner Brockway's suspension from the House. The blend of radicalism, nationalism, contempt for parliamentary conventions and deepening scepticism about the feasibility of democracy should have made him a likely sympathiser with Mosley. However he insisted in retrospect that he never had faith in Mosley's character. Eventually, following a visit to Italy, he suspended his disbelief and joined the British Union of Fascists. His suspension was brief; he left to join two further right-wing groups before sharing Mosley's fate in 1940.[43]

The earlier expectations and subsequent disappointments of the Labour recruits were evident in their letters of resignation. Brown argued that Labour as a minority government could have pursued a socialist programme, thereby maintaining its integrity and the faith of its supporters. Alternatively, the Government could have carried through 'the most energetic and far reaching policy of national reconstruction which the balance of Parties in Parliament permitted'. Instead, the Government's weakness had put the Liberals 'well on our left flank'. Such choices meant that Labour 'had ceased to be the apostle of a new order without becoming the energetic utilisers of the possibilities of the present order'. Beyond his claims of failed policies Brown indicted the party structure. The PLP was continually faced by decisions already made; when MPs voiced criticisms they were ignored. The party conference was stifled by the overlap between Ministers and the major unions. 'The Party caucus is the most powerful, the most rigid and the most unresponsive of any caucus in the country.' The stark portrait was without nuance, the damning verdict of the disillusioned. For Brown there was no hope of reform. Strachey focused on the failure to pursue a socialist programme. Snowden was guilty of obstinacy, his cabinet colleagues of lethargy. The cost would be borne by the workers.[44]

Mosley's agenda evoked sympathy hedged with substantial reservations amongst some sections of Labour's rank and file. George Catlin, the husband of the feminist Vera Brittain, was a professor of political science at Cornell; he would become a Labour candidate. He had carried out research work for Mosley and found Mosley's position both appealing and problematic. 'I want to preach social discipline and I ask as a Socialist, upon what basis I am to do it popularly if I am to preclude myself from a certain Mosleian national appeal.' He acknowledged to Mosley the need for a drastic reorganisation based on national unity with a strengthened executive, but remained insistent that the wider context must be one of international co-operation. He hoped in late March 1931 that he and Mosley shared these principles. Ian Mikardo was a Labour activist in London's East End. He agreed with Bevan's assessment that Mosley's programme met immediate needs; he participated in 'a ferment of discussion' following Mosley's Llandudno speech despite doubts about Mosley's authoritarian aspects. Unlike Bevan, his sympathy appears to have continued into the New Party.[45]

Within the Labour Establishment reaction to the New Party was angry and derisory. Beatrice Webb dismissed the venture as 'an amazing act of arrogance, a melodramatic defection'. Her appraisal of Mosley contrasted with her portrait eight years earlier. 'Mosley has bad health, a slight intelligence and an unstable character – I doubt whether he has the tenacity of a Hitler. He also lacks genuine fanaticism. Deep down in his heart he is a cynic. He will be beaten and retire.' Yet she admitted that he was the only orator in the labour movement apart from MacDonald. He could never return. 'Not even Uncle Arthur will be able to let him in again, not even as a prodigal son.' Dalton was predictably triumphant.'We will bomb the traitors out of their holes!... The air seems cleaner already.'[46]

From his distinctive position within the ILP left Frank Wise detected a withering of Mosley's radicalism. The boldness of the Birmingham proposals had gone; now he was guided by a desire not to quarrel with vested interests. Wise suggested an ambiguity in his position. This 'Discreet Buccaneer' apparently sought a business government that would patch up the existing system, yet Wise, although presumably unaware of the more radical memorandum of autumn 1930, was uneasy. 'But of Mussolinis and Pilsudskis we are suspicious.' The political character of the New Party remained unresolved. Strachey and Young were committed socialists; Mosley's socialism had been a rhetorical currency for Labour audiences. His references to the 'modern movement' could have very different implications; his language referred typically to nation rather than to class. Beatrice Webb felt that the episode was indicative of a wider turbulence. 'In the chaos of our political life to-day there will be many meteors passing through the firmament.'[47]

The project's future depended not just on the verdicts of politicians and intellectuals, but also on the responses of local activists. The Chairman of Smethwick Trades and Labour Council and the Agent were summoned to London for a meeting with Mosley on 24 February. They consulted the Trades Council Executive and then accepted the invitation. Mosley informed them that he intended to form a new party which would eventually attract significant Labour support including the ILP. He anticipated 400 candidates at the next election and 100 victories. Here was an absurdly ambitious prospectus pitched at Labour. The pitch was accompanied by offers. The Chairman could be the Smethwick candidate, the Agent could be appointed as a regional organiser.

The Smethwick party's response was unambiguous. Their support for Mosley was dependent on his remaining within the party. The TLC's subsequent assessment combined loyalty to the party with a sense of betrayal:

> The Member to whom they in Smethwick had looked with such hope, the man of whom such fine things had been said from many a platform, that he was the future Prime Minister of England; the man for whom they had done what they had done, for whom they had worked as they had worked, had taken this step and now they found that they were simply left high and dry.

One of those who had met Mosley in London presented their choice as the triumph of proletarian integrity over patronage. 'We were met at the station by a splendid Rolls Royce... we came away on the bus, aye, and we paid our own fare.'[48]

George Shepherd, Labour's National Agent, and Ben Shaw, his Scottish counterpart, rapidly collected material on the Divisional Parties affected by the exodus. The principal doubt concerned Stoke, where Cynthia Mosley was believed to have a strong personal following. Elsewhere, local parties seemed robust. Visiting Birmingham in mid March, Dalton reported no sign of support for Mosley at his meetings. However, he felt that 'behind the scenes the local movement is rather perturbed'. This was evident at the ILP's Easter Conference when delegates discussed the compatibility of ILP and New Party memberships. The National Administrative Council had previously stated that they were not. A Birmingham delegate claimed that this had been 'a bombshell and would cause considerable difficulty in the Midlands' – a claim denied by another Midlands delegate. Some perturbation was predictable, whatever the formal repudiations of the New Party by local and national Labour bodies. Mosley's connections, not least financial, with the Birmingham and Black Country labour movements had been substantial. Some high-profile West Midlands Labour figures accepted his offers of New Party posts. These included Dan Davies, Strachey's Agent in Aston, and Bill Risdon, the ILP's Midlands Organiser. Most significantly, Allan Young became the New Party's National Organiser. [49]

The departure of the Mosleyites intensified Labour loyalists' animosity towards all critics. Immediately after the exodus Charles Trevelyan resigned from the cabinet. The destruction of his Education Bill on the altar of denominational education was the occasion; this provoked his broader criticism of government policy and the lack of socialist measures. MacDonald's private response noted how 'our greatest troubles are coming from those who were the latest converts, whose study of Socialism is the least thorough, and whose knowledge of the Movement is the least intimate'. Such sentiments were widely shared in the PLP. The backbench response to Trevelyan's criticisms was largely unsympathetic. Frank Wise might praise his 'magnificent and courageous statement'. Many more shared the response of the venerable loyalist Will Thorne – that many of Trevelyan's statements were 'uncalled for, especially at the present time'. Trevelyan's cousin, Phillips Price, confirmed to him that many resented his attack on MacDonald. Defections and resignations, especially perhaps by baronets, served only to strengthen the resolve of Labour loyalists.[50]

8
Rejections

March 1931 might appear as a favourable moment to launch a new political party. The failure of the government to respond effectively to the economic crisis and the uncertainties and divisions of the established opposition parties could suggest the possibility of political space. But the meagre response to Mosley's initiative amongst parliamentarians demonstrated the strength – both visceral and material – of established ties. Mosley was ill and unable to participate in the initial programme of meetings. The burden of the campaign was borne by Cynthia Mosley and Strachey. Audiences were typically large; many were curious, some were hostile. Meetings, however crowded and spirited, carried minimal legacy for the party's prospects. The party's base was meagre: it owed something to discontented ILP members. Subsequently, the emphasis on 'action' attracted some university hearties, most notably Peter Howard, the England rugby player. The party initially secured support from a few public figures. Harold Nicolson had resigned from the Foreign Office to work for Beaverbrook. He saw in Mosley and the New Party an escape from the compromises and vulgarities of popular journalism. He agreed with Mosley that 'democracy is dead... The people must be treated humanely and firmly.' In contrast, Cyril Joad, the populariser of philosophical arguments, was a recruit from the left. Whatever the political variety amongst its adherents, the New Party was an elite initiative.[1]

Late in March, the death of the Labour Member for Ashton-under-Lyne offered an opportunity for a campaign against the established, and hopefully discredited, parties. Three weeks later, Allan Young became the first – and it would prove the only – New Party by-election candidate. Ashton, a cotton constituency a few miles east of Manchester, had been devastated by that industry's slump. In April 1931, half of its mills stood idle; the local unemployment rate was 46 per cent. Here was an opportunity to demonstrate the Government's failure to committed Labour voters. Metropolitan journalists, and perhaps New Party strategists, could see Ashton as quintessential Labour territory. Yet, in the cotton towns the ranks of mill chimneys and rows of terraced houses could mislead the outsider. Cotton workers traditionally included many Conservatives who were allegedly antipathetic to puritanical Liberalism, and to that party's association with the Irish. Edwardian Liberalism and respectable Labour had eroded those attachments, but Ashton had a recent history of electing Conservative 'personalities'.[2]

In December 1910 a Canadian millionaire had arrived in Ashton sponsored by another Canadian, Bonar Law. Max Aitken had established his headquarters in Manchester's luxurious Midland Hotel, recently the venue for the first meeting of Mr Rolls and Mr Royce. Once elected, Aitken visited Ashton sporadically; he moved to the Lords as Lord Beaverbrook in 1916. His successor, Albert Stanley, had been appointed President of the Board of Trade in Lloyd George's new government. An effective demonstration of the Premier's policy of appointing businessmen to Whitehall, Stanley, although born in Derby, was educated in the United States. He had established himself as a dynamic manager in the street-car business, and had returned to London in 1908 to rescue the ailing tube railways developed by the American tycoon Charles Tyson Yerkes. Post-war, Stanley left Whitehall to further his business interests and in 1920 quit the Commons to become Lord Ashfield.[3]

His Ashton successor Sir Walter de Frece brought glamour, not because of his theatrical interests, but because of his wife, the music hall star Vesta Tilley. In the 1890s she had been Britain's highest earning woman. Her act had offered a self-consciously respectable rejection of bawdiness and innuendo. Appealing more to women than to men, she promenaded Ashton's recently enfranchised women voters, asking that they bring a little sunshine into her life. De Frece was successful in straight fights against Labour in the 1920 by-election and in 1922. In 1923 he won a three-cornered contest with the Liberal in second place. The 1923 Labour candidate, Ellen Wilkinson, a Distributive Workers' official, had dual Labour and Communist membership, an ecumenism permitted until the following year. De Frece, having attacked her as a Bolshevik sympathiser, faced legal action. He quit Ashton, recapturing Blackpool from the Liberals in the 1924 Red Letter election.[4] Ashton's dalliance with high-profile and affluent Conservatives was over. De Frece's successor, Cornelius Holman was young; his time in Ashton was brief. He was declared a bankrupt in 1928. The consequential vacancy gave Labour its opportunity. Albert Bellamy was a solid citizen. Once a locomotive driver on the London and North Western Railway, and a union activist, he had become President of the Amalgamated Society of Railway Servants in 1911, the year of the industry's first major stoppage; he was subsequently first President of the National Union of Railwaymen. Like Jimmy Thomas, but without his showmanship, he epitomised the cautious, respectable culture of railway trade unionism. For a decade from 1917 he served on the Soldiers' and Sailors' Pensions Appeal Tribunal. A Stockport magistrate from 1906, his career marked the ascent of the decent and dutiful working class into political and administrative responsibilities.[5]

Bellamy was opposed in Ashton by the previous local Liberal candidate and by a local Tory, Colonel Broadbent. Coming from Stockport he was the outsider. Parochial in its candidates, the by-election attracted widespread attention. Ashton was precisely the type of seat Labour needed to win for any hope of a parliamentary majority; Liberals looked for recovery from the nadir of 1924; Tories needed reassurance that the majority they had won four years before was not disintegrating. Amongst the outside speakers, as so often in the late 1920s was Sir Oswald Mosley. Electoral turnout in Ashton was traditionally high, lubricated, so it was claimed pre-war, by problematic practices. The 1928 contest produced a record by-election poll of over 89 per cent and Ashton's first Labour Member. Bellamy took just over 40 per cent of the vote and increased his share by 4 per cent in May 1929. He established himself as an assiduous constituency Member, available monthly to his constituents at the Weavers' Institute. This success could be read as an example of Labour's gradual advance in industrial Britain, its extent and pace shaped by local industrial experiences and political and cultural identities. Labour would attempt to capitalise on Bellamy's quiet decency-'a level-headed broadminded and tolerant man with honesty of purpose and gentlemanly demeanour'.[6]

The worsening economic climate from late 1929 had weakened Labour's electoral position. Its by-election performances were affected by whether a Liberal stood. When the Liberals withdrew from the field the 1929 Liberal vote went heavily in favour of the Conservatives. This had been evident in Labour losses in two very different Labour seats, West Fulham and Sunderland. In contrast, at Shipley the Labour vote had fallen by 10 per cent, the Liberal share had increased and the Conservatives had taken the seat. Only Tory division over Empire Free Trade had saved East Islington for Labour, two months before the Ashton contest.

Trade unions naturally wished to retain seats that they had funded and which had provided parliamentary representation. The NUR was very active in local Labour Parties, but had few geographical concentrations of membership. It succeeded in retaining the Ashton candidacy. John Gordon had been born in Dublin, and had worked on the Great Western before becoming a union employee in 1912 and its Chief Accountant three years later. A practising Catholic, his religion inevitably highlighted an acrimonious controversy over the Government's Education Bill. The Government had recently dropped the Bill following defeats in the Lords. In a humiliating prelude, Ministers in the Commons had lost out to a revolt of Labour MPs, both Catholics and those sensitive to the demands of their Catholic constituents. Emotions over Labour's position on the funding of denominational education became inflamed on both sides. Ashton included an estimated 4,000 Catholic electors; two Labour Catholic councillors had quit the party over the issue.[7]

The Conservative Association re-nominated Broadbent. He felt that, given the catastrophic state of the cotton trade, even in Free Trade Lancashire, Protection's hour had come. Conservatives rented a shop, displaying in its window the cheap imports that had displaced home produced textiles and allegedly shut down Ashton's mills. Economic crisis energised the Conservatives; in contrast despite previous credible polls in Ashton, no Liberal stood. Perhaps recent by-elections had engendered pessimism, perhaps local Liberals lacked funds. The fate of the 1929 Liberal vote seemed vital. Gordon proclaimed his virtue as the only free trade candidate, but the heavily Nonconformist character of local Liberalism might engender reluctance to vote for a Catholic. The Liberal organisation circulated seven questions to the candidates. Their content hinted at an aspiration for a Progressive understanding, but the Liberal Association simply invited Liberal voters to make their own judgment on the candidates' responses.[8]

Gordon's difficulties with the Government's economic record and Broadbent's demands for Protection and retrenchment were complemented by the education controversy. On the Sunday before the poll, Gordon attended Mass at St Ann's Church. The priest informed the congregation that Gordon's responses on education were 'evasive' and 'unsatisfactory', in contrast to those given by Broadbent and Young. The choice for 'loyal Catholics' was clear. They must vote for candidates who would exercise freedom of conscience when 'Catholic principles conflict with Party discipline' and who would support a Catholic claim for financial assistance for their schools. Gordon was unapologetic. The claim of evasiveness did not refer to his response to a questionnaire, but to a questioner at a meeting. He resented his religion being dragged into the contest, and felt that many Catholics objected to the priest's intervention. Perhaps those who prioritised the Schools question would be more likely to vote Tory anyway, but the altercation illuminated the complexities of Ashton politics where some believed that ethnic and religious identities still mattered.[9]

The New Party entered the contests two weeks before the poll with Allan Young's adoption on 16 April. Its local branch claimed 40 members. The party's Manchester organisation divided acrimoniously over the lack of consultation about the nomination. More fundamentally, the New Party's insistence that the only issue was unemployment had to reckon with a complex and, to its strategists, unfamiliar political terrain. Liberalism retained a presence and free trade loyalties died hard, despite the devastation of what had once been King Cotton. Voters could be cross-pressured between the appeals of class loyalty and cultural identity, or between established partisanship and the corrosive consequences of recent economic experience. In Ashton the spell of a talented, rich and glamorous outsider could be attractive. The New Party's opening meeting was crowded. The town hall was packed to hear Cynthia Mosley. How much was inquisitiveness and how much a more substantive interest that could end with a vote puzzled both strategists and observers. The New Party campaign was sustained by lavish poster displays, by evening meetings and by street corner agitation.[10]

Young was not a persuasive platform speaker. His talents were more suited to the drafting of policies. 'Very able but completely humourless' was one verdict. Mosley's arrival demonstrated that he was the *de facto* candidate who could complement his wife's casting as the glamorous outsider. Harold Nicolson on stepping off the London train in Manchester found himself in a giddy whirl that had parallels with Aitken's intervention two decades earlier. 'Go to the Midland Hotel, where I find Tom and Cimmie, Allan Young and Joad, Maureen Stanley, Eckersley, Bruce and other hangers-on.' They travelled east from Midland opulence to impoverished Ashton and found a packed audience. Mosley, having warmed up the meeting, raised the emotional temperature. 'England is not yet dead... it is for the New Party to try and save her.' The contrast with Young's erudite disquisitions on New Party policy was stark. Mosley offered himself as 'an impassioned revivalist speaker, striding up and down the rather frail platform with great panther steps and gesticulating with a pointing, and occasionally a stabbing, index'. Such pyrotechnics could fire optimism. Mosley's peroration, in Nicolson's assessment, could convince almost all the audience, at least for the moment. Canvassers reported 50 per cent of the canvass backed Young. Mosley was sceptical, but Nicolson, the excursionist from King's Bench Walk and Sissinghurst, felt certain that 'we shall get in above Labour... it would be an enormous triumph'.[11]

A contrasting perspective, admittedly in retrospect, came from Jack Jones, a politically experienced campaigner from the south Wales coalfield. Short of money, he worked in Ashton as a New Party organiser, attempting to compensate for the party's lack of a local base. He engaged two ex-Communists from Manchester, and together they carried out the daily grind of street meetings, not least the appeals to the unemployed outside the Labour Exchange. Jones recalled the contrast between this agitation by the poor bloody infantry and the life of the New Party high command. The latter kept in touch by telephone, discussing how to secure the Liberal or the Catholic vote. Some motored over for morning meetings with the Agent before returning for lunch at the Midland. They appeared in cavalcade for the set-piece evening meetings. Mosley and Strachey prepared their speeches and looked important in front of reporters. Only Cynthia Mosley spoke in the streets, not least at the many 'In Our Street Meetings' for women.[12]

Young achieved significant support but well below that suggested by an emotional rally as endorsed by a political day-tripper.

Ashton-under-Lyne By-Election April 30 1931

Electorate		34,784	
Turnout			80.2%
J. Broadbent	Conservative	12,420	44.6%
J.W. Gordon	Labour	11,005	39.4%
A. Young	New Party	4,472	16.0%
		1,415	5.2%

Compared with May 1929, Labour's share had fallen by 5 per cent and the Conservative vote had risen by 11.6 per cent. The Liberal poll in 1929 had been 22.6 per cent. Although turnout had fallen by 5 per cent, the poll of 80 per cent was still remarkably high, reflecting Ashton's tradition of high electoral participation rather than the New Party's impact. The rise in the Conservative vote probably indicated support from former Liberals and some disillusioned Labour voters. Labour's loss would have involved shifts to both other candidates. The New Party would certainly have secured backing from former Liberal and Labour voters, but in all probability failed in its declared ambition to win over many Conservatives. Labour supporters at the declaration vented their anger at Mosley and his coterie.[13] Their assessment that the New Party had cost Labour the seat was understandable but mistaken. The decline in the Labour vote was typical of the party's by-election performance in the first half of 1931. Some contests saw much worse results. Manchester Ardwick in late June would see the Labour share drop by almost 10 per cent.

Mosley's immediate response to defeat was dismissive of his Labour adversaries and of the broader political arrangements. 'The New Party will take no part in the utterly futile proceedings of the present Parliament until we have from the country a demonstration of opinion behind us to go back to Parliament and tell them they must wake up because the country is sick of them.' Mosley nevertheless appeared before the Select Committee on Procedure on 4 June to present the party's policy on institutional reform; this had developed from the January 1930 Mosley Memorandum through the December Manifesto and the February 1931 policy statement. The proposals should be located within a broader disquiet about the efficacy of political institutions. Strachey and Joad captured this concern in their presentation of the case for reform.

> Every few weeks Parliament had debated Unemployment... The endless futile speeches have all been made – and re-made. To those who care for the future of Great Britain nothing is more horrible than to sit through these debates. In the ornate and hideous Chamber the nation's breath seems to grow fainter, speech by speech.

Damaging continuity of policy was blamed in part on parliamentary decadence.[14]

The Select Committee had heard a succession of witnesses claiming that the alleged decline of Parliament was attributable to the diminishing influence of the Private Member. Mosley emphasised that his case was based on a different diagnosis that was informed by contrasting priorities. 'We think that the right of the individual to talk is not quite as great as the right of the nation to live.' He anticipated a radical change through the ballot box. 'I believe that the people of this country... will in time elect a Parliament prepared to take such action, but I quite agree that it would be a very different Parliament from the present.' He dismissed any suggestion of an exemplar from elsewhere. 'I certainly should not imitate foreign movements. I notice that we are always accused of imitating Rome by people who spend their whole time imitating Moscow.'[15]

Despite such denials the New Party's political identity remained unclear, not least amongst its leading figures. A weekend at Savehay Farm in early June resolved nothing. Strategy was discussed, papers were read. Strachey delivered 'a good old fashioned Marxian speech'. Young squirmed impatiently while Mosley spoke 'soulfully of the Corporate State of the future'. Discussion of the party's developing Youth Movement clearly troubled Allan Young. A few days later he expressed concern to Nicolson that the party might shift too far to the right and be 'forced into Hitlerism'. He was opposed to any suggestion that communist force be met with fascist force, a prospect seemingly implied by the Youth Movement.[16]

Strachey, despite his own concern about the party's direction, remained keen to develop links with the left. There were rumours that Arthur Horner, a talented, young South Wales Communist already prone to heretical ideas, was a possible recruit, Conversation with the Miners' General Secretary, A.J. Cook, had led by late June to a thoroughly unrealistic scenario. Strachey claimed that Cook, although supportive of the New Party, could not as yet declare openly in its favour. Any public commitment must await a breach between the Miners' Federation and the Labour Party. Cook supposedly was confident that this breach would occur and would lead to the New Party securing at least 40 miners' seats. Whatever the disenchantment of miners with the Labour Government, not least over mining issues, this expectation, whether suggested by Cook or exaggerated by Strachey, was fantasy. By 1931, mining communities were firmly embedded in the Labour Party. In many villages union and party were two faces of Labour hegemony; together they offered a defence against the excesses of coal capitalism. Political, industrial and social networks intertwined. This dominance had been long in the making. There could be no space for the New Party. The suggestion, however fanciful, troubled Nicolson. He hoped that the day would never come when 'the Party would be completely swamped by purely sectional interest'. Yet he seemed untroubled by Mosley's search for financial backing from rich businessmen.[17]

An Interim Report from the Royal Commission on Unemployment published late in June brought a return by the New Party to the Commons. The majority report recommended cuts in benefit payments and in the period of entitlement, increased contributions, the introduction of means tests for specific categories and the ending of 'abuses', relabelled as 'anomalies'. The labour movement committee members produced a minority report. This recommended no significant changes be made until the Commission had completed its work. The only exception concerned some 'anomalies'. The Government, most Labour MPs and the TUC united behind the so-called 'Anomalies Bill', whilst putting all the other proposals on ice. The proposed legislation was particularly severe on the payment of unemployment benefit to married women. In the eyes of many, their employment, and therefore their status as unemployed, was 'anomalous'. For the TUC and many Labour back-benchers postponement of the majority's proposals was preferable to implementation, and the removal of 'anomalies' was a price worth paying; for Snowden and at least some of the cabinet, the imminence of the May Committee's Report would mean substantial retrenchment anyway. This characteristic ministerial response left the ILP left unmoved; they tabled an amendment at Second Reading.[18]

The New Party leadership discussed the legislation. The discussion was in Nicolson's view unsatisfactory. There were significant tensions within the party. Mosley returned to the Commons for the Second Reading for the first time since he left the Labour Party. He crossed the floor and took his seat behind the Conservatives. He expressed no interest in the detail and merits of the so-called 'anomalies'. His opposition was exclusively founded on the proposition that the legislation resulted from a failed policy. He had no objection to the proposed procedure. 'The Regulations made by the Minister are to be laid on the Table of the House, and if unchallenged, are to have the force of law.' Mosley was unapologetic. 'I have no objection to the methods; I object only to the end.' Walter Elliot noted that this procedure showed similarities with Mosley's recent evidence to the Select Committee. Above all Mosley's indictment was aimed at the record of the Labour Government. Wage cuts and reductions in social services meant the deterioration of the home market, the last hope for British industry. The trade unions in their loyalty to the Government were forced to collaborate in the destruction of what they existed to defend. Mosley condemned the concordat between Government and TUC which had produced the Bill. 'By this measure you buy until the autumn, another short lease of your own miserable lives.'[19]

Mosley and his New Party colleagues joined the ILP left in opposing the Bill at Second Reading. The following week, the latter, already facing disciplinary sanctions, subjected the Bill to an all-night Committee session on the floor of the House. This demonstration by the awkward squad angered loyalists who were kept in attendance trooping through endless divisions until breakfast. The rebels had minimal support from other Labour Members; only the former Mosleyite Bevan and the ex-minister Trevelyan were notably sympathetic. In contrast Allen, Forgan, Cynthia Mosley and Strachey were active in the all-night resistance. So was W.R. Brown and to a lesser degree, Oliver Baldwin. They could share and express the anger of the ILP left. Sir Oswald Mosley was a notable absentee. His case against the legislation had been made; he stayed aloof from the detailed and passionate exploration of working-class poverty.[20]

The character and purpose of the Youth Movement remained contentious. Nicolson reflected that Mosley 'at the bottom of his heart really wants a fascist movement, but Allan Young and John Strachey think of the British working man. The whole thing is extremely thin ice.' The ice cracked quickly. The immediate cause was a basic disagreement over the party's policy towards the Soviet Union. Strachey's maiden speech in the Commons had emphasised the need to expand Anglo-Soviet trade; in the summer of 1930 he had visited the Soviet Union with Bevan and George Strauss. They had subsequently produced a pamphlet arguing that this untapped market could contribute significantly to a solution of Britain's economic problems. Thereafter, Strachey attempted to balance Mosley's emphasis on imperial development with the insistence that trade pacts should be made outside the empire and in particular with the Soviet Union. Mosley's attitude towards the Russian experiment had always been critical; facing pressure from Strachey for a more pro-Soviet policy Mosley encouraged him to write a memorandum.[21]

The result was 'The New Party and Russia'. Strachey claimed that the development of trade with Russia and the New Party's broader policy on insulation and planning would mean 'a progressive breach' with those powers, especially France and the United States, who were attempting 'to restore the pre-war form of International Capitalism'. Such a re-alignment, involving closer co-operation with Russia, was inconsistent with old-style imperialism. 'When we have built up an economic system capable of satisfying our own economic wants for ourselves, we shall not need an Imperial tribute drawn from the exploitation of colonial races.' India should therefore be assisted to establish a self-sufficient economic system. Strachey concluded that 'co-operation with Russia is a logical consequence of the New Party's whole policy'. Nicolson characterised the memo as 'idiotic'. Forgan, characterised by Nicolson as 'sensitive, shrewd, determined, experienced, amicable', was distancing himself from his ILP past, and was endorsing a nationalist basis for his new allegiance. He dismissed Strachey and Young as 'embittered bolsheviks' who would join the Communist Party. The New Party council rejected Strachey's memorandum by five votes to two; Strachey and

Young resigned from the party. Nicolson noted that 'they both minded dreadfully severing this link with old associates. Poor old Allan Young is on the verge of tears.' Their indictment of Mosley covered the Youth Movement, Unemployment Insurance, India and Russia. Together his positions within these controversies demonstrated 'a fascist tendency'. The indictment was rapidly endorsed by Joad's decision to quit the party on similar grounds, much to Nicolson's mystification.[22]

Strachey in retrospect claimed that their long and close collaboration with Mosley had encouraged increasing self-deception in order to avoid or postpone a painful breach. 'We pretended to ourselves that his talk about Fascism did not mean anything.' This diagnosis is persuasive but does not illuminate the complexities and instabilities within Strachey's own politics. Impatient with both the Labour Government and the ILP's insistence on socialist rectitude, he had been prepared to envisage cross-class co-operation in pursuit of a national solution to an immediate crisis. His close friend for whom the New Party had been a step too far, Aneurin Bevan, attributed Strachey's travails to his distance from the class struggle. Strachey was an intellectual with 'a tendency to dominate and shape these things arbitrarily'. In contrast, Bevan claimed for himself 'the security of metaphysics based on a social struggle upon which to rely in moments of doubt and uncertainty'. Boothby, who knew Strachey very well, subsequently understood him as a figure of their generation. 'In a very real sense he mirrored the desperate times in which we have had to live. He spent most of his life in search of a faith and a leader; and never found either.'[23]

Mosley in all probability welcomed the exit of the New Party's left luminaries, but not the timing. Immediately prior to the breach he had envisaged the prospect of a National alliance with Lloyd George and Churchill. If Labour and conventional Conservatives failed to manage the crisis, this collaboration could provide the basis for an alternative government. Mosley appreciated that his involvement in such an alliance would antagonise Strachey and Young. He hoped any resignations could be postponed until the autumn. As Nicolson noted 'he wishes to use them a little more before he flings them aside'. The National option was explored at a dinner hosted by the Liberal, and close associate of Churchill, Archibald Sinclair. His guests included Cynthia and Oswald Mosley, Nicolson, Lloyd George and Megan Lloyd George, Churchill and Brendan Bracken. After the women, including two MPs, had retired, Lloyd George conjured up the prospect of a National Opposition, as a response to the formation of a MacDonald–Baldwin coalition that would be precipitated by a threat to the pound. He suggested that once formed it would move rapidly from opposition to office. Nicolson portrayed a virtuoso performance inclusive of all his audience. 'The impression was that of a master-at-drawing sketching in a fig-leaf, not in outline, but by means of the shadows around it.' The sketch included nothing of the mechanics through which such a coalition might take office. The discussion left a sense that 'the Great Coalition had been formed'; Mosley seemed pleased, but as Nicolson reflected, 'nothing has been said'.[24]

August Bank Holiday saw a New Party spectacular. A gala and demonstration was held at Renishaw Park. the North Derbyshire home of Sir George Sitwell. An eccentric who had moved to the Florentine Castello di Montegufoni, his remodelling of the Renishaw gardens provided an impressive backdrop. Advertised as 'the biggest and cheapest attraction in the whole of Great Britain', 40,000 responded. The menu included athletics and boxing and the Sheffield Orpheus Male Voice Choir. Shooting galleries and roundabouts provided the rhythms of the fairground. Two brass band contests attracted 31 bands. The prizes were provided and presented by Mosley. The prize winners were almost all from the Yorkshire coalfield. Here at least he could still meet members of the organised working class without the risk of disorder.

All the entertainments paused for Mosley's oratory. He launched a scathing attack on the Labour Government. Its lack of courage had facilitated the recommendations of the May Report published a few days earlier. 'The Government was economising at the expense of the worker.' Snowden was 'the flunkey of the bond holder and the banker'. His indictment was unashamedly nationalist. 'Why was it necessary to look after foreign countries before anything was done at home?... .You can't get anything done in Britain unless you are a foreigner. Why if a man was drowning today, he would have to shout for help in German.' Trade unionism was endemically Protectionist, but the Government's internationalism blinded them to this imperative. Economic security was postponed indefinitely. 'When every Hottentot is in a trade union, you will be better off.'[25]

Three years earlier on a July Saturday Mosley had entertained Smethwick and Stoke Labour Party members at Savehay. Those guests had represented a well-established political party with over 150 MPs. In 1928 Mosley had mattered politically because he belonged to a party which in urban areas could claim a significant presence. In contrast, Renishaw Park was a Bank Holiday entertainment. Although allegedly organised through the New Party's Sheffield branch it had originated as an initiative by the party leadership and owed much to Sitwell's

support. The New Party with its four MPs had minimal local organisation. The crowds came to be entertained. The prize winners in the band
competitions took Mosley's cups and congratulations. They left his
politics at Renishaw.

Mosley travelled from north Derbyshire to the beaches and sunshine
of the Cap d'Antibes. Bevan, in welcoming Strachey's breach with
Mosley, had prophesied that 'looking at the political situation in this
country… the cards are not yet dealt with which the final game will
have to be played'. This holiday month would see a financial and political crisis that would transform the British party system into a pattern
that would last for almost a decade. Mosley had referred at Renishaw
to the Report of the May Committee. The majority report provided a
sombre narrative of escalating debt; the accompanying recommendations demanded the sacrifice of significant social provision on the altar
of sound finance. Labour ministers' response was to use the summer
Recess to pursue accommodations with the Trades Union Congress and
with sympathetic Liberals. Labour backbenchers' doubts would be met
by TUC acquiescence, leaving the ILP critics, and anyone who chose to
join them, in impotent isolation. Collaboration with sufficient Liberals
would produce a Commons majority. The agenda was one more act in
a drama of political bargaining that had maintained the Government
for more than two years. Its putative viability as unemployment rose,
electoral support withered and demands for robust economies esca-
lated, offers a tantalising counterfactual. But in August 1931, any cho-
reographed response was stillborn as the May Committee majority's
strident proclamation of budgetary disaster became intertwined with
an international financial crisis that threatened to drive Britain off the
Gold Standard. Guardians of economic orthodoxy, not least Snowden,
prophesied chaos.[26]

Ministerial panic was evident as they met, initially in a committee of
five, and then in full cabinet, to discuss possible economies. The intensity of the crisis and the Government's minority position meant that
consultation with Conservatives and Liberals began early in the process. Predictably, Opposition leaders criticised government proposals
for economies as insufficient. Apart from their shared belief in retrenchment, political priorities indicated that the Government should bear the
odium for any cuts, thereby offering a valuable overture to an election.
On the Riviera, Mosley could feel that the crisis was confirming the
New Party's rejection of 'old gang' politics and its prognostications of
economic disaster. 'Everything is moving towards us, few movements
have been so speedily or dramatically justified' was his assessment

on 16 August. Four days later, Nicolson responded that the situation seemed likely to ease. The TUC would accept proposals for economies, markets would calm and ministers would resume their holidays. This expectation died on the same day. When MacDonald and Snowden met the TUC General Council on 20 August they faced opposition, articulated forcefully by Bevin and less aggressively by the TUC General Secretary, Walter Citrine. Their attack was levelled not just against specific economies, but against the Government's deflationary strategy. In part the challenge reflected the insights of the TUC Research Department. These had been expressed in a memorandum suggesting that the language of crisis was hyperbolic. Any cuts should be socially progressive; perhaps a tariff should be introduced. More radically, development schemes could be funded by borrowing; devaluation should be considered. Bevin's self-confidence on economic matters had been boosted by his recent work on the Macmillan Committee on Finance and Industry, not least through his collaboration with Keynes. Many on the General Council, unsure of the economic arguments, followed his forceful lead; they felt a visceral antipathy to ministers' proposals. Not for the first time, trade union leaders felt patronised by Labour ministers. They were alienated by MacDonald's supercilious demeanour and by Snowden's inflexibility and dismissive response to any criticism. All too often the Government had been given the benefit of escalating doubts, not least over the treatment of the unemployed.[27]

Proposals from within the TUC demonstrated that alternative economic policies were not the monopoly of individuals marginalised by the mediocrity of established party mentalities and the drilled conformity of machine politics. However, the General Council's response was founded not so much on a distinctive policy as on a collective identity informed with a sense of what Labour politicians should and should not do. This sentiment had damned ILP critics and pronounced anathema on Mosley. Its decisive impact in August 1931 came within the cabinet where Henderson, always sensitive to union priorities and prejudices, emerged as a focus of opposition to the economy proposals. Over the next three days the cabinet failed to resolve its dilemma; the final symbolic event was a split vote of 11 to 9 in favour of a 10 per cent cut in unemployment benefit. The resignation of the Labour Government on August 24 was followed not, as widely anticipated, by an interim administration of Conservatives and Liberals, but by a National Government headed by MacDonald. He was joined from the Labour cabinet by Snowden, Thomas and two peers. Other posts in the small cabinet and almost all in the wider administration went to Conservatives and Liberals. The expectation was that the National Government would have a brief life. Once the crisis had been addressed by an adequate programme of cuts, the parties would resume their normal alignments and presumably fight an early election.

This unexpected development precipitated a rapid, vigorous and hostile response from the Labour Party and the TUC. Very few Labour backbenchers backed the new government. None of them was a trade unionist; almost all had entered the PLP in 1929. They were peripheral figures and official pronouncements, both national and local, rapidly ensured that they joined the Mosleyites as renegades. Yet the Labour condemnation of the National Government and of its Labour members and supporters necessitated amnesia. Almost all ministers had endorsed, or reluctantly accommodated to, the deflationary agenda, until the TUC had cried foul. Some ministers had continued their support after that fateful meeting. Six of the eleven who had voted for the 10 per cent cut subsequently came out as opponents of the National Government. Their recent actions required sagacious revisions.

The denouement of August 1931 had its roots in the policy pursued since June 1929. Few within the PLP had been openly critical; the rebellious few had met with mounting hostility. Both the PLP and the wider party responded to the National Government with similarly apparent solidarity. Yet for many Labour MPs the transition was difficult. They had remained loyal and sometimes affectionate supporters of MacDonald and Snowden through all the disappointments and compromises. Notably, the enforcement of the new line was directed not just against Labour supporters of the National Government; loyalists also attacked long-standing critics who could contrast the established and vindicated rectitude of the few with the Damascene conversion of the many. When the PLP met on 28 August, Dalton, now a forceful critic of MacDonald, noted the impatience shown to a former Mosleyite and to a vigorous and knowledgeable ILP critic. 'Aneurin Bevan, very ill received, makes incoherent complaint, as does Buchanan.' Sankey, who had continued as Lord Chancellor in the new Government, defended his position to this unreceptive audience. The PLP might be impatient with established critics but he felt that the bitterness of recent days had bred a broader radicalisation. 'They have gone mad and talk about class war.' The status of the new political arrangements remained opaque, but unequivocally Labour had placed itself in opposition to the National Government, thereby restricting the political space for other potential critics.[28]

The formation of a National Government unsettled many Conservatives. All the electoral indicators had pointed to a Conservative majority at the next election. The Conservative predominance amongst the new government's parliamentary support was not matched in the distribution of ministerial posts. Any claim for proportionality lost out to the argument that the allocation should express the Government's claim to be national. The new government could be viewed suspiciously as a threat to cherished Conservative policies. The party's progress towards Protection could be jeopardised by collaboration with Liberals. The Conservative right, already angered by Baldwin's position on India, could only be discouraged by the partisan diversity of the government's senior membership. Yet such tensions were largely containable by agreement on the urgency of the crisis and by the prudential judgment that desired economies could be achieved without tarring the Conservatives as the party of heartless retrenchment.

Creation of the National Government offered respite to Liberals who had been so often divided over their attitude to an increasingly unpopular Labour Government, and all too aware of their own electoral vulnerability. The alacrity with which Liberals moved to support and join the National Government was facilitated by Lloyd George's fortuitous illness. In his absence, senior Liberals could forget their recent, and in several cases unconscious, flirtation with a more radical economics and their interest in a Progressive arrangement, to launch an unqualified defence of economic orthodoxy. Such zeal facilitated an unexpected return to office. For a one-time Asquithian such as Sir Herbert Samuel, the return was to a ministerial world he had left in December 1916. The Liberal opportunity was expected to be brief, and the party's benefits from this National interlude seemed uncertain. The new government, by concentrating on the immediate crisis, had delayed the choice between Protection and Free Trade. Yet any credible Liberal future necessitated that this issue be confronted.[29]

These dramatic developments were welcomed by Mosley; his diagnosis of the imminence of crisis seemed vindicated, but his political independence with its lack of resources had meant isolation from the drama. Once the TUC had effectively disowned the Labour Government Nicolson pondered whether Mosley should return immediately. Mosley's silence contrasted with the flood of comments by significant and available politicians. The political crisis was the preserve of a small group; backbenchers were dispersed on holiday. Nicolson's advice was perhaps realistic. 'I do not see what you would do were you here at this moment... it is more dignified to be absent and aloof, than to be present and not consulted.' Nevertheless two days after the formation of the National Government, Mosley reached Dover. He argued that, having been proved right on the crisis, the New Party must continue on the same path and avoid any co-operation with Labour. By the end of August he had abandoned hope of any appeal to the Labour vote. 'Henderson and the machine have transformed the crisis into a class conflict. But all those who dread inefficiency and drift will look to us for guidance and initiative. We shall hit the black coat vote.' Such sentiments would have been strengthened by a meeting with Randolph Churchill, clearly acting as the messenger for his father. The latter had wanted to know whether Mosley 'would join him and the Tory toughs in opposition'. Such opposition would be directed against both the National Government and the Labour Party. Mosley saw the New Party's prospects as heavily dependent on avoidance of an early election; delay would allow both the strengthening of the party and accumulating evidence of ministerial incompetence.[30]

When the Commons met on 8 September the alignment of National versus Labour was assumed by most politicians and commentators to be temporary. The National Government had a parliamentary majority, it would pass a package of economies, calm the markets and then normal partisanship would be resumed. How far such normality would differ from the pre-crisis pattern was obscure. MacDonald and his allies would face serious difficulties in returning to Labour. The bitterness of early Commons exchanges between recent colleagues suggested a diminishing inclination on both sides to envisage such a reunion. MacDonald commended the Government as composed of 'men belonging to all parties who believe that until this emergency is over party strife should not appear'. Henderson's riposte to MacDonald's national appeal expressed Labour's new mood. 'We appeal to that part of the country that we have tried to represent, and I hope that we will appeal on high, strong Socialist grounds.' Labour's response was too mild for Maxton and the ILP left. He insisted that capitalism no longer functioned and Labour was 'rapidly approaching a revolutionary situation'.[31]

Mosley's hope was that the end of the National Government would be precipitated by its failure to address the crisis; the consequence would be political fluidity on the political centre and right. This might leave space for a tough, modernising nationalist party with a cross-class appeal. He insisted that the budgetary crisis was not the basic issue. 'The continual decline and collapse of the industries of this country makes completely illusory any attempt to balance the Budget.' He scornfully dismissed Labour claims that they had been the victims of 'a bankers' ramp'. The crisis was the consequence of a long-term financial policy, implemented by Snowden and underwritten by the PLP and the party conference. 'They did not walk out of the bankers' palace till it fell about their ears.' Contempt for Labour's record was complemented by support for Protection, backed by 'stringent guarantees' on industrial efficiency and reconstruction. Leo Amery responded positively. He welcomed Mosley's 'very good fireworks'. He had made 'the speech I should have liked to make, pouring contempt on the whole of the economy nonsense and insisting on the urgency of the trade and industrial situation'. Mosley voted against the Government at the end of the debate, but subsequently offered support for a General Powers Bill. Such backing was consistent with his arguments for political and administrative reform. It could also strike a chord with Tory Protectionists who favoured more decisive state intervention to address the crisis. Mosley's parliamentary interventions received a positive press response. There were affable exchanges with Conservative Members. He professed optimism about the New Party's prospects, but feared the Tories would try and force an early election. New Party resources were few; a rally in Trafalgar Square four days after his Commons *tour de force* found Mosley speaking in a fine mist to a small crowd, his oratory pitted against hecklers and damp umbrellas.[32]

John Strachey also contributed to the September Commons debates. He shared Mosley's dismissal of the National Government and claimed that former ministers remained in denial about the crisis's character. He believed the National Government's budget to be 'the signal for an all-round reduction of costs by a reduction in wages'. Whilst welcoming Labour's opposition to this agenda he insisted that Labour's front bench had not grasped its implications. To resist cost-cutting was 'to challenge the whole existence of British capitalism'. The appropriate response was to mobilise the working class on a programme of specific demands – shorter hours, higher wages, work or maintenance. This strategy would require an awareness of the need to 'struggle for the overthrow of the capitalist system by whatever means history and destiny may propose'. The two former comrades sought to mobilise on contrasting bases, class and nation. Strachey was on the next stage of his political journey. He read *Capital* and corresponded with the luminaries of British Communism, Harry Pollitt and R. Palme Dutt. By the end of the year he would acknowledge his inability 'to deny the accuracy of the Communist diagnosis and correctness of the Communist line in Great Britain'. Mosley responded to alleged Communist violence at a Glasgow meeting by asserting the necessity of fascism. 'We need no longer hesitate to create our trained and disciplined force.'[33] But the weekend of the Glasgow affray was a decisive moment in the resolution of the financial and political crisis.

Speculation about an early election had fostered financial uncertainty. Gold and foreign exchange continued to be withdrawn from London. On 15 September a mutiny within the Atlantic Fleet anchored at Invergordon intensified the withdrawals. A cabinet committee sought credits from New York and Paris. The attempt failed. The only option was to quit the Gold Standard. The National Government had failed in its proclaimed primary objective. Devaluation was finessed by bankers and ministers. This need not be painted as the threatened catastrophe of a month earlier, but as an acceptable response, since the budget would be balanced. The prevention of currency depreciation necessitated continuing implementation of economies. The Commons passage of the enabling legislation for the suspension of the Gold Standard exposed Labour divisions on the desirability of any cross-party collaboration. Henderson agreed with MacDonald to facilitate the legislation's passage; he spoke from the Opposition front bench in non-partisan terms about the need to manage the crisis. Many Labour Members dismissed such consensual sentiments. The Government had failed; it must be criticised. Christopher Addison, once the target of Mosley's demands for retrenchment, had shifted from Coalition Liberal to Labour. As Minister of Agriculture he had been amongst the minority opposed to the 10 per cent cut in unemployment benefit. His front-bench speech, in contrast to Henderson's, was forceful. 112 Labour MPs, a cross-section of the PLP, voted against the government. Subsequent rumours suggested Henderson's unhappiness at the party's mood, and less convincingly the possibility of his joining a reformed National Government. Such speculation neglected the balance within the party, not least the influence of the unions and the outlooks of some significant politicians.[34]

The episode strengthened the feeling within the National Government that any possibility of a Labour Government, however remote, threatened financial stability. An election could exorcise the spectre. Labour was not just a political opponent, but a national peril that must be comprehensively defeated. The dichotomy of National and Labour was transformed from a short-term device to a long-term prospectus. Initial electoral plans were for a Protectionist platform headed by MacDonald and Baldwin; it could embrace those Liberals connected with Sir John Simon who were prepared to subordinate their free trade faith to the need to defeat Labour. Within such expectations Mosley could still have a credible position. He had made a measured contribution to the Gold

Standard debate; he welcomed the abandonment of a system that he had consistently opposed. Freedom from its straitjacket could lead to disaster or progress. The currency must not be allowed to depreciate; its stabilisation must be linked with industrial development. He could make an electoral claim as a Protectionist and a drastic moderniser.

The crisis had inflamed Nicolson's endemic elitism. 'The submerged classes are in fact foreigners... The working class have no sense of fair play and no common sense; they think only of their own grievances and of the rich; education has ruined this unhappy country.' In a subsequent memorandum he emphasised the polarisation of politics between National and Labour, and the consequential difficulty for the New Party. Whilst acknowledging that much could be learned from Italian fascism, he insisted that this did not offer a feasible option; it would frighten conservatives and make no immediate appeal to their opponents. Rather the weakness of the New Party suggested that an attempt should be made to join the politically heterogeneous National alliance as 'an Action Group'. Mosley approached his old adversary, Neville Chamberlain. In late September he was hopeful of a deal that would allow the New Party a few candidacies as the National opponent of Labour, presumably in constituencies where Conservative hopes were minimal. F.M. Box, the New Party Chief Agent, went into negotiations with his Conservative counterpart. There was a suggestion of six or possibly 12 seats.[35]

Any negotiations were unproductive; by early October the New Party had lost whatever limited appeal it had once possessed for Tory strategists. A much more significant electoral arrangement became credible. The firmly Free Trade Liberals under Samuel were persuaded to fight an election under the National umbrella. The appeal would not be overtly Protectionist but instead a request for a 'doctor's mandate' to prescribe whatever measures seemed appropriate. Success for this strategy would mean a National majority which would be predominantly Conservative and Protectionist. Nevertheless, in a fevered atmosphere Samuel's Liberals saw the medical metaphor as the most effective means of retaining their seats and in some cases their ministerial posts. They feared displacement by Sir John Simon's group, who were already abandoning their free trade credentials. Many Liberals were anxious about Labour's strengthened emphasis on class and socialism. An inclusive National alliance, however much it was a blatant obfuscation for electoral purposes, offered the best guarantee of a thorough Labour defeat. Obvious disagreement on a key policy could be swamped in a tide of rhetoric stressing nation and crisis, and vilifying Labour as unpatriotic.

Within little more than a month the political uncertainty of August had been transformed into two unequal adversaries. No political space remained. This settlement marginalised both Mosley and Lloyd George. The latter, recovering from illness, led a very small Liberal group opposed to the National Government. Its few candidates sought local support from Labour. In 1931 the hope for a Progressive alliance were finally extinguished. Mosley had hoped for political fluidity, instead the old gang had remained in control.[36]

New Party fantasies of 400 and later of 100 candidates withered to 24. Only Forgan and Mosley from the parliamentary group were candidates. Brown and Strachey stood as Independents. Mosley moved from Smethwick where he faced the implacable hostility of local Labour to Stoke, where Cynthia Mosley had decided not to contest on health grounds. When the dissolution was announced, the New Party gained an unexpected recruit. Cecil Dudgeon, once the admirer of Robert Cecil, had announced the previous year that he would retire from Galloway at the next election. He had cited the plight of Liberalism and his personal affairs. He had remained active in the parliamentary Liberal party and had been identified with the group around Sir John Simon. The Liberal response to the National Government had rendered them even more fragmented. 'The crew went into three separate boats and pulled for three different ports.' Even a national crisis could not restore unity. In contrast the New Party offered country before party. He abandoned his thorough support for free trade in favour of scientific protection. Mosley visited Galloway accompanied by his 'minders', the boxer, Ted 'Kid' Lewis, and the rugby player, Peter Howard. He attracted large crowds and commended Dudgeon as 'a practical agriculturist'. Perhaps such an episode was what a local newspaper meant when it claimed that Dudgeon's candidacy 'on behalf of that fantastic new party... may add to the gaiety of the election'.[37]

Mosley's visit to Castle Douglas and Dalbeattie was not unique. Much of his time was spent away from Stoke touring New Party battlegrounds. Sometimes this characterisation was more than figurative; Mosley's stewards took on vociferous opponents, most violently at an abandoned meeting in Birmingham's Rag Market. In contrast, the rural Galloway audiences were attentive. His Stoke meetings were peaceful and enthusiastic as he presented the New Party programme for economic success and reform of political institutions. His Labour opponent, Ellis Smith of the Patternmakers, insisted that the issue was the perpetuation of capitalism or the advent of socialism. There could be no middle way.

In contrast, the Conservative candidate, Ida Copeland, wife of the head of the china manufacturer Spode and Copeland, appealed to her local connections rather than to 'all sorts of Utopian promises that could never be fulfilled'.[38]

James Lees-Milne was Mosley's cousin. He would have an eminent career as an architectural historian and conservationist. In October 1931 he had recently come down from Oxford and went to Stoke as a family favour. His retrospective portrait of Mosley was far removed from Wertheimer's stylish recruit of 1924 or Ellen Wilkinson's 'Valentino in real life'. 'The posturing, the grimacing, the switching on and off of those gleaming teeth, and the overall swashbuckling, so purposeful and calculated were more likely to appeal to Mayfair flappers than to sway indigent workers in the Potteries.' The empathy of this product of Eton and Magdalen with the sentiments of the Stoke working class may be questionable. Certainly, erstwhile Labour allies had been well aware of Mosley's style as a platform performer. Recognition of artifice had not detracted from his popularity at the Durham Miners' Gala nor as a by-election campaigner. Was context vital? Did his limitations become more apparent or viewed more critically with his political marginalisation?[39]

Mosley polled just under a quarter of the vote in Stoke, 10,534 compared with 13,264 for Ellis Smith and 19,918 for Ida Copeland. Mosley's response was that they had made great headway since the New Party was formed. Yet other New Party candidates, including Robert Forgan, had attracted derisory votes. Dudgeon's 986 supporters would have gratified the local critic who had dismissed him as a 'political acrobat'. The only exception was in Merthyr where Sellick Davies, previously the Liberal candidate at Evesham in 1929, secured 300 more votes than Mosley. Merthyr was the only constituency where the New Party had a straight fight with Labour and could function as a *de facto* National candidate. Davies emphasised 'scientific protection'; this was sufficient to win the support of the local Conservative Association. The Merthyr Liberals, torn between anti-socialism and antipathy to Protection quizzed the candidates but seem to have offered no recommendation. Davies seems to have secured much of the limited anti-Labour vote. Unfortunately for Davies, the south Wales coalfield was Labour's one success story in 1931. Some candidates were unopposed including Aneurin Bevan; others found that their vote increased compared with 1929, both in percentage terms and arithmetically. The Labour Member for Merthyr, R.C. Wallhead, had been ill and barely appeared in the campaign. Lack of visibility proved no handicap in this Labour stronghold. Yet Merthyr might suggest that similar straight fights in less unfavourable seats would have given the New Party a parliamentary bridgehead.[40]

The election marginalised the discordant and the iconoclastic. A majority of electors opted for the National cocktail of patriotism, caution and anti- Labour vitriol. Labour's representation was reduced to 46 plus five on the ILP left who had refused to accept the Labour position on internal discipline. In addition, Josiah Wedgwood survived in the Potteries, having been returned unopposed as the Independent and individualistic representative of his community. The party was largely driven back to the coalfields and to working-class districts of London. Elsewhere, the party had one representative each from Bristol, Leeds and Liverpool. Glasgow provided two more, plus three of the ILP contingent. Birmingham was once again a Conservative monopoly. The city's turnover of majorities had been huge. Jim Simmons had won Erdington in 1929 by 133 votes; in 1931 he lost by almost 19,000. Labour's eleven-vote majority in Ladywood had become a Conservative one of 14,000. Strachey stood in Aston as a left-wing independent and lost his deposit. The rout of Birmingham Labour would not be reversed until political alignments had been shifted by the trauma of 1940. Labour disappeared from the Black Country. W.J. Brown stood as an Independent Labour candidate in West Wolverhampton and was decisively beaten.[41]

The fragmentation of Labour was evident in the fates of the quartet who had been entrusted with Labour's unemployment policy. Mosley's marginalisation contrasted with Thomas's landslide victory at Derby on the National ticket. Tom Johnston's defeat in West Stirlingshire was by a narrow margin. Lansbury's roots in Poplar meant that he was the only member of the 1929 cabinet to retain his seat. The second-generation aspirants who had seen Mosley as a rival, criticised his proposals and rejoiced at his apostasy were largely defeated. Dalton, Morrison and Greenwood lost their seats; only the discreet Attlee was successful as part of the East End resistance to the National deluge. When Mosley spoke at the Durham Miners' Gala in 1929 Labour held all but one of the county's eighteen seats; in 1931 they retained only two. All the county's industrial constituencies were lost and most of the mining seats. The latter defeats were attributed by some to Ramsay MacDonald's National candidacy at Seaham; more weight should perhaps be accorded to the residual strength of Durham Liberalism. Three of the coalfield seats were lost to Liberals in straight fights; elsewhere in Durham, Liberals stood down in the National interest.

In contrast, Mosley's erstwhile Conservative associates all fared well in the election. Stanley was appointed to the initial National Government and enjoyed an unopposed return. Elliot, also firmly established as a man with a ministerial future, and Boothby, equally firmly established as an outsider, saw their majorities escalate. Macmillan had had severe health problems precipitated in part by the pain of his private world. Under treatment at a German clinic he returned to contest deeply depressed Stockton. He profited from the absence of a Liberal; his majority was more than 11,000. He remained a marginal figure throughout the thirties, collaborating in progressive initiatives and producing his agenda for a planned economy, *The Middle Way*. Like Sidney and Beatrice Webb he visited the Soviet Union in 1932. His travelling companion was Allan Young who would support Macmillan with the research skills that he had once provided for Mosley. Young's concern with planning and modernisation no longer seemed fired by a socialist commitment.[42]

The election had essentially been Labour against the rest. The National majority in terms of seats was overwhelming; in terms of the popular vote it was unique, but Labour's vote remained credible. In the complex party politics of the twenties the electoral system had favoured Labour; in 1931 with Labour faced by a united opponent the system had the opposite effect. The electoral cataclysm had produced a party system whose durability was as yet unknown. The National alliance had been a product first of economic and political crises and then of electoral pressures and calculations. The issue of Free Trade or Protection remained unresolved, although the new Commons had a Protectionist majority. Any solution would necessarily pose difficulties for the Government's cohesion. Equally, Labour in the Commons was not only small in numbers but limited in leadership. One reaction to the traumas of office and the polls could be to move to the left. Beyond questions of political strategy lay the basic economic issue. Could the government cope with challenges that seemed unmanageable, not just in Britain, but most dramatically in Weimar Germany and in Herbert Hoover's United States? Mosley's expectation was that the government and by extension the established method of muddling through would fail. His message at Stoke after his defeat was based on the premise that deepening economic crisis would precipitate political polarisation and transformation. 'Our time is not yet but it will come.'[43]

9
Options

The formation of the National Government, and more permanently the consequences of the electoral tsunami, had elevated the respectable and cautious and had marginalised the radical and deviant; as Boothby had warned, all the 'shits' really were in one basket, and they would remain there throughout the thirties. A battered Labour Party had been radicalised by its trauma but only within firmly constitutional and electoral limits. Its political recovery would prove insufficient to revive credible hopes of office when faced with a united anti-Labour front that retained strong electoral support. Those who would be condemned as 'Guilty Men' dominated the political landscape. Critics unsuccessfully sought counter-strategies; only Mosley responded by founding a fascist organisation.

The October 1931 election had severed any residual ties that Mosley retained with conventional party politics and parliamentary procedures. The liquidation of the New Party's fragments, a visit to Mussolini and a summer spent writing *The Greater Britain* culminated in the inauguration of the British Union of Fascists almost a year to the day after Mosley's negotiation's for a minor role in the National electoral alliance had proved sterile. In October 1932 he stepped outside the pale of political respectability, never to return. The death of Cynthia Mosley, the following May marked the end of both personal and political chapters; her attachment to fascism had been at best tenuous and reluctant.

This singularity has invited explanations in terms of Mosley's character. A familiar portrait is of talent subverted by fatal flaws. These are held to have prompted gross misjudgements at critical moments – his resignation from the Labour Government, his forming of the New Party, his apocalyptic reading of the political prospects after the 1931 election. Such disastrous errors allegedly demonstrated impatience, arrogance, an unwillingness, or inability, to accept the necessary discipline and frustration of political bargaining. In sum, he revealed himself as unable to play the political game effectively. Supportive evidence is provided not least by his changes of party, successive dalliances that led him into an ultimately ignominious marginality.

Thomas Johnston had worked with Mosley and Lansbury as members of the ill-fated trio; having become a member of the Labour cabinet in its final months, he had voted amongst the minority in the August 1931 vote on a cut in unemployment benefit. He lost his seat in the subsequent election and, with Mosley shifting towards fascism, he offered a nuanced assessment of his former colleague. Mosley should not be dismissed as a 'word druggist'; he had 'ability, industry, courage, youth, and money as well as skill in histrionics'. This portrait had similarities with that penned by Beatrice Webb nine years earlier. Johnston acknowledged that Mosley had been treated badly by senior Labour ministers:

> He could get no outlet whatever for his energies. Thomas and Mosley were a sadly ill-matched couple and the wily old man of the world kept the young assistant out of mischief drafting reports until he discovered that his reports never led to anywhere but the waste paper basket. In his irritation and disgust a potential Mussolini was born.

So far, this appraisal could offer material for later revisionist assessments of Mosley. Johnston however added a qualification to this relatively sympathetic portrait. 'Whether his adherence to any particular cause can last long enough for him to get fully acquainted with it, before he moves on is another matter.'[1]

The claim that Mosley's attachment to any political party was loose must be placed in context; party politics between 1918 and 1931 was characterised by instability. The massive expansion of the electorate in 1918 was followed by a smaller one a decade later. Many voters and several politicians shifted allegiances. Significant Liberals shifted to Labour. Some had been disillusioned by the Liberal Government's entry into war in August 1914 or by the illiberalism of the war years. Trevelyan and Noel Buxton brought these experiences and their patrician liberalism into the 1924 and 1929 cabinets. In contrast, Addison had been a social Liberal voice in the Lloyd George Coalition and subsequently a victim of post-war demands for economy to which Mosley had made his contribution. Wedgwood Benn had been a robustly anti-Lloyd George Liberal who only joined Labour after Asquith's resignation as leader. Equally, many shifted formally or in effect to the Conservatives whilst often insisting that they remained principled Liberals. The Lloyd George Coalition offered one such conveyor belt; another came with the formation of the National Government. Anti-socialism and distaste for any Progressive project that gave a major place to the trade unions were articulated through liberal tenets.

Most shifts of allegiance were single journeys. Liberals abandoned their tribal home claiming that their principles could be better pursued elsewhere, as could their careers. Such blends of rectitude and opportunism contrasted with Mosley's serial partisanship. Yet, by late 1924 Churchill, as he later acknowledged, had 'ratted' twice; from 1930–31 India and broader disagreements with official Conservatism under Baldwin and Neville Chamberlain marginalised him for almost a decade. By the late twenties Lloyd George was nominal leader of a nominally reunited Liberal Party; in 1931, ill-timed hospitalisation and the preferences and antipathies of those who had benefited from his fall from the premiership combined to exclude him from the National Government. Nevertheless, his intentions and talents would remain sources of intermittent concern for those who prized partisan predictabilities. The conclaves of 1930 demonstrated that there were younger politicians across the ideological spectrum who differed on policy but agreed that existing party leaderships and cultures stifled new and necessary initiatives. Perhaps Mosley should be viewed as a distinctive exemplar of a politically plastic decade.

His style combined emotion, impatience, manipulation and dismissiveness. His platform performances, at least during his Birmingham period, aroused comparisons with Joseph Chamberlain; they proclaimed that he, and not Chamberlain's sons, was the proper heir to a city's distinctive political legacy. The comparison perhaps illuminates Mosley's singularity, compared with his contemporaries. Some politicians, for example Attlee, have personified their party, seeking to articulate its ethos and to secure compromises between disputatious factions. Some have combined symbolic fidelity with attempts to shift party priorities; Baldwin and, many years later, Macmillan offer example of prime ministerial attempts to ride simultaneously two horses in the circus. A few, capitalising on the relative freedom afforded by successive electoral disasters, have overtly attacked an established party ethos, most spectacularly Blair in the prelude to 1997. These diverse strategies all rested on a common assumption that effective leadership necessitated a dependable party base and therefore to some extent toleration of its eccentricities and limitations. Although abundant evidence supports the credibility of this maxim, it has not always been followed. Lloyd George at the height of the battle over Lords reform in 1910 was widely perceived as thoroughly partisan, yet, to a few he revealed a contrasting evaluation of the place of party. He explored with some Conservatives the possibility of a coalition that would implement an agreed programme of national modernisation, necessitating the mutual abandonment of some partisan icons. His post-war coalition had hoped to pursue such a strategy but had been wrecked on the rocks of economic orthodoxy and tribal loyalties. Lloyd George's lack of an assured party base made him vulnerable in 1922 and subsequently helped to ensure his marginality. Joseph Chamberlain had divided the Liberals over Irish Home Rule and the Conservatives over tariff reform. Like Mosley, he had shown a reluctance to bargain, preferring at critical moments rupture to reconciliation. Mosley shared with Chamberlain and Lloyd George an instrumental view of party. It offered a tool for the pursuit of objectives and should be discarded if deemed to have failed the test. Mosley's induction into any party culture had been minimal; the jettisoning of any party attachment was relatively easy.[2]

Neither the Birmingham industrialist nor the Welsh-speaking solicitor had been socialised through appropriate educational institutions and informal networks into the values and mores of the traditional governing class; hence, perhaps, their scepticism about established mentalities, their affinity with 'men of push and go' and their oratory which could cause panic amongst the privileged. Whatever their differences over methods they could agree on the need to pursue the Edwardian objective of 'National Efficiency'. Mosley in the twenties evinced similar characteristics and provoked similar responses. Skidelsky's portrait of the feudal enclave that was Rolleston might be overdrawn, but that pre-war society as recalled by Mosley offered suggestions of an effective response to the challenges of obsolescence and international competition. David Cannadine has provided a darker vision. He portrayed Mosley's attempt to recreate a lost world as in part revenge for a class defeat, but also as expressing a belief in the merits of a consensual society where all were cared for but most in return accepted authority. Cannadine presented Mosley as at war with economic liberalism, plutocracy and press lords, party caucuses, democracy, socialism, the mob, and the stifling routines of parliament. This image of Mosley *contra mundum* collapses the complexities of Mosley in the twenties into the marginal figure of 1932 and beyond.[3]

Mosley's sense of himself as an outsider arguably owed more to his understanding of the war than to his social origins. His construction of the war generation and of his role as its tribune raises important questions about the salience and impact of this experience for post-war politics. Military titles were frequently used by politicians. Some argued that the essential priority was to return to the pre-war world; others, often but not wholly on the left, insisted that wartime imperatives had produced models of economic and social organisation whose subsequent abandonment had been to the detriment of many who had served. That the heroes of 1914 had become the impoverished and often unemployed of the early twenties became a refrain on Labour platforms. These legacies were epitomised by the Mayor of Stepney, Major Attlee, complete with medals and officer's cane, as he went with other London mayors to meet Lloyd George on behalf of the unemployed. Yet such demonstrations indicated the extent to which any political agenda of a war generation had been integrated and perhaps submerged within existing party structures. There was no significant British conflict within the returned servicemen's organisations about their political character; such struggles were at their most fevered where armies had finished on the losing side or where diplomats at Versailles had failed to meet popular expectations about territorial expansion. For Mosley, the great betrayal lay in the pursuit of a return to the chimera of 1914; he dismissed this as a disastrous obsession epitomised for him by the return to the Gold Standard.

The resilience of the political system that increasingly fed Mosley's hostility owed much to military victory and the consequential complacency in governing circles and beyond about the viability of existing institutions. The franchise had been expanded to include effectively all men over 21 and most women over 30; constituency boundaries had been redrawn to reflect demographic changes since 1885. Otherwise, in the context of political upheaval across much of Europe, the regime was notable for its continuity. The House of Lords remained unelected and unreformed, the voting system, despite the fleeting prospect of the alternative vote, retained the disproportionality of first past the post, the attenuated female franchise discriminated against the less well-off and those seen as rootless. Even the unanticipated worked in favour of the right; the formation of the Irish Free State, by removing most Irish Members from Westminster, made it much easier to form a Conservative Government.

Continuity in state institutions was not complemented by continuity in party politics. The pre-war Progressive alliance between Liberals and Labour had always been contested amongst and within its constituents. Social Liberals had disputed with their more traditional colleagues about the proper scope of state intervention; Labour politicians had debated the merits of a more aggressively independent strategy. The degree of compatibility between the partners had depended on sufficient agreement on policy and the readiness of Labour to remain as the junior partner. Sources of potential conflict were evident, but by 1914 Progressive electoral success had pushed the Conservative towards intransigence on Ireland and sulphurous rhetoric on much else. How effectively the Progressive alliance would have survived in the absence of war is opaque. Increasing trade union membership was boosting Labour's self-confidence, but unions were reluctant to spend money on speculative candidacies. Electoral prudence might have facilitated a renegotiation of the relationship which would have strengthened the position of Labour.

Liberal divisions, Conservative wartime resurgence and Labour unity based on union solidarity that inhibited potentially destructive disputes over the war meant that by 1918 the Progressive alliance was effectively dead. The last credible hope for its survival went with the failure of the proposal for the alternative vote. Instead, there began the search for a viable partisan configuration that could accommodate the demands of a massively expanded electorate. Above all, many politicians and voters became concerned with the challenge of Labour. Trade union strength eroded with post-war depression in the staple industries; 'Black Friday' could be viewed within the labour movement as treachery or prudence; the General Strike, five years later, was an unambiguous defeat. Yet, until 1931 many politicians remained concerned with the containment of Labour.

Mosley's parliamentary career developed in the context of successive responses to this challenge. These were shaped by the largely unreformed institutional structure, the complexities and unpredictability of three party battles under the first past the post electoral system, and the choices of key actors. The durability of many politicians and voters' attachment to free trade, despite mounting evidence against its familiar justifications, hampered co-operation between anti-socialists. The post-war Lloyd George Coalition could be understood as an attempt to combat the challenge of Labour through a putative Centre Party. This innovation would replace outmoded Liberal–Tory conflict with a programme of pragmatic modernisation that could contain any challenge from the left. Mosley, in his initial months in parliament, found this ambitious agenda attractive. Many on the government benches whose partisan identities had been formed pre-war were at best reluctant subscribers. A substantial number of Coalition Liberals hoped for a future reunion with their estranged former colleagues. Many Tories became increasingly disenchanted with what they characterised as the Coalition's penchant for liberal solutions, not least the Irish settlement. By early 1922 Conservatives were increasingly optimistic that their party could provide the decisive core for an anti-socialist politics. The Carlton Club vote in October wrote the death certificate not just for the Coalition but for any Centre Party project. The immediate consequence was a period of political uncertainty, with three elections in less than two years. The eventual outcome seemed decisive; after the October 1924 election, the Liberals had been reduced to a rump of 40 Members; Labour had experienced a brief spell as a minority government; Baldwin's Conservative Party had emerged apparently as the party for all anti-socialists. Its 1924 campaign emphasised the constitutional threat posed by the Labour left, the evils of Bolshevism, and in contrast the credibility of the Conservative Party as custodian of all that was decent; the blend of self-conscious respectability and hysteria attracted many Liberal voters.

This period of uncertainty could have had several outcomes; it was concurrent with Mosley's journey from a lightly worn Conservatism through informal Liberalism to Labour Party membership. His Harrow candidacies as an Independent charted this shift. In November 1922, despite his support for free trade, he retained some credibility as an independently minded Conservative; he was helped by the official party candidate's preference for retention of the Coalition. A year later, Mosley was in many respects an unofficial Liberal candidate. These Harrow years perhaps strengthened a belief that there was scope within the party system for independent initiatives, an assessment that could neglect the distinctive volatility of party identities and alliances that characterised the transition between the Carlton Club meeting and the Zinovieff letter.

The Conservative Party was increasingly dismissed by Mosley as unimaginative and reactionary. Such indictments could play well in partisan campaigning, but neglected how effectively that party was adapting to the demands and uncertainties of a mass electorate. Under Baldwin's leadership the internal divisions resulting from the end of the Coalition were mended, the leader's reasonableness and a-political style could attract votes from the unsure and the barely interested. Yet, Baldwin's welcome to the Conservative big tent was complemented by diatribes and caricatures against supposedly dangerous minorities. These vilifications were usually purveyed by colleagues, thereby maintaining the leader's distance from unseemly partisanship. Many

within Labour ranks might be decent members of the national community, but intellectuals and extremists were destructive of basic values.
Conservatism was not just the party of property, however small, but of
the family, the constitution and the nation. Here were the origins of a
dominance that would shape British politics for much of the twentieth
century. The presentation of Conservatism as common sense was rooted
in local organisations that in many small towns and rural areas were
effectively statements of community identity; such networks expressed
and sustained local hierarchies and offered the building blocks for
electoral hegemony. The inclusivity of the big tent restricted political
space for the left and denied it to the radical right. Like many of his
contemporaries Mosley seemed unaware of the appeal and durability of
Baldwin's party.

Mosley's brief involvement with Liberalism owed much to his association with an independently minded Conservative; Lord Robert Cecil's
criticisms of the Coalition often were at one with liberal principles and
values. Mosley's attacks on reprisals in Ireland first brought him into
alliance with Liberals; his demands for cutting public expenditure were
shared with many Conservatives but nevertheless accorded with traditional liberal economic prescriptions. Understandably, a young politician from Mosley's background reacting against Conservative prejudices
and limitations might easily connect with the Liberals. Yet many within
post-war Liberalism hoped for a return to the pre-war world. For Mosley
this prospect was irretrievable, its pursuit was damaging.

Perhaps Mosley's Liberal period was no more than the opportunistic
embrace of a partisan possibility at a moment of uncertainty; perhaps
it indicated an intellectual attraction to complete systems of thought
that in this case meant an endorsement of Free Trade. Whatever the
basis for this attachment, the result of the 1923 election and the arrival
of MacDonald in Downing Street precipitated Mosley's rapid shift to
Labour. The Liberals could make or destroy governments, but even
on the favourable territory of Free Trade versus Protection they had
finished third. Mosley's response might have demonstrated a concern
with his own career, but it also suggested a realistic assessment of Liberal
prospects. Many Liberal victories had been in unexpected places where
their support had been buoyed by Conservative voters backing Free
Trade against the gamble of Protection; often the Liberal margin of
victory had been small. This vulnerability was accompanied by Liberal
failure to make much advance in urban seats that had once been theirs
but which had now become Labour strongholds. The party no longer
had credibility as a potentially governing party, a predicament that

many senior Liberals who had once held office, refused to accept. This lack of realism, fed by nostalgia for lost eminence, hampered the development of other Liberal strategies. Liberals with strong local bases could win seats based on their championing of local grievances; this appeal seemed effective in some agricultural districts, or in urban areas where Labour remained weak. Frank Gray's victories in Oxford City in 1922 and 1923 demonstrated the potential of this strategy which he memorialised in his appropriately titled *The Confessions of a Candidate*. Such a politics was at odds with the dreams of the party's leaders; at best it could offer a vocal parliamentary presence. It had no appeal for Mosley.[4] Yet there were Liberals who understood the impossibility of any return to a mythologised pre-war liberal age. Intellectuals, most notably Keynes, were painfully aware of liberalism's predicament, both in terms of ideas and political strategy. The basic diagnosis and the quest for new ideas were shared by Lloyd George. Yet his leadership of the party from 1926 faced not only electoral marginality, but the distaste of so called colleagues who remained trapped in a web of economic orthodoxy and animosity masquerading as principle.[5]

When Mosley joined the Labour Party the labour movement's industrial challenge had largely been contained. 'Black Friday,' the subsequent rout of the miners, the Engineers' defeat in the 1922 lockout together demonstrated the destruction of post-war trade union optimism. Unemployment in the staple trades had weakened the unions; their agenda had withered to defence of what had been achieved. Mosley had certainly not come to Labour through his support on industrial matters. In the 1921 coal crisis his distance from and antipathy to Labour were obvious. Ireland had brought him into progressive circles; eventually the lack of credible alternatives and the hope that Labour's strength would grow had brought him into the party. Nevertheless, he supported the General Strike despite scepticism about 'Direct Action', and was a prominent advocate of the miners' case throughout the lockout. He believed the former was a mistake and the latter a heroic resistance. Industrial action could be only defensive. Rather, the way forward must be through political action: this assessment raised the critical question of the Labour Party's effectiveness as instrument.

Labour remained very much the second party; compared with pre-war, its position had been transformed, but its brief tenure in office owed much to the vagaries of a three party contest under the unreformed electoral system. Although from 1922 the party had established secure electoral bases in a minority of seats, employment in these strongholds was often dominated by well unionised occupations. Expansion beyond this territory remained a challenge. Apart from the party's weakness in rural areas, many urban areas and much of the working class remained tantalisingly out of reach. Mosley's Ladywood campaign was a bid for success in a constituency that in its social composition seemed natural Labour territory, a 'must win' seat if Labour was to achieve a parliamentary majority. Baldwin's resounding victory in 1924 meant that such a prospect seemed an ambitious target for the next election. The party's by-election performance, at first modest, strengthened during 1926; Mosley's Smethwick victory was typical of this advance. Nevertheless, down to the end of the parliament electoral expectations remained uncertain.

Mosley sought influence within a party whose identity was becoming less accepting of diversity. Communists were gradually excluded; by 1927 the line between Labour and Communist was firmly drawn and tightly policed. Left critics within the Independent Labour Party were increasingly cast as troublemakers or as 'characters'; responses therefore ranged from disciplinary threats to a limited toleration of eccentricity. The distinctive claims of women in the party were subordinated to a vision of Labour defined in economic and social terms that appeared gender-neutral but which ghettoised women's experiences. Bureaucratic processes became more intrusive; appeals to loyalty could capitalise on widespread pride in the party's achievements. These were the years of Ramsay MacDonald's eminence, his iconic status evident in the huge crowds that had greeted his unsuccessful prime ministerial election tour in 1924. MacDonald's vision of the party as the home for a broad progressive alternative to Baldwin's blend of cautious social reform and reassuring prejudices could promote tensions with trade unionists. They felt that such an agenda risked insensitivity towards the priorities of those whom they represented. However, the defeats of 1926, persistent depression in some industries, and deepening hostility within the unions between Labour loyalists and a left increasingly equated with Communists all combined to strengthen an alliance between MacDonald and his party allies, and a majority within the unions' leaderships. They could agree that all should work together for the election of a Labour Government. The consummation of this strategy came at the party's 1928 conference where critics of *Labour and the Nation* were marginalised. What many in the audience and beyond wanted from a Labour Government was unclear. Beyond the feasibility or otherwise of alternative economic policies and the imprecise but reassuring rhetoric of socialism lay an elementary issue of respect. The miners' lockout of 1926, with its aggressive policing and the insensitive bureaucratic treatment of the unemployed, inspired a common refrain; strikers defending their conditions and workers claiming benefits should be treated not as potential criminals but as equal citizens.

This celebration of unity and suppression of reasonable doubt was observed by Mosley from the 1928 conference platform as a silent member of the party's National Executive. He and a few colleagues had had their own concerns during the production of this acclaimed statement. Since Mosley had joined the party he had worked assiduously to influence policy. His money had funded the Birmingham party, he had explored the prospects of the Independent Labour Party as an influential body, he had been elected to both that party's National Administrative Council and to Labour's National Executive. He had campaigned assiduously and effectively not least at by-elections. He had courted MacDonald, provoking the enmity of those with ambitions who failed to secure such access. His popularity as a campaigner in the wider party was evident. Amongst MPs with their pecking orders, networks based on mutual favours and patronage, and occupationally based fiefdoms he was much less successful. Amongst the unions he was well regarded by many within the Miners' Federation; like others from outside the organised working class he was viewed by other union leaders with a mixture of suspicion and pragmatic assessment of his utility.

The 1929 election demonstrated the vulnerability of Baldwin's Conservative Party as the basis for an anti-socialist majority. Lloyd George money revived many local Liberal organisations from the depths of 1924. The Liberal programme to combat unemployment offered a challenging agenda which was not seriously endorsed or perhaps understood by many of the party's candidates. The Liberal revival was limited in terms of seats won, but the recovery of the Liberal vote was heavily at the expense of the Conservatives. The parliamentary cohesion of the anti-socialists was destroyed. Membership of the resulting Labour Government offered Mosley his opportunity to try and implement the ideas on employment policy that he had argued for in opposition. That he would meet with frustration was predictable given the configuration of the state, the dominance of orthodox economic ideas and the balance of mentalities and priorities within the Parliamentary Labour Party and the trade unions.

His resignation from the government was understandable; his justificatory speech in the Commons was a lucid presentation of his case which did not ascribe blame to former colleagues. Even before his resignation from the government, he was meeting with malcontents from the Conservative Party to conjure up programmes of co-ordinated action;

subsequently such discussions intensified. Eventually he rejected the Labour Party as an effective instrument for his favoured initiatives. The party's institutions, including the unions, were characterised as purely defensive. Therefore they were not resources for a progressive politics but obstacles. In part, the verdict could reflect Mosley's experiences within the Parliamentary Party – the ranks of loyalists, often sponsored by trade unions, who came not to listen to the arguments but to vote out of a visceral loyalty against intellectuals, trouble-makers, incomers from another class. Such rejections could strengthen the criticism that trade unions were sectional organisations that could fragment the community and as such were antithetical to conceptions both of socialism and of the nation. Such sentiments could be found in the ethos of the ILP, they had been evident in MacDonald and Snowden's critique of syndicalism and 'Direct Action' before and after the war. MacDonald's distaste for what he dismissed as union sectionalism would be evident in August 1931. Two political generations in the future, similar sentiments would inspire the Wilson Government's abortive *In Place Of Strife*.

The formation of the National Government involved the assembly of a much more effective anti-socialist majority; its permanence was guaranteed by an electoral landslide and by the subsequent introduction of Protection. Some Liberals were alienated, but more significantly a long-standing basis for division amongst anti-socialists was removed. This settlement, together with the passage of Labour into opposition in August 1931, left minimal political space for others. The crystallisation of this party system raises the counterfactual as to whether Mosley could have acted differently and more effectively during the critical months of 1931. The survival of the New Party necessitated its entry into the National ranks. Some evidence suggests that this option was feasible until it became clear that virtually all Liberals would subscribe to the National campaign. Many at the time thought that such Liberal acquiescence was far from certain, but desire for office and fidelity to economic orthodoxy proved decisive. Mosley became immediately irrelevant. Unlike the Liberals, he added no electoral resources to the National campaign.

An alternative counterfactual would be rooted in the early weeks of 1931. No New Party would have been formed; Mosley would have remained a critical presence within Labour. Following the defections of MacDonald, Snowden and Thomas, his position in the PLP and the wider movement would have been strong. 'Oh if Oswald had only waited' lamented George Bernard Shaw in the aftermath of the electoral disaster.[6] The argument is not persuasive. Most Labour Members who had gone into opposition had loyally supported MacDonald and the Government against their internal critics. Leading figures in what had become the Opposition had held ministerial posts. Such vulnerability bred anger against those who recalled the recent and uncomfortable past and claimed that the government's collapse had vindicated their earlier criticisms. Such claims for prescience, whether by the ILP left or Bevan, were unwelcome. The basis of anti-National sentiment was loyalty to Labour. Remaining with Labour was unlikely to have strengthened Mosley's position.

The distinctiveness of Mosley's post-1931 trajectory can be appreciated by a consideration of the subsequent careers of those who were close or sympathetic to him in the months prior to the formation of the New Party. Cynthia Mosley publicly backed his shift to fascism, but credible evidence suggests that she was deeply unhappy about Mosley's new political venture. Harold Nicolson had recorded in December 1931 that she 'wants to put a notice in *The Times* to the effect that she dissociated herself from Tom's fascist tendencies'.[7] Nevertheless she dutifully accompanied Mosley to Rome and to Mussolini. In contrast Robert Forgan became committed to the British Union of Fascists as director of organisation and deputy leader. He energetically promoted the BUF; a publicity campaign was complemented by private meetings to secure support from business. He resigned in autumn 1934, perhaps feeling that the organisation had jettisoned whatever radicalism it had once claimed. The growing association of the BUF with violence and anti-Semitism was decisive for him. He returned to medicine and effectively abandoned politics.[8]

W.E.D. Allen gave his literary talents to the BUF. The columns of *The Blackshirt* were enlivened by his 'Letters of Lucifer'; more significantly, under the pseudonym 'James Drennan', he published in 1934, *BUF: Oswald Mosley and British Fascism*. This justification indicted liberal individualism as a failed model for society and instead commended fascism as a collectivist model inspired by the Elizabethans. He, too, quit the BUF. Subsequent war service in the Household Cavalry, including under Wingate in Abyssinia, was followed by government posts abroad and, post-war, a career that blended the family firm with writing that demonstrated his expertise on Georgia and the Caucasus.[9]

W.J. Brown, having refused to join the New Party, remained the eternal gadfly. Twice defeated as an Independent Labour candidate at West Wolverhampton in 1931 and 1935, he still retained many of the ideas that had marked his time in the 1929 parliament. At the 1935 election he campaigned for a public works programme, a national investment board, extensive nationalisation and an inner cabinet for economic reconstruction. When the Transport and General Workers' Union responded unsympathetically to the 1937 London busmen's strike, Brown became involved in sponsoring the breakaway National Passenger Workers' Union. This initiative predictably provoked the TGWU leader, Ernest Bevin. The position of Brown's union within the TUC was damaged. His departure from the Labour Party in 1931 had involved a thorough indictment of the party caucus. By 1942, when he won a wartime by-election at Rugby as an Independent, any residual socialism was minimal. He had become a robust individualist arguing for a more efficient prosecution of the war; for 1942, he was unfashionably anti-Communist. He represented, in a highly personalised fashion, elements in the rejection of 'Guilty Men' and the radicalism of the People's War. Retaining his seat in 1945, but defeated in 1950, his final intervention was to stand unsuccessfully at West Fulham in 1951, ostensibly as an Independent but supported by local Conservatives. The Cold War and the Attlee Government had moved him further to the right.[10]

In contrast, two of Brown's one-time associates amongst the PLP's Mosleyites would hold senior office in that government. John Strachey spent the thirties as a prolific and readable advocate of Marxism; his initial exposition, *The Coming Struggle for Power* was published in 1932. Robert Boothby praised 'a superb intellectual performance... The margins are scored with indignant exclamation marks... Of course it's no good trying to refute you. As well try to argue with the Pope about the Immaculate Conception.' Strachey's crusade continued through the decade but eventually he decided that his basic proposition that the choice lay between communism and barbarism had been subverted by Keynesian theory and by the practice of the New Deal. Strachey held office from 1945 as a born-again gradualist.[11] In contrast, Aneurin Bevan, returned unopposed for Ebbw Vale in 1931, spent the thirties as a crusader for his economically devastated constituency and a scathing critic of the timidity and cringing respectability of Labour Party and trade union leaders. The crisis of May 1940 did not mean his incorporation into an inclusive coalition, but a new career as the most effective and often isolated critic of an administration that included many of his own party. His inclusion in the post-war government could seem a gamble by the supposedly cautious Attlee; if so, like Campbell-Bannerman's inclusion of another Welshman almost forty years earlier, it proved a spectacular success.[12]

Robert Boothby and Harold Macmillan were similarly marooned by the 1931 settlement. More amenable erstwhile critics of the Conservative leadership, most notably Walter Elliot, were incorporated into the National Government. In contrast, Boothby and Macmillan spent the decade as at best semi-detached members of their party, critical of the government's inadequacies in the economic and social spheres, and increasingly hostile to Neville Chamberlain and his policy of appeasement. Macmillan worked in cross- and non-party organisations seeking a feasible progressivism. He wrote and published on this theme; his works never achieved the popularity of Strachey's, but proved more anticipatory of the shape of things to come. Allan Young, once Mosley's political secretary, fulfilled a similar role for Macmillan. *The Middle Way*, published in 1938, was perhaps the definitive statement of Macmillan's politics in a decade when occasional gossip suggested he might shift to Labour. Macmillan acknowledged that this work, still available in paperback through his firm three decades later, owed much to the one-time New Party candidate for Ashton-under-Lyne. *The Middle Way* was 'a task I could not have completed amid so many private and public distractions, without the devoted assistance of my friend Allan Young'.[13]

May 1940 broke the party alignment that had marginalised dissenters and dangerous thinkers eight and a half years earlier. For Bevan and Strachey, the ambiguous radicalism symbolised by 'Guilty Men' and Labour involvement in the Churchill coalition offered a route out of a seemingly permanent minority status. Within the Conservative Party, those previously marginalised as critics joined the new establishment. The Churchillians were in the ascendancy. Macmillan and Boothby secured government posts; characteristically, Boothby – after a highly impressive start – soon had to resign after an enquiry into his involvement in the complex financial affairs of Czech emigres. He returned to his established role as semi-detached critic. In 1945 he and Strachey celebrated their Scottish election victories with champagne on the night sleeper to London. Macmillan's prospects improved through the war; his politics had retained a tribal edge and after the devastating defeat of 1945 he would employ an impressive talent for selective and effective partisanship.[14]

The subsequent careers of the Mosleyites of 1930–31 demonstrate diversity and talent; one prime minister, two cabinet ministers, and distinctive, sometimes idiosyncratic individualists. Yet their post-1931 achievements, other than the demonstration of qualities in opposition, required the denouement of May 1940, with its thorough discrediting of post-1931 governments. That the party settlement of 1931 would have eroded eventually is a reasonable claim; that it shattered so rapidly and with such far-reaching consequences was not predictable.

Even after this political earthquake, any prophecy of the subsequent eminence of some former Mosleyites would have been derided as fantasy. Mosley's pessimism about the viability of conventional politics is understandable; many from diverse political positions felt similarly. The disaffiliation of the Independent Labour Party from the Labour Party in July 1932 was based on an expectation that capitalist crisis would enhance the prospects for a socialist left that was not Communist. The action proved disastrous for the ILP. The critical question from the vantage point of the early thirties is not the intelligibility of Mosley's pessimism but his fascist response to this diagnosis.

Mosley's political career until the brief and troubled life of the New Party can be explored and analysed without any significant reference to fascism or to any alleged burgeoning sympathy for fascist doctrines. Some traces could be seen as suggestive – passing references in late-night discussions and the rhetoric of the private document circulated amongst Conservative would-be accomplices in late 1930. Within the Commons there were occasional criticisms of Mosley as an unattractive nationalist, complemented by a journalist's October 1930 characterisation of him as 'the English Hitler'. What the fragments amount to is unclear. Simplistic hindsight might claim the prefiguration of the road to Olympia, Cable Street and wartime internment. This assessment would neglect both the choices that had yet to be made and the crucial issue of context. The 'English Hitler' comment was made in the aftermath of Hitler's dramatic success in the 1930 Reichstag elections. It may indicate no more than a claim about oratory, electoral appeal and radical nationalism. The proposals in the private memorandum appear to have provoked no hostility from those who read them. This silence suggests that they were not regarded by Macmillan and others as a decisive step beyond what was politically acceptable. Arguably, Mosley's escalating rhetoric was yoked with proposals that were not distinctively fascist; or perhaps such a simple demarcation may in itself be misleading.

Such traces must be located within broader British responses to Italian fascism. Initially, Mussolini's regime puzzled some sections of the British left. The connection between Italian syndicalism and the corporate state and, for some, the alleged similarities between the Italian system and the aspirations of the Guild Socialists, could evoke sympathy. The murder of the socialist deputy Matteotti in 1924 and the subsequent destruction of what remained of an independent labour movement removed much of this uncertainty. Despite such repression the left's interest in state planning as a rational alternative to the market could readily lead intellectuals and the administratively minded to prioritise apparent efficiency rather than a formal political democracy that, in the view of some, was demonstrably failing and was arguably an anachronism. The collapse of the Labour Government inspired pilgrimages to Moscow, most famously that of Sidney and Beatrice Webb. If they discovered a future that worked, so did Mosley in Rome. Mosley's Labour rival, Hugh Dalton, secure in the post-1931 Labour hierarchy, visited both cities. He met Mussolini and professed admiration for what he viewed as his regime's energetic pursuit of modernisation. Cordiality was complemented by a diary entry. 'There is no living man it would have thrilled me more to meet.' The Italian model also attracted enthusiasm from some on the British right who claimed that liberal politics and liberal capitalism had failed. They insisted on the need for an effective response to the destructiveness of Bolshevism. The last sentiment had an affinity with the democratic socialist insistence that a qualitatively better society could not be born out of collapse and destruction. Crucially, fascism understood essentially through the Italian case should not be dismissed as either an exotic episode or a barbarism doomed to an early disaster; rather it was viewed by many contemporaries as a significant response to the crisis of stabilisation across much of post-war Europe.[15]

The Greater Britain showed substantial continuities with Mosley's earlier indictments of Conservative and Labour Governments, perhaps most thoroughly with his private memorandum of late 1930. The diagnosis of the economic problem emphasised rapid technical change and the transformation of productive techniques and organisation. Specifically British vulnerabilities were exacerbated by an inability to recognise that the old pillars of pre-eminence had gone. Lost export markets could not be regained; the dominance of the financial sector was a powerful obstacle to reform of industry; political institutions, well suited to the nineteenth century, had become a crippling anachronism. Some remedies were familiar – planning, insulation, the construction of an imperial trading bloc and the streamlining of the executive. Yet, such proposals were preceded by a robust justification of the 'modern movement', now ostentatiously identified as fascist.[16]

In part, his justification for fascism rested on his diagnosis of the left's inadequacies. He acknowledged the logical appeal of the Webbs' case for evolutionary socialism; perhaps he recalled their earlier discussions at Passfield Corner. But peaceful gradualism was untenable and irrelevant. There could be no 'natural evolution' to socialism. Mosley claimed that the socialist agenda assumed a static society and was incompatible with 'the hard facts of a dynamic age'. Equally, the

Independent Labour Party's 'Socialism in Our Time' programme with its 'Living Wage' was dismissed as disastrously inconsistent. Its policy for the transition involved the scrapping of existing institutions, inevitably a recipe for chaos; a high-wage policy unaccompanied by any form of protection was absurd. These left agendas in their inconsistency and irrelevance meant that the field was abandoned to the Communists who were prepared, in Mosley's view, to embrace chaos in the name of a subsequent emancipation. 'The position is at any rate clearer-headed and more honest than the performances of the theoretical Socialists of Labour and the ILP, who gallop up to the fence of class struggle and then stop short of the logical conclusion, leaving the nation to fall into the Communist ditch.'[17]

The specifically fascist content within Mosley's programme was predicated on a belief that economic decline and eventual collapse would provide the opportunity for Communism, and that established parties would be incapable of an effective response. Fascism, in contrast, offered the prospect of a constructive revolution through the corporate state, the 'suppression of chaos'. A constructive response necessitated the subordination of sectional concerns, including those of finance or labour, to the national welfare. Disputes would be resolved by administrative machinery and *in extremis* by the intervention of the state. Elaborate planning mechanisms were complemented by radical reform of parliament. The Lords would be replaced by a National Corporation, effectively a Parliament of Industry; the successor to the Commons would be elected preponderantly on the basis of an occupational franchise supplemented by a geographical one. How democratic this 'rationalised democracy' would be remained obscure. Mosley's characteristic rhetoric suggests that debate would be limited by the tyranny of 'facts'. 'The essence of Fascism is the power of adaptation to fresh facts... The steel creed of an iron age it cuts through the verbiage of illusion to the achievement of a new reality.'[18]

One intolerance was absent from *The Greater Britain*. The text contained no overtly anti-Semitic references. Although the fascist model remained significantly Italian, and therefore lacking in anti-Semitic content, the sensational growth of the Nazis meant that by mid 1932 Mosley also claimed an affinity with Hitler's movement. He insisted both privately and in the text that British fascism would be shaped by indigenous political traditions. Yet, casual anti-Semitism was common, not least in Mosley's social circle, and political instances had been significant. Anti-Semitic campaigns in London's East End had been a staple of pre-war politics; the Anti-Aliens Act of 1905 had articulated a broader prejudice.

The Marconi scandal had licensed the association of Jewish politicians with alleged financial malpractices. Mosley had witnessed the furore on the Conservative right over the Coalition's condemnation of General Dyer's responsibility for the Amritsar massacre. Anger on the Tory backbenches, aimed at the Secretary for State for India, Edwin Montagu had been overtly anti-Semitic. On the left, hostility to financiers could occlude anti-capitalist and anti-Semitic caricatures. *Revolution by Reason* had contained such a hint. The references in *The Greater Britain* to sectionalism and decadence could hint at what was to come.[19]

Mosley claimed that the implementation of the fascist agenda through constitutional means was preferable but that such a transition could well be forestalled by the threat of economic and social disintegration

> To drift much longer, to muddle through much further is to run the risk of collapse. In such a situation, new ideas will not come peacefully; they will come violently as they have come elsewhere. In the final economic crisis to which neglect may lead, argument, reason, persuasion vanish, and organised force alone prevails. In such a situation, the eternal protagonists in the history of all modern crises must struggle for mastery of the State. Either fascism or Communism emerges victorious; if it be the latter, the story of Britain is told.[20]

This projected apocalypse misrepresented what had happened in Italy and was happening in Germany. In neither case was there a simple confrontation with the Communists; the Italian Communist Party had been small in 1922, its German counterpart, although much more significant, secured the support of less than 17per cent of German voters in the November 1932 Reichstag election. Fascist violence was directed against all organisations of the left, Socialist, Communist and trade unions of any political persuasion. As a bemused Antonio Gramsci conjectured on the rise of Mussolini, fascism was an attempt to solve the problem of production and exchange by machine guns and pistol shots. For frustrated capitalists, paranoid bourgeois, ex-combatants who felt their sacrifices had been in vain, and social and ideological conservatives, fascism could be a regime of last resort, not without risk, but seemingly better than any credible alternative. Such choices indicated failures by more traditional parties of the right and centre-right that had left a space for a more radical alternative.[21]

In contrast, Baldwin, having succeeded MacDonald as Prime Minister, won a decisive election victory in November 1935. The anti-Labour majority constructed in crisis four years earlier had survived despite a limited and uneven economic recovery. Baldwin personified reassurance and unspectacular decency; the reality was a coalition that attracted some on economic grounds, many on the basis of a visceral conservatism and others scarred by Labour's record in office, both real and imagined. Fear supplemented economic calculation. Labour's recovery was limited both geographically and occupationally. Labour's radicalism in response to 1931 had been limited and was diminishing. Whatever some Conservatives might claim, Labour's aspirations were contained within a shared constitutionalism. The unreality of Mosley's apocalyptic expectation was underscored by the uniqueness of the Communist Party's electoral victory in West Fife.[22]

Fascism was neither necessary nor feasible. British politics was notable for the strength of its centre-right party in an environment where political argument was increasingly about economic and social issues and identities. Unlike much of southern and eastern Europe, the right was not divided over issues of church and state nor, as in Germany, was there a significant political separation between Protestant and Catholic. The Conservative Party, resting as it did on a variety of formal and informal networks, prospered under a mass electorate; its limited attachment to a programmatic politics was perhaps seen by many as a virtue. This partisan achievement was made possible by continuities within the political system which for Mosley, and to some degree for other radicals, were sources of frustration. The regime had not been discredited by military defeat or by subsequent nationalist vitriol against alleged diplomatic failure. In contrast, the formation of the Irish Free State was viewed widely as evidence of political wisdom rather than ineptitude. Mosley might have claimed to be the tribune of the war generation; there was no such constituency and no politics of the piazza. The war and its economic aftermath precipitated no ideological crisis. To the frustration of Mosley and others across the ideological spectrum, Baldwin's folksy wisdom resonated more than the agendas and rhetoric of his critics.[23]

Underpinning Baldwin's success was the relative mildness of the British economic crisis, at least compared with the last years of the Weimar Republic and Herbert Hoover's United States. The rate of unemployment was lower; even with the cuts of 1931 the welfare system lessened the misery of the unemployed. Electoral democracy and a liberal state were not widely viewed as expensive luxuries. 1931 had demonstrated that they were compatible with a politically viable right-of-centre solution. Labour had been contained both industrially and politically, yet such qualified integration had not opened up space for more radical initiatives on the left. Mosley's assertion that the inadequacies of the National Government would produce a crisis only illuminated the primitive determinism that underpinned his position and expectations after 1931. Equally, his insistence that fascism offered the only effective response to communism was falsified by Roosevelt's New Deal. 'Do we need a Dictator?' asked *The Nation* on the eve of the President's inauguration in March 1933. Given the prominence of Mussolini and Stalin and the recent appointment of Hitler to the Chancellorship, the question is understandable. The New Deal's achievements, however ambiguous, gave a negative answer. Keynes wrote to Roosevelt in December 1933; 'You have made yourself the trustee for those in every country who seek to mend the evils of our condition by reasoned experiment within the framework of the existing social system.' The preceding April, Keynes had given a lecture in Dublin entitled 'National Self-Sufficiency'. His apparent rejection of liberal verities had been welcomed by Mosley. Keynes's response, in the wake of *The Greater Britain,* had been unaccommodating. His purpose was 'not to embrace you but to save the country from you'.[24] Keynes's commendation of Roosevelt and hostility to Mosley raise the feasibility of a British New Deal, a grand coalition of the marginalised, voters, politicians and intellectuals that could offer an alternative to the National Government's blend of conservatism and unspectacular amelioration.

The feasibility of such an alternative depended on the availability of sufficient partisan resources. Any New Deal coalition would have been effectively a successor to the Progressive Alliance that had secured a precarious electoral dominance in the immediate pre-war years. Any equivalent in the 1920s was improbable; the much more likely and eventually achieved coalition was an anti-socialist one whose innovations were limited and often disguised. There would have been few Liberal adherents to such a New Deal alternative; Liberal responses in August 1931 were almost monolithically orthodox. Mosley's meetings with Conservative malcontents demonstrated both the shallowness of much of their dissatisfaction and serious disagreement about the substance of what should be done. Within much of the Labour Party coalitions were viewed always with suspicion and after 1931 often with visceral hostility. Some within the trade unions might have been attracted by a New Deal strategy, but, as a document from the TUC research department noted in August 1931, there was no political majority for an alternative economic policy, a proposition as true of the electorate as of parliamentarians. Here was a society marked by damaging inequalities where a majority of the electorate made conservative choices; from 1931 the configuration of parties ensured that this sentiment was effectively demonstrated in electoral outcomes.[25]

Baldwin's superficially apolitical homilies gave way to Neville Chamberlain's abrasive partisanship in May 1937. Shortly afterwards, George Orwell returned from the traumas of the Spanish Civil War. Viewed from the boat train, southern England and then official London epitomised the England over which Baldwin had presided.

> The industrial towns were far away, a smudge of smoke and misery hidden by the curve of the earth's surface. Down here it was still the England I had known in my childhood: the railway-cuttings smothered in wild flowers, the deep meadows where the great shining horses browse and meditate, the slow-moving streams bordered by willows, the green bosoms of the elms, the larkspurs in the cottage gardens; and then the huge peaceful wilderness of outer London, the barges on the miry river, the familiar streets, the posters telling of cricket matches and Royal weddings, the men in bowler hats, the pigeons in Trafalgar Square, the red buses, the blue policemen.

All epitomised for Orwell 'the deep, deep sleep of England'. He feared that an awakening would come only with 'the roar of bombs.'[26]

Orwell was right. May 1940 destroyed the anti-socialist coalition and what little was left of Mosley's reputation. In the last pre-war years Mosley had rented Wootton Lodge, a property in the foothills of the Peak District. Between his campaigns he spent time there with his second wife Diana, one of the Mitford sisters. A photograph of Hitler stood by their bed. In August 1938 with the Czech crisis a few weeks away, while Mosley was fishing for trout in the lake, she wrote to her sister Unity in Germany. 'The Fuhrer is the kindest man in all the world isn't he?... We are having such *heavenly* hols.'[27] Wootton offers a Gothic version of *The Remains of the Day*, not least because both the aristocratic characters in Ishiguro's novel and Mosley and his circle were firmly rooted in their social milieu and sympathetic to fascism. This summer idyll was close to Rolleston and to Curzon's Kedleston; it was also near to Hazelwood where Edith Maude Hull had written *The Sheik*.

Against this rural image of the big house and a leisured class at summer play, stood A.J. Cook, the radical from the Rhondda, the personification of pre-war syndicalism and, in the 1920s, of the miners' resistance to lower wages and longer hours. In 1931 Cook was terminally ill; he would die a few days after Labour's electoral disaster. One afternoon Walter Citrine, the TUC General Secretary, visited him. He found that Cook already had two visitors, the Rhondda Communist, Arthur Horner, and Mosley. Many years later, Citrine considered this a curious bedside trio. In the world of the tidy trade union administrator and with the benefit of hindsight it might seem so, but the gathering illuminated something of the complexity of Oswald's odyssey.[28]

The kaleidoscope reveals the young Tory rebel, the apostle of liberalism, the darling of labour crowds and the elegant exemplar of the resigning minister. It also offers ambition, volatility, inflexibility, entitlement and authoritarianism. In the end was the anathema of the renegade who had placed himself outside the bounds of political decency. Such diversity allied to shifting contexts licenses alternative Mosleys. Post-1931, the marginalisation of all those with dangerous ideas facilitated his isolation; the military disaster of May 1940 severely damaged the anti-socialist coalition; a People's War followed by a Peoples' Peace suggested that victory over fascism had ushered in a viable social democratic settlement that would demonstrate the value of unostentatious British methods of amelioration and reform. Macmillan, once the outsider, as Prime Minister endorsed much of this concordat. For him, principle and electoral prudence were complementary. Once again, Mosley was at best irrelevant and more frequently the subject of a morality tale about a 'flawed character'. Growing scepticism about the viability of the social democratic settlement coupled with inevitable questioning of received wisdoms precipitated Mosley's rediscovery as the lost radical and generated considerable controversy about the character of Mosley's pre-1931 agenda and its feasibility. These exchanges often neglected the complexities and uncertainties of the party system within which Mosley acted for 13 years. Yet these experiences shaped his and others' expectations about the feasible and desirable. In the contemporary context of political volatility and estrangement, Mosley's journey through a partisan landscape may have more than historical interest.

Notes

Overture: Guilty Men

1. 'Cato', *Guilty Men* (London, 1940); Kenneth O. Morgan, *Michael Foot: A Life* (London, 2007) pp. 72–82.
2. 'Cato', *Guilty Men*, pp. 17–21 for political scene setting; pp. 32–4 for Bevin and Lansbury.
3. Winston Churchill, *The Second World War*, Volume 1, *The Gathering Storm* (London, 1948); C.L. Mowat, *Britain Between the Wars, 1918–1940* (London, 1955) p. 142. The contingency of the Guilty Men myth's appeal is analysed in Philip Williamson, 'Baldwin's Reputation: Politics and History 1937–1967' *Historical Journal* 47:1 (2004) 127–168.
4. See the profile in *Oxford Dictionary of National Biography* (hereafter *ODNB*) online http://www.oxforddnb.com/index/56/101056984/ (accessed 8 June 2014).
5. HC Deb 5th Series Volume 290 Columns 1930, 1932, 14 June 1934.
6. Mowat, *Britain Between the Wars*, p. 361; A.J.P. Taylor, *English History 1914–1945* (Oxford, 1965), p. 285. Mosley's own contribution can be found in *My Life* (London, 1968).
7. Robert Skidelsky, *Politicians and the Slump: the Labour Government of 1929–31* (London, 1967); *Oswald Mosley* (London, 1975). The latter includes the 'lost leader' comment at p. 13.
8. Peter Clarke, *Lancashire and the New Liberalism* (Cambridge, 1971).
9. Ross McKibbin, *Parties and People: England 1914–1951* (Oxford, 2010); Duncan Tanner, 'Class Voting and Radical Politics: the Liberal and Labour Parties 1910–1931', in Miles Taylor and Jon Lawrence (eds.), *Party State and Society: Electoral Behaviour in Britain since 1820* (Aldershot, 1997), pp. 106–30.
10. Oswald Ernald Mosley was born 19 November 1896 and succeeded to the baronetcy on 21 September 1928. He was frequently referred to as 'Tom Mosley'.
11. Mosley, *My Life*, p. 10; the Vicar's blessing is in *Derby Mercury*, 20 August 1873.
12. Image from Skidelsky, *Oswald Mosley*, pp. 33–4, the recollection of a Rolleston woman; George Eliot's perceptions are assessed in Raymond Williams, *The Country and the City* (London, 1973) Chapter 16.
13. For the developing railway network see Robin Leleux, *A Regional History of the Railways of Great Britain*, Volume IX, *The East Midlands* (Newton Abbot, 1984); Anslow's comment is in *Railway Gazette*, 16 February 1912.
14. David Cannadine, *The Decline and Fall of the British Aristocracy* (New Haven, CT, 1990), Chapters 10–11. These are entitled, 'Lost Causes and Disappointed Hopes' and 'The Politics of Paranoia'. Rolleston's farmland, 3,800 acres, was sold off in two sales in 1919 and 1920; the hall and 204 acres of parkland were sold in 1923–4. Nigel J Tringham (ed.), *A History of the County of Stafford*, Volume X, *Tutbury and Needwood Forest* (Woodbridge, 2007) p. 199.

15. Mosley, *My Life* Chapter 3; Skidelsky, *Oswald Mosley*, pp. 67–8; Adrian Gregory, *The Last Great War: British Society and the First World War* (Cambridge, 2008).
16. Robert Rhodes James, *Anthony Eden* (London, 1986), Chapter 2; Kenneth Harris, *Attlee* (London, 1982), pp. 34–40.
17. Simon Ball, *The Guardsmen: Harold Macmillan, Three Friends and the World They Made* (London, 2005); Anthony Sampson, *Macmillan: A Study in Ambiguity* (London, 1967); Alastair Horne, *Macmillan, 1894–1956* (London, 1988); D.R. Thorpe, *Supermac: The Life of Harold Macmillan* (London, 2010).
18. Curzon to his second wife, Grace, 21 March 1920, cited in Skidelsky, *Oswald Mosley*, p. 85.

1   Apprenticeships

1. Mosley, *My Life*, p 90. In the post-1918 period the terms 'Conservative' and 'Unionist' were used interchangeably and this practice is followed in the text.
2. J. Turner, *British Politics and the Great War: Coalition and Conflict 1915–1918* (New Haven, CT, 1992) Chapters 9–12.
3. For Henderson see Fred Leventhal, *Arthur Henderson* (Manchester, 1990); Chris Wrigley, *Arthur Henderson* (Cardiff, 1990); Ross McKibbin, 'Arthur Henderson as Labour Leader' *International Review of Social History* 23 (1978) 79–101. More generally, Ross McKibbin, *The Evolution of the Labour Party 1910–1924* (Oxford, 1974). The Coalition Labour members were Barnes, Parker, Roberts and Wardle.
4. For Milner see A.M. Gollin, *Proconsul in Politics: A Study of Lord Milner in Opposition and in Power* (London, 1964); J.O. Stubbs, 'Lord Milner and Patriotic Labour 1914–18' *English Historical Review* 88 (1972), 717–54; for Tillett see Jon Schneer, *Ben Tillett: Portrait of a Labour Leader* (London, 1982).
5. For pre–war Harrow see Henry Pelling, *Social Geography of British Elections, 1885–1910* (London, 1967), pp. 62, 66–7; for Harrow 1918 election Skidelsky, *Oswald Mosley*, pp. 69–75; *Harrow Gazette* 22, 29 November 1918. Chamberlayne had stood as a Liberal Unionist at Glasgow St Rollox in January and December 1910; his identity at South Shields in 1906 had been ambiguous. F.W.S. Craig, *British Parliamentary Election Results 1885–1918* (London, 1974). The local Labour recommendation to abstain is in *Harrow Gazette* 13 December 1918.
6. *Harrow Observer* 29 November 1918.
7. *Harrow Gazette* 22 November 1918.
8. *Harrow Gazette* 20 December 1918.
9. Kenneth O. Morgan, *Consensus and Disunity: The Lloyd George Coalition Government 1918–22* (Oxford, 1979).
10. McKibbin, *Labour Party*; David Marquand, *Ramsay MacDonald* (London, 1977), pp. 234–7 for MacDonald's defeat in West Leicester.
11. Trevor Wilson, *The Downfall of the Liberal Party, 1914–35* (London, 1966); Michael Bentley, *The Liberal Mind, 1914–29* (Cambridge, 1977); Michael Hart, 'The Decline of the Liberal Party in Parliament and in the Constituencies, 1914–1931' (Oxford DPhil thesis, 1982).
12. Chris Wrigley, *Lloyd George and the Challenge of Labour: The Post–War Coalition, 1918–1922* (Hemel Hempstead, 1990) Chapter 2.

13. Colin Coote, *Editorial: The Memoirs of Colin Coote* (London, 1965), pp. 102–3; G.R. Searle, *Country Before Party. Coalition and the Idea of 'National Government' in Modern Britain 1885–1987* (London, 1995) pp. 117–20.

14. K.O. Morgan *Consensus and Disunity*, p. 130.

15. HC Deb Volume 132 Columns 2689–2723 (Allocation of Time), 2723–2808 (Second Reading), 2847–2964 (Committee and Third Reading), 5, 6 August 1920.

16. Charles Townshend, *The British Campaign in Ireland 1919–21: The Development of Political and Military Policies* (Oxford, 1979); Peter Hart, *The IRA and Its Enemies: Violence and Community in Cork 1916–1923* (Oxford, 1998); D.M. Leeson, *The Black and Tans. British Police and Auxiliaries in the Irish War of Independence* (Oxford, 2012).

17. HC Deb Volume 133 Columns 1008–13, quotation at 1011.

18. Quotations HC Deb Volume 133 Columns 1008, 10–11.

19. 18 HC Deb Volume 135 Columns 487–601. Greenwood at Column 495, Mosley at Columns 518–23, quote at 523.

20. *Harrow Gazette* 15 October 1920.

21. Skidelsky, *Oswald Mosley*, p. 95; for Mosley's advocacy of the League of Nations as essential to a stable international system see HC Deb Volume 125 Columns 339–41, 12 February 1920, Volume 130 Columns 1590–93, 17 June 1920.

22. Robert Cecil to H.H. Asquith 11 May 1922, Cecil of Chelwood Papers ADDMSS 51073, 16–29; for profile of Cecil see Martin Ceadel, *ODNB* Volume 10, pp. 721–4. Note also the comment of Lord Northcliffe, 'One difficulty with Robert Cecil is his modesty and diffidence. Others are his lack of business–like habits and making speeches at times and places either unknown to the Press beforehand or difficult of access.' Letter to H.W. Massingham 2 April 1922 Mosley Papers B/2/1. Also Morgan, *Consensus and Disunity* Chapter 8.

23. HC Deb Volume 133 Column 984, 20 October 1920.

24. Bottomley candidates were successful in by–elections at Dover, 12 January 1921, and twice at The Wrekin, 7 February and 20 November 1920.

25. Maurice Cowling, *The Impact of Labour 1918–24: The Beginning of Modern British Politics* (Cambridge, 1971), pp. 74–5; *Harrow Gazette* 21 January, 25 February 1921; for Bottomley *ODNB* Volume 8, pp. 768–70, and for Rothermere Volume 25, pp. 347–9.

26. Kenneth O. Morgan and Jane Morgan, *Portrait of a Progressive: The Political Career of Christopher, Viscount Addison* (Oxford, 1980) Chapters 5, 6.

27. Ewen Green, *Ideologies of Conservatism. Conservative Political Ideas in the Twentieth Century* (Oxford, 2002) Chapter 4.

28. Robert Cecil to Austen Chamberlain 20, 27 April 1921, cited Wrigley, *Lloyd George and the Challenge of Labour*, pp. 306–7.

29. Oswald Mosley to Robert Cecil 17 April 1921, Cecil of Chelwood Papers ADDMSS 51163, 4–5.

30. Robert Cecil to J.R. Clynes (copy) 11 June 1920, Cecil of Chelwood Papers ADDMSS 51162, 117. Cecil's concern was to explore whether Labour would not run candidates against those Conservatives who took a strong line on the League of Nations.

31. Scott Diary, 9 August 1921 in Trevor Wilson (ed.), *The Political Diaries of C.P. Scott 1911–28* (London, 1970) p. 400; Robert Cecil to Lord Grey 12 April 1921 (copy), Cecil of Chelwood Papers ADDMSS 51073, 79–81; Cowling, *The Impact of Labour* Chapters III, V; Michael Bentley 'Liberal Politics and the Grey conspiracy of 1921' *Historical Journal* 20 (1977) 461–78; Keith

Robbins, *Sir Edward Grey: A Biography of Lord Grey of Fallodon* (London, 1971), pp. 355–8.

32. Robert Cecil to Lord Cowdray (copy), 9 July 1921, Cecil of Chelwood Papers ADMSS 51163 6–9.

33. Robert Cecil to J.A. Spender 30 August 1921 (copy), Spender response, 2 September 1921, Cecil of Chelwood Papers ADDMSS 51163, 12–14, 17–18.

34. Robbins, *Sir Edward Grey*, p. 358.

35. C.P. Scott to Robert Cecil, cited Skidelsky, *Oswald Mosley*, p. 112; Herbert Gladstone to Robert Cecil 18 November 1921 Mosley Papers OMN/B/2/1.

36. Robert Cecil to Reginald Berkeley (copy), 2 May 1922 Cecil of Chelwood Papers ADDMSS 51163, 80; Robert Cecil to H.H. Asquith 9 October 1922 Cecil of Chelwood Papers ADDMSS 51073, 30–333; Asquith's reply, 19 October 1922 insisted that Liberal Party sentiments had to be taken into account, 34–39.

37. *Dumfries and Galloway Standard* 26 April, 10 May 1922.

38. Eddie Hartington to Robert Cecil (no date) Cecil of Chelwood Papers ADDMSS 51163, 23–4.

39. *Harrow Gazette* 1 October 1920.

40. *Harrow Gazette* 24 September 1920, 11 March 1921.

41. *Harrow Gazette* 15 April 1921.

42. *Harrow Gazette* 12 November 1920.

43. *Harrow Observer* 18 February 1921.

44. *Harrow Observer* 4 August, 15 September, 13 October 1922.

45. *Harrow Observer* 21 July 1922.

46. Cowling, *Impact of Labour* Chapter XI.

47. *Harrow Observer* 27 October, 10 November 1922, cited in Skidelsky, *Oswald Mosley*, p. 117.

48. Mosley, *My Life* for Cowdray p. 165; *Harrow Observer* 27 October 1922.

49. Mosley's commendation of 'Safety First' is in *Harrow Observer* 27 October 1922. For Asquithians see Hart thesis, pp. 194–204; for Law, Robert Blake, *The Unknown Prime Minister: The Life and Times of Andrew Bonar Law* (London, 1955) pp. 461–75.

50. *Harrow Observer* 17 November 1922; for Ward–Jackson see Michael Kinnear, *The Fall of Lloyd George. The Political Crisis of 1922* (London, 1973) p. 66. *Harrow Observer* 3 November 1922 for his election address.

51. J.A. Spender to Mosley 26 November 1922 Mosley Papers OMN/B/2/1; Asquith comment 29 May 1923 in *HHA: Letters of the Earl of Asquith To A Friend, Second Series 1922–1927* edited by Desmond Macarthy (London, 1934), pp. 61–2; Sir John Simon to Mosley 17 August 1923 Mosley Papers OMD/K/1; Kathleen Simon to Cynthia Mosley 21 November 1922 Mosley Papers OMN/A/5/5.

52. For Mosley speeches see HC Deb Volume 161 Columns 1358–66, 13 March 1923; Columns 2426–34, quote at 2433–4, 20 March 1923; Volume 163 Columns 2726–33, 10 May 1923; Volume 167 Columns 1820, 1823–8.

53. Beatrice Webb Diary 8 June 1923, in N. and J. Mackenzie (eds.), *The Diary of Beatrice Webb*, Volume 3, *1905–24, The Power to Alter Things* (London, 1984), p. 418.

54. See Victor Cazalet Journal 12 May 1923, in Robert Rhodes James, *Victor Cazalet: A Portrait* (London, 1970) p. 90; Robert Rhodes James, *Memoirs of a Conservative: J.C.C. Davidson's Memoirs and Papers, 1910–37* (London, 1969) p. 177.

55. Philip Williamson, *Stanley Baldwin: Conservative Leadership and national Values* (Cambridge, 1999); Philip Williamson and Edward Baldwin (eds.), *Baldwin Papers: A Conservative Statesman, 1908–1947* (Cambridge, 2004); Maurice Cowling, *The Impact of Hitler: British politics and British policy, 1933–1940* (Cambridge, 1975), pp. 259–61. Sian Nicholas, 'The Construction of National Identity: Stanley Baldwin, "Englishness" and the Mass Media in Inter–war Britain', in M. Francis and I. Zeiwniger–Bargielowski (eds.), *The Conservative Party and British Society, 1880–1990* (Cardiff, 1996) pp. 127–46.
56. *Harrow Observer* 23, 30 November 1923; Margot Asquith to Mosley 6 December 1923 (telegram) Mosley Papers B/2/1.

2 Renegade

1. HC Deb Volume 169–72, quotes at 367, 370, 17 January 1924.
2. *Harrow Observer* 29 February 1924; Oswald Mosley to Ramsay MacDonald, 21 December 1923, Ramsay MacDonald Papers 1169; Stansgate Diaries 21 February 1924 ST 66.
3. *Harrow Observer* 28 March, 4 April 1924; Oswald Mosley to Ramsay MacDonald, 7 April 1924, Ramsay MacDonald Papers 1169.
4. Margot Asquith to Oswald Mosley 7 April 1924, Mosley Papers OXM/D/4/1; Robert Cecil to Lord Grey 10 April 1924, Cecil of Chelwood Papers ADD MSS 51073, 84–6. Churchill comment is in Winston Churchill to Robert Cecil, 23 March 1924, Cecil of Chelwood Papers ADD MSS 51073, 107–9.
5. Beatrice Webb Diary 8 June 1923; Ramsay MacDonald to Cynthia Mosley 17 August 1923, Mosley Papers OXM/D/4/1.
6. Beatrice Webb Diary 24 March 1924 in N. and J. Mackenzie (eds.), *The Diary of Beatrice Webb*, Volume 4 (London, 1985), p. 20.
7. *Independent Labour Party Conference Report* 1924 p. 136; Dalton Diary 19–22 April 1924 in Ben Pimlott (ed.), *The Political Diary of Hugh Dalton 1918–1940, 1945–60* (London, 1986), p. 39; Stansgate Diaries 8 May 1924, ST 66.
8. Egon Wertheimer, *Portrait of the Labour Party* (London, 1929), pp. vii–xii. For a detailed analysis see Nicholas Owen '"MacDonald's Parties" The Labour Party and the Aristocratic Embrace 1922–31' *Twentieth Century British History* 18:1 (2007), 1–53.
9. Ellen Wilkinson, *Peeps at Politicians* (London, 1930). Unlike Fairbanks, Valentino's sexuality was contested by contemporaries. For a literary representation see John Dos Passos, 'Adagio Dancer' in his *USA* (Harmondsworth, 2001) pp. 883–6. This section was published initially in 1936 as *The Big Money*. For cultural context see Billie Melman, *Women and the Popular Imagination in the Twenties: Nymphs and Flappers* (London, 1988) especially Chapter 6; Alison Light, *For Ever England. Femininity, Literature and Conservatism Between the Wars* (London, 1991) especially pp. 175–6.
10. *Birmingham Town Crier* 18, 25 July 1924.
11. For the culture of Birmingham politics see John Boughton, 'Working Class Politics in Birmingham and Sheffield 1918–1931' (unpublished PhD thesis, University of Warwick, 1985). For the Ferguson affair and its aftermath see David Howell, *MacDonald's Party: Labour Identities and Crisis 1922–1931* (Oxford, 2002), pp. 390–96.
12. *Birmingham Town Crier* 25 July 1924.

13. For Joseph Chamberlain see P.T. Marsh, *Joseph Chamberlain: Entrepreneur in Politics* (New Haven, CT, 1994); for pre–1914 Birmingham electoral politics see Pelling, *Social Geography of British Elections*, pp. 179–84.
14. *Birmingham Town Crier* 12 September 1924.
15. Austen Chamberlain to Ida Chamberlain 2 November 1924, Austen Chamberlain Papers AC5/1/339 – In Robert Self (ed.), *The Austen Chamberlain Diary Letters 1916–1937* (Cambridge, 1995) p. 259; Robert Self, *Neville Chamberlain A Biography* (Aldershot, 2006) pp. 77–8, 86.
16. Self, *Neville Chamberlain*, pp. 80, 97, 103.
17. For complaints after the 1923 election see Report of Management Committee to Birmingham Conservative and Unionist Association 15 February 1924, Birmingham Central Library Archives 5915781; Neville Chamberlain to Ida Chamberlain, 1 November 1924 in Robert Self (ed.), *The Neville Chamberlain Diary Letters*, Volume 2 *The Reform Years, 1921–1927* (Aldershot, 2000), p. 257; for disillusioned cleric see Rev. John Lewis to Oswald Mosley 7 June 1926, Whiteley Papers UL 6/3.
18. Neville Chamberlain to Ida Chamberlain 1 November 1924 in Robert Self (ed.), *Diary* Volume 2, p. 256; his subsequent comment was from the chair at a meeting of the Birmingham Conservative and Unionist Management Committee 14 November 1924; the Amery comment in D. Faber, *Speaking for England: Leo, Julian and John Amery – the Tragedy of a Political Family* (London, 2005) p. 179; *Birmingham Town Crier* 7, 14, 21 November, 19 December 1924, 6 January 1925 for post–poll responses including comments on the conduct of the count. For the wider context see Bill Schwarz, 'The Language of Constitutionalism Baldwinite Conservatism' in *Formations of Nations and Peoples* (London, 1984), pp. 1–18.
19. Hugh Thomas, *John Strachey* (London, 1973); Michael Newman, *John Strachey* (Manchester, 1989).
20. Raymond A. Jones, *Arthur Ponsonby the Politics of Life* (London, 1989).
21. Ladywood accounts for 1926, Whiteley Papers UL 6/3.

3   Elect

1. Note Skidelsky's portrait of Bondfield in *Politicians and the Slump*, pp. 71–2, and his treatment of the episode in *Oswald Mosley*, p. 157 footnote.
2. Labour Party National Executive Committee (NEC) Organisation Sub–Committee Report 23 June 1925; for A.A. Purcell see Kevin Morgan *Bolshevism, Syndicalism and the General Strike. The Lost Internationalist World of A.A. Purcell* (London, 2013)
3. NEC 24 June 1925; *Birmingham Town Crier*, 26 June 1925. The Birmingham Borough Labour Party Executive, 23 June 1925 reports Mosley as claiming that the Forest of Dean miners were unanimous in his support. The Executive opposed Mosley leaving Birmingham with one dissentient.
4. See by–election report 28 July 1925 in NEC minutes, same date.
5. Pelling, *Social Geography of British Elections*, pp. 184–99.
6. For contemporary portraits see Bracher, *The Herald Book of Labour Members* (London, 1924), p. 36, J.E. Davison; p. 165, Alfred Short; p. 166, Charles Sitch.
7. *Smethwick Telephone*, 27 November 1926.
8. *Birmingham Town Crier*, 26 November 1926, Oswald Mosley, 'Why I am fighting Smethwick'; 3 December, 'The Truth about Smethwick'.

9. NEC, 24 November 1926; Bernard Donoughue and G.W. Jones, *Herbert Morrison: Portrait of a Politician* (London, 1973) pp. 96–7; Ben Pimlott, *Hugh Dalton* (London, 1985), pp. 150–57; Rennie Smith Diary, 29 November 1926, Eng. Hist. Mss. d 287; J. Johnson, 'Birmingham Labour and the New Party', *Labour Magazine*, April 1931, p. 535.

10. NEC, Emergency meeting of London members, 27 November 1926.

11. John Shepherd, *George Lansbury: At the Heart of Old Labour* (Oxford, 2002); Jon Schneer, *George Lansbury* (Manchester, 1990); *Smethwick Telephone*, 4 December 1926. Lansbury following his weekend visit to Birmingham reported to another Emergency meeting of NEC London members, 29 November 1926; Mosley also attended to present his position. The meeting reaffirmed NEC disapproval of the Smethwick procedure.

12. NEC, 1 December Emergency meeting, 3 December Full meeting 1926; *Smethwick Telephone*, 4 December 1926. Dalton Diaries, December 1926.

13. Jim Simmons, *Socialist Evangel* (Birmingham, 1971), pp. 68–9; the purpose of Mosley's research agenda was 'to cover the whole field of politics & be able to produce information on any subject likely to arise in political debates'. Memorandum on the Proposal for a Research Department, 1929, Baron Noel Baker Papers NBKR 2/2, file on Society of Labour candidates.

14. *Smethwick Telephone*, 18, 25 December 1926, the latter including claim of deliberate disorder made by Ian Fraser MP; *Birmingham Post*, 23 December 1926; *Manchester Guardian*, 12, 17 December 1926; Skidelsky, *Oswald Mosley*, pp. 157–63; *Smethwick Telephone*, 14 May 1927 for Smethwick Conservative Association Annual Meeting.

15. NEC, 22 December 1926. Minutes include Smethwick by–election report.

16. NEC, 23 March 1927. MacDonald Papers 1172 contains a memorandum by Mosley on his funding of the Birmingham and other local parties.

17. Herbert Morrison, *New Leader*, 28 January 1927.

18. Dalton Diary, 5 October, 19 December 1928, Pimlott (ed.), *The Political Diary of Hugh Dalton*, p. 46.

19. Sidney Webb to Beatrice Webb, 1 December 1926, Passfield Papers II 3 I file 23.

20. Whiteley Papers UL 6/3 contains material on this dispute, for example Mosley to Whiteley, 25 January, 20 April 1928, 28 March, 24 April 1929.

21. *Smethwick Telephone* 1928, 14 January for invitation, 14 July expectations, 21 July account, 28 July photographs.

22. Pelling, *Social Geography of British Elections*, pp. 270–74; Roy Gregory, *The Miners in British Politics, 1906–14* (Oxford, 1968), pp. 168–73.

23. Bracher, *Herald Book*, p. 16 for Bromfield, pp. 117–18 for McLaren.

24. For John Ward see entry in *ODNB* Volume 57, pp. 318–19. Ward Papers, 4/13 for correspondence from Conservative Central Office; 18 November, 29 December 1927 about Ward's intentions; Percy Shelly to Ward, 13 August 1928 about pledges and Conservative support; *Staffordshire Sentinel*, 25 October 1924 for Ward biography; 1 November for Duke of Sutherland.

25. Percy Shelley to John Ward, 13 August, 13, 18 November 1928, Ward Papers 4/3; for authenticity see Simmons, *Socialist Evangel*, p. 69: 'She was so natural and sincere and never made you feel uncomfortable in her presence.' For scepticism, John Beckett, unpublished autobiography, Chapter 8.

26. Oswald Mosley to Wilfrid Whiteley, 20 January 1928, Whiteley Papers UL 6/3.

4   Networker

1. Howell, *McDonald's Party*, Part II.
2. G.A. Phillips, *The General Strike: The Politics of Industrial Conflict* (London, 1976).
3. Skidelsky, *Oswald Mosley*, pp. 156–7; *New Leader*, 28 May 1926.
4. *Trades Union Congress Report* 1926, pp. 423–6. For John Bromley see *Dictionary of Labour Biography* Volume 13 (London, 2010) pp. 42–62.
5. *Labour Party Conference Report* 1926, p. 197. Beatrice Webb commented acerbically that 'the ILP contingent made themselves look ridiculous by putting up Mosley to support the miners in a passionate speech'. Mackenzie (ed.) *The Diary of Beatrice Webb*, Volume 4, p. 197, entry for 12 October 1926.
6. For "incompetent", see Ramsay MacDonald to A.J. Cook, 14 January 1927, MacDonald Papers 1173; for Beatrice Webb see Margaret Cole (ed.)*Beatrice Webb's Diaries 1924–1932* (London, 1956), p. 116, entry for 10 September 1926; Wertheimer, *Portrait of the Labour Party*, p. 153; Paul Davies, *A.J. Cook* (Manchester, 1987) offers a rounded portrait.
7. Huw Beynon and Terry Austrin, *Masters and Servants: Class and Patronage in the Making of a Labour Organisation. The Durham Miners and the English Political Tradition* (London, 1994), Chapter 9; Hester Barron, *The 1926 Miners' Lockout. Meanings of Community in the Durham coalfield* (Oxford, 2010); Mosley, *My Life*, pp. 214–15, 306.
8. Howell, *MacDonald's Party*, pp. 126–9.
9. *Durham Advertiser*, 18 August 1927; *Durham* Chronicle, 19 August 1927.
10. The men on 6s 8d were the lowest-paid; the figure - 33 p - refers to the payment per shift. Thirty shillings - £1.50 - broadly indicates their wage for a full week. George Harvey in *The Mineworker*, 23 September 1927; Ramsay MacDonald to James Robson, 13 February 1928, MacDonald Papers 1173.
11. *Labour Party Conference Report* 1927, p. 249; 1928, p. 228; Davies, *Cook*, Chapter 6.
12. Wertheimer, *Portrait of the Labour Party*, p. 183.
13. Alan Bullock, *The Life and Times of Ernest Bevin*, Volume 1, *Trade Union Leader 1881–1940* (London, 1960); Peter Weiler, *Ernest Bevin* (Manchester, 1993); See Morgan, *Bolshevism, Sydicalism and the General Strike*, Chapter 6, for the claim that accounts of Bevin during the General Strike have been insufficiently critical. Howell, *MacDonald's Party*, p. 272 illuminates his hostility to the ILP'S Living Wage; the retrospective indictment of intellectuals is taken from a letter to G.D.H Cole, 31 December 1935, copy in Transport and General Workers' Union Archive, MSS 126/TG/61195/TEMP44.
14. *Birmingham Town Crier*, 25 July 1924.
15. For background see Howell, *MacDonald's Party*, Chapters 15–17; Marquand, *Ramsay MacDonald*, pp. 450–62.
16. Arthur Marwick, *Clifford Allen: The Open Conspirator* (Edinburgh, 1964), Martin Gilbert (ed.) *Plough My Own Furrow: The Story of Lord Allen of Hurtwood as Told Through His Writings and Correspondence* (London, 1965); Fred Leventhal, *The Last Dissenter: H.N. Brailsford and His World* (Oxford, 1985).
17. Oswald Mosley to Clifford Allen, 20 September 1924, Allen Papers Box 5; the text of Allen's 1924 conference speech is in *Independent Labour Party Conference Report* 1924, pp. 88–100.
18. *Birmingham Town Crier*, 12 September 1924.

19. See Skidelsky, *Oswald Mosley*; Thomas, *John Strachey*, pp. 49–52; Newman, *John Strachey*, p. 16. For positive comments on Strachey's book see letters from Hugh Dalton, 3 January, J.M. Keynes, 5 January, Ramsay MacDonald, 29 January, all 1926 although MacDonald letter dated 1925, Strachey Papers Box 1. For a discussion of both Mosley's pamphlet and Strachey's book see Noel Thompson, *Political Economy and the Labour Party* (London, 2006), pp. 47–9.

20. For Young's appointment see Birmingham Borough Labour Party Executive, 31 March 1924, Party meetings 3 April, 10 July 1924; also Allan Young to Wilfrid Whiteley, 1927, Whiteley Papers UL 6/3; for Young's resignation see Birmingham Borough Labour Party Executive, 17 October, 29 November 1926.

21. J. Johnson, 'Birmingham Labour and the New Party', p. 534.

22. Oswald Mosley, *Revolution by Reason: An Account of the Birmingham Proposals, Together with an Analysis of the Financial Policy of the Present Government Which has Led to Their Great Attack on Wages.*

23. *New Leader*, 17 April 1925.

24. Birmingham Borough Labour Party, Meetings 11 June, 2 July 1925, Executive 23 June 1925; *Birmingham Town Crier*, 19 June, 10 July 1925; John J. Jennings to Wilfrid Whiteley, 24 September 1926, Whiteley Papers UL 6/3; Mosley presented the proposals to MacDonald as 'a piece of research... and by no means a cast iron policy to which we are in any way bound', 3 September 1925 (incomplete) MacDonald Papers 1170. He spoke on the scheme at the subsequent party conference: *Labour Party Conference Report*, 1925, pp. 264–5.

25. Gilbert (ed.) *Plough My Own Furrow*, pp. 191–200; Leventhal, *The Last Dissenter*, pp. 197–203; Gordon Brown, *James Maxton* (Edinburgh, 1986), Chapters 20–26; Fenner Brockway, *Inside the Left* (London, 1942) p. 157.

26. *Birmingham Town Crier*, 14 November 1924; see entry on Simmons in *DLB*, Volume 13, pp. 339–52.

27. *Birmingham Town Crier*, 24 October 1924.

28. Mosley, *My Life*, p. 174.

29. I.S. Wood, *John Wheatley* (Manchester, 1990); Howell, *A Lost Left: Three Studies in Socialism and Nationalism* (Manchester, 1986), pp. 229–80; the Brockway comment is in *New Leader*, 13 August 1926, in response to Wheatley's argument, as reported 6 August.

30. Allan Young to Wilfrid Whiteley, 6 March 1927, Whiteley Papers UL6/3; Allan Young to Cynthia Mosley, 16 April (no year given but is 1928) Mosley Papers A/2/21/2.

31. *New Leader*, 6 July 1928 for discussion of Cook–Maxton campaign on NAC; two meetings of the ILP Parliamentary Group were held on 6, 13 December 1928. For detailed account see 'Note of Discussion at the Special Meeting of the ILP Parliamentary Group', Maxton Papers. For bemusement and exasperation see Ponsonby Diary 16 December 1928, Dalton Diary 13 December 1928 in Pimlott (ed.) *The Political Diary of Hugh Dalton*, pp. 50–51.

32. For atmosphere and decisions at 1929 ILP Conference see Howell, *MacDonald's Party*, pp. 284–7.

33. HC Deb Volume 222 Column 303, 8 November 1928.

34. For composition of PLP Committee see Howell, *MacDonald's Party*, pp. 33–40; Beatrice Webb Diary 5 April 1927, Mackenzie (eds) *The Diary of Beatrice Webb*, Volume 4, p. 120.

35. Charles Trevelyan to Molly Trevelyan, 30 September 1925, Trevelyan Papers Ex MSS 119; Ramsay MacDonald to Oswald Mosley, 9 March 1925, MacDonald Papers 1170; Dalton Diary, 20 July 1928, in Pimlott (ed.) *The Political Diary of Hugh Dalton*, p. 45.
36. Beatrice Webb Diary, 24 December 1928, in Mackenzie (ed.) *The Diary of Beatrice Webb*, Volume 4 pp. 155–6; James Johnston, *A Hundred Commoners* (London, 1931), p. 125.
37. India comment in Skidelsky, *Oswald Mosley*, p. 133; for Debs, Eugene Debs to Florence Hall, 2 February 1926, Debs to Oswald and Cynthia Mosley, 10 March 1926, Mosley Papers OMNA/A/4/6/1; Ray Ginger, *The Bending Cross: A Biography of Eugene Debs* (New York, 1949); Nick Salvatore, *Eugene Debs: Citizen and Socialist* (Urbana, IL, n.d.). For Mosley's initial impressions see his letters to John Strachey, 15 January, 15 February 1926, Strachey Papers Box 1, largely included in Skidelsky, *Oswald Mosley*, pp. 147–9.
38. Skidelsky, *Oswald Mosley*, pp. 146–50; for the United States before the Great Depression see David M. Kennedy, *Freedom from Fear: The American People in Depression and War, 1929–1945* (Oxford, 1999), Chapter 1.
39. For the fortunes of the American labour movement, see David Montgomery, *The Fall of the House of Labor: The Workplace, the State and American Labor Activism* (Cambridge, 1987).
40. Oswald Mosley, 'Is America A Capitalist Triumph?', *New Leader*, 2 April 1926.
41. Allan Nevins and Frank Ernest Hill, *Ford: Expansion and Challenge, 1915–1933* (New York, 1957) Chapters VIII–XIII, XX; for Edmund Wilson's interviews with Ford workers see 'Detroit Motors', in Lewis M. Debney (ed.) *The Portable Edmund Wilson* (Harmondsworth, 1983) pp. 203–19; Mosley's relationship with the Labour Party is placed in context in Kevin Morgan, *The Webbs and Soviet Communism*, Chapter 5.
42. Crawford Diary, 2 June 1929, in John Vincent (ed.) *The Crawford Papers. The journals of David Lindsay, Twenty–Seventh Earl of Crawford and Tenth Earl of Balcarres* (Manchester, 1986), p. 528.
43. *Labour Party Conference Report*, 1927, pp. 181–2 for MacDonald; Labour Party National Executive Committee, 26 October 1927.
44. For Cramp see *ODNB* Volume 13, pp. 981–2; for Wilkinson Volume 58, pp. 994–7.
45. *Labour Party Conference Report*, 1927, p. 181.
46. Oswald Mosley to Ramsay MacDonald, 8 November 1927, MacDonald Papers 1172.
47. Charles Trevelyan to Molly Trevelyan, 11 November 1927, Trevelyan Papers Ex MSS 121; Dalton Diary, 6 February 1928, in Pimlott (ed.) *The Political Diary of Hugh Dalton*, p. 41; Mosley to MacDonald, 'Monday', MacDonald reply, 21 February 1928, MacDonald Papers 1173.
48. Sidney Webb to Beatrice Webb, 24 February 1928, Passfield Papers II.3. I file 24. Labour Party NEC, 2 May 1928.
49. Labour Party NEC, 2 May 1928.
50. *Labour Party Conference Report*, 1928, passim.
51. 'Report of the Sub–Committee on the First Session's Administrative and Legislative Programme', Passfield Papers iv. 21. See discussion in Philip Williamson, *National Crisis and National Government: British Politics, the Economy and Empire, 1926–32* (Cambridge 1992), pp. 40–41.

52. *Birmingham Town Crier*, 17, 24 May 1929.
53. *Staffordshire Evening Sentinel*, 16, 24 May 1929; Percy Shelly to John Ward, 31 May 1929, for reference to 'dollar princess'; Lancelot Hart to John Ward on proposed leaflet 29 April 1929, Ward Papers 4/13; *Birmingham Town Crier*, 31 May 1929.
54. *Smethwick Telephone*, 1 June 1929; *Birmingham Town Crier*, 14 June 1929.

5 Minister

1. Crawford Diary 2 June 1929, in Vincent (ed.) *Crawford Diaries*, p. 528; J.L. Garvin to Mosley 15 June 1929, Mosley Papers 2/1/32.
2. Poster in Skidelsky, *Politicians and the Slump* facing p. 67. Mosley's ministerial experiences are examined in Skidelsky, *Oswald Mosley*, Chapters 9–10.
3. David Howell, *Respectable Radicals. Studies in the Politics of Railway Trade Unionism* (Aldershot, 1999), Chapter 7 especially pp. 238–47.
4. 'Rumours about A.J. Cook', Citrine Papers 1/6.
5. John Shepherd, *George Lansbury* Chapter 14; Memorandum by Lansbury, 22 July 1929 'An Outline of a Plan of National Reconstruction', Lansbury Papers III c 81–94.
6. Graham Walker, *Thomas Johnston* (Manchester, 1988); J. Johnston, *A Hundred Commoners* (London, 1931), pp. 156–8.
7. Marquand, *Ramsay MacDonald*, pp. 488–93 on cabinet making.
8. Howell, *MacDonald's Party*, Chapter 5.
9. Michael Kinnear, *The British Voter* (London, 1981), pp. 48–9.
10. Skidelsky, *Politicians and the Slump*, Chapters 6–7; Ross McKibbin, 'The Economic Policy of the Second Labour Government 1929–1931' *Past and Present* 65 (1975) 95–123; Duncan Tanner 'Political Leadership Intellectual Debate and Economic Policy during the Second Labour Government, 1929–1931', in E.H.H. Green and D.M. Tanner (eds) *The Strange Survival of Liberal England. Political Leaders, Moral Values and the Reception of Economic Debate* (Cambridge, 2007), pp. 113–50; George Lansbury to Oswald Mosley (copy), 25 September 1929, Lansbury Papers III d 177.
11. HC Deb Volume 229 Columns 91–110 for Thomas, 163–5 for Maxton, 3 July 1929; Volume 230 Column 98 for Wheatley, 15 July 1929. The subject was the partial restoration of a housing subsidy introduced by Wheatley as minister in 1924. Brockway, *Inside the Left*, pp. 197–8 for Wheatley's reception at the new parliament's first PLP meeting.
12. HC Deb Volume 229, Columns 206–14 for Lansbury, 3 July; 255–70 for Mosley, 4 July 1929.
13. HC Deb Volume 229 Column 259 for Mosley giving Liverpool Street figure and query by Worthington Evans, see latter again at 279–80, Samuel at 307–8, with response from Thomas; Mosley, *My Life*, p. 234; Ponsonby Diary, 13 July 1929; Beatrice Webb Diary, 28 July 1929, in Mackenzie (ed.) *Diary of Beatrice Webb*, Volume 4, pp. 183–4.
14. For Mosley on hard work and the underdog see entry for 9 July 1929 in Kenneth Young (ed.) *The Diaries of Sir Robert Bruce Lockhart*, Volume 1, *1915–1938* (London, 1973) p. 95; HC Deb Volume 230 Columns 516–25, 1156–61, 17, 23 July 1929; *Durham Advertiser*, 1 August 1929, *Durham Chronicle*, 2 August 1929.

15. HC Deb Volume 229 Columns 1123–128, 11 July 1929, Volume 230 Columns 130–59, 15 July 1929.
16. *Labour Party Conference Report*, 1929, p. 228 (Snowden), pp. 176–86 for Thomas and accompanying discussion, Citrine Papers 7/8.
17. *Labour Party Conference Report*, 1929, debate at pp. 171–6, 187–90, Lansbury at 189.
18. *Labour Party Conference Report*, 1929, pp. 234–5 for NEC elections. Dalton's vote was 1,575,000, Morrison polled 1,693,000.
19. Skidelsky, *Politicians and the Slump*, pp. 91–5, *Oswald Mosley*, pp. 184–6; George Lansbury to Oswald Mosley, 25 September 1929, Lansbury Papers III d 177.
20. Lansbury Papers III d 220–29, note also George Lansbury to J.H. Thomas, 23 October 1929, emphasising ministerial support for temporary pension scheme, Lansbury Papers III d 233. Thomas sent a copy of this letter to Snowden, 24 October 1929; he expressed concern lest social policy jeopardise industry's capacity to offer employment. J.H. Thomas Papers Section C 123.
21. Skidelsky, *Politicians and the Slump*, pp. 95–101. The Report of the Retirement Pensions Committee CP 366(29) includes W.R. Smith's note of dissent, 19 December 1929, CAB 24/207/57; Thomas's comments are in CP 341(29) 'Report on Retirement Pensions, Report of Sub–Committee of Inter–Departmental Committee on Unemployment 26 November 1929', CAB 24/207/32. His comments concluded with the proposal for a small ministerial committee.
22. Skidelsky, *Politicians and the Slump*, pp. 129–34; Ponsonby Diary 17 February 1930; Wertheimer, *Portrait of the Labour Party*, p. 188; Beatrice Webb Diary, 2 November 1929, Mackenzie (ed.), *Diary of Beatrice Webb*, Volume 4, p. 200.
23. For Henderson's concerns see Beatrice Webb Diary, 2 December 1929, and for her picture of ministers at the banquet, 21 December 1929, in Cole (ed.) *Beatrice Webb's Diary*, pp. 230, 232.
24. HC Deb Volume 231 Columns 762–9, (Mosley), 4 November 1929; for ILP left dissatisfaction *New Leader*, 8 November 1929.
25. Skidelsky, *Politicians and the Slump*, pp. 122–31; Howell, *MacDonald's Party*, pp. 41–3.
26. *New Leader*, 29 November 1929.
27. Will Thorne to Ramsay MacDonald, 3 December 1929, MacDonald Papers 440.
28. Nicolson Diary, 20 January 1930.
29. For Keynes see Donald Moggeridge (ed.), *The Collected Writings of John Maynard Keynes* Volume XX (Cambridge, 1981), p. 312; Mosley to MacDonald, 23 January 1930, Tom Johnston to MacDonald, 24 January 1930 MacDonald Papers 446.
30. MacDonald to Mosley, 19, 25 February 1930, Mosley Papers OXM/D/4/1; see also material in J.H. Thomas Papers, MacDonald to Thomas, 1 January 1930, Thomas to MacDonald, 19 February 1930, MacDonald to Thomas 20 February 1930.
31. *ODNB* Volume 23 pp. 617–20 (Greenwood), Volume 50 pp. 126–7 (Shaw). Ponsonby Diary 8 February 1930.
32. Copy of Mosley Memorandum in MacDonald Papers 446.

33. Herbert Morrison to J.H. Thomas, 2 February 1930, text in Skidelsky, *Politicians and the Slump*, pp. 405–7.
34. Cabinet Paper CP 134(30) in MacDonald Papers 446.
35. CP145(30) Unemployment Policy, George Lansbury, 6 May 1930, CAB 24/211/44.
36. PLP Minutes, 12, 19, 26 March, 9 April 1930; Ponsonby Diary, 12 March 1930; Lansbury to MacDonald, 10 April 1930, MacDonald Papers 446.
37. The meetings of 13, 19, 20 May are recorded in considerable detail in Keith Middlemass (ed.), *Thomas Jones Whitehall Diary*, Volume II, *1926–1930* (London, 1969), pp. 257–61 and in MacDonald Diary 20–21 May 1930. For Mosley's expectations see entries for 13, 20 May 1930 in Kenneth Younger (ed.), *The Diaries of Sir Robert Bruce Lockhart*, p 121.

6 Critic

1. Beatrice Webb Diary, 29 May 1930 in Mackenzie (ed.), *The Diary of Beatrice Webb*, Volume 4, pp. 217–18.
2. Lord Snell, *Men Movements and Myself* (London, 1938) pp. 226–34, reference to Mosley p. 232; note the entry on Snell in *Dictionary of Labour Biography*, Volume 13, pp. 352–62.
3. George Lansbury to Ramsay MacDonald, 21 May 1930 MacDonald Papers, John Rylands University Library; Dalton Diary, 20, 21 May 1930 in Pimlott (ed.)*The Political Diary of Hugh Dalton*, pp. 110–11, but note also Johnston's earlier expression of anger to Dalton at Government lethargy, 13 May 1930, p. 107.
4. HC Deb Volume 239 Columns 55–175, Thomas's contribution is at Columns 97–107, Lansbury's at Columns 164–72, 19 May 1930; *New Leader*, 25 April 1930.
5. *New Leader*, 23 May 1930; Dalton Diary, 20 May 1930, in Pimlott (ed.) *The Political Diary of Hugh Dalton*, p. 110.
6. HC Deb Volume 239 Columns 404–5, 21 May 1930; Dalton Diary, 21–22 May 1930 in Pimlott (ed.) *The Political Diary of Hugh Dalton*, pp. 111–14.
7. PLP Minutes, 22 May 1930; for accounts of discussion see Dalton Diary as in fn 6; Transcript interview G.R. Strauss, 19 January 1962, Nuffield College Oxford, Oral History Project.
8. For Hayday, see *ODNB*, Volume 26, pp. 3–5.
9. Ernest Thurtle, *Time's Winged Chariot* (London, 1953), pp. 101–3 for retrospective comment on Mosley.
10. *Birmingham Town Crier*, 30 May 1930.
11. Dalton Diary, 22 May; Philip Noel Baker to Oswald Mosley, 26 May 1930, Mosley Papers 2/1/33; Headlam Diary, 23 May 1930 in Stuart Ball (ed.), *Parliament and Politics in the Age of Baldwin and MacDonald: The Headlam Diaries 1923–35* (Cambridge, 1992), pp. 188–9; Edwards would become secretary of the MFGB following A.J. Cook's death in November 1931, see entry in *ODNB*, Volume 17 pp. 915–16.
12. HC Deb Volume 239 Columns 1317–1444, Mosley's contribution is at 1348–72. For an analysis of Mosley's economic programme see Daniel Ritschel, *The Politics of Planning: The Debate on Economic Planning in Britain in the 1930s* (Oxford, 1997), Chapter 2; 'Why Was There No Keynesian

Revolution under the Second Labour government? A Reassessment of Sir Oswald Mosley's Alternative Economic Agenda in 1930–31', in John Shepherd, Jonathan Davies and Chris Wrigley (eds), *Britain's Second Labour Government 1929–31: A Reappraisal* (Manchester, 2011) pp. 55–84.

13. Neville Chamberlain to Ida Chamberlain, 1 June 1930 in Robert Self (ed.) *The Neville Chamberlain Diary Letters,* Volume 3, *The Heir Apparent, 1928–1933* (Aldershot, 2002), p. 187. Press comments are summarised in Skidelsky, *Oswald Mosley,* p. 216 footnote.

14. See entry in *ODNB,* Volume 59 pp. 831–2; E.M.H. Lloyd Papers 13/1, Material for biography of Wise, collected 1934; Patricia Hollis *Jennie Lee: A Life* (London, 1997) Chapter 3, see also p. 69 footnote citing Beatrice Webb Diary, 24 April 1931 on Wise 'a rough person doing rough things in a "rough way"'; Kevin Morgan, *The Webbs and Soviet Communism* (London, 2006) pp. 190–93; Wise presented his position on the Living Wage, along with J.A. Hobson, to the Joint Committee on the Living Wage, see Minutes of Evidence, 8, 14 December 1927, TUC Archive MSS 292/117/10. Wise's use of American comparisons is striking.

15. E.M.H. Lloyd to Frank Wise, 12 April 1921, Lloyd Papers 7/6; Robert Williams was secretary of the National Federation of Transport Workers and an early and brief member of the Communist Party; Wise's contribution to the debate on 28 May 1930 is at HC Deb Volume 239 Columns 1414–20.

16. Jennie Lee to Frank Wise 12 October 1930 cited Hollis, *Jennie Lee: A Life,* p. 51; Ponsonby Diary, 29 May 1930.

17. *Birmingham Town Crier,* 13 June 1930; Birmingham Borough Labour Party Meeting 12 June 1930, the motion was ruled out as the initiative of an individual, not of an affiliated organisation; the history of the Doncaster resolution can be traced in the records of the Doncaster Divisional Labour Party, Executive, 25 May, 16, 30 July, Quarterly Meeting, 1 June 1930, Special Delegate Meeting, 14 September, 9 November 1930, DS/7/2/4, Annual Report 1930 DS7/1/1.

18. HC Deb Volume 231 Columns 417–22, quotation at 421.

19. For W.J. Brown see his autobiography *So Far* (London, 1943) and entry in *Dictionary of Labour Biography* Volume 10 (London, 2000), pp. 29–35; smoking room image in John Beckett, unpublished autobiography, Chapter 16; Dai Smith, *Aneurin Bevan and the World of South Wales* (Cardiff, 1993); Michael Foot, *Aneurin Bevan, 1897–1945* (London, 1962), Chapter 4; John Campbell, *Aneurin Bevan and the Mirage of British Socialism* (London, 1987), Chapter 3; Note Bevan 'Will the Government Fail? The Coming Storm', *New Leader,* 27 June 1930; Aneurin Bevan to John Strachey, October 1930, Strachey Papers Box 1; for Forgan see *Dictionary of Labour Biography* Volume 6 (London, 1982); for Oliver Baldwin, entry in *Dictionary of Labour Biography* Volume 12 (London, 2005), pp. 7–13, his autobiography *The Questing Beast* (1932), *New Leader,* 6 June 1930 for W.J. Brown's comment.

20. HC Deb Volume 241, Mosley's contribution is at Columns 1347–57, quote at 1356 (16 July 1930).

21. Note articles by Allan Young, *New Leader,* 4, 11, 18 July 1930.

22. Amery Diary 16 July 1930 in John Barnes and David Nicholson (ed.), *The Empire at Bay: The Leo Amery Diaries 1929–1945* (London, 1988), p. 77; HC Deb Volume 241 Columns 1400–1409 for Wise, MacDonald is at 1422–9; and his Diary, 17 July 1930; *New Leader,* 18 July 1930.

23. PLP Minutes, 8, 16, 30 July 1930.
24. *Labour Conference Report*, 1930, pp. 179–85 for MacDonald's speech, his responses to critics, 192–3; Dalton Diary, 3 October 1930; Pimlott (ed.) *The Political Diary of Hugh Dalton*, p. 122.
25. *Labour Party Conference Report*, 1930, pp. 186–200.
26. *Labour Party Conference Report*, 1930, pp. 200–204; for one account of why the MFGB opposed the Doncaster resolution see Gordon Macdonald's report to Lancashire Miners' Conference, 1 November 1930, Lancashire and Cheshire Miners' Federation Reports, 1930.
27. *Manchester Guardian*, 8 October 1930.
28. P.J. Grigg to Winston Churchill, 18 October 1930, in Martin Gilbert (ed.) *Winston Spencer Churchill Companion* Volume 5 Part 2 *The Wilderness Years, 1929–1935* (London, 1981), p 195.
29. *Labour Party Conference Report*, 1930, p. 229.
30. Dalton Diary (Unpublished), 19 November 1930; for an account of the episode see Howell, *MacDonald's Party*, pp. 297–8.
31. Labour Party NEC, 25 November 1930.
32. See material in Dalton Diary, 7, 10, 20 November 1930, in Pimlott (ed.)*The Political Diary of Hugh Dalton*, pp. 127, 130.
33. Marion Phillips to G. Ford (Sunderland), 2 December 1930, Phillips Papers; nevertheless, Mosley addressed the Society of Labour Candidates, 18 December 1930 on 'The Unemployment Situation'. See the society's *Report for 1930*, Baron Noel-Baker Papers NBKR 2/2.

7 Explorer

1. W.P. Crozier, editor of the *Manchester Guardian*, interview with Baldwin, 12 June 1934, cited in Cowling, *Impact of Hitler*, p. 33; Phillip Williamson, *National Crisis and National Government*, pp. 118–32; the original comment was by Sidney Dark, editor of *The Church Times*, see Williamson, *Stanley Baldwin*, p. 345.
2. Stuart Ball, *Baldwin and the Conservative Party: The Crisis of 1929–1931* (New Haven, CT, 1988); for the Lloyd George initiative see Williamson, *National Crisis and National Government*, pp. 109, 124–5.
3. John Campbell, *Lloyd George. The Goat in the Wilderness* (London, 1977), Chapters 9–10; Wilson, *The Decline of the Liberal Party*, Chapter 19.
4. Beaverbrook to Oswald Mosley, 17 July 1930, Mosley Papers OXM/D/4/1.
5. Green, *Ideologies of Conservatism*, pp. 158–9 with particular emphasis on Macmillan; for a view from the left see Frank Wise, 'The Young Tories Start to Think. Facing Facts at Last', *New Leader*, 15 April 1927.
6. Robert Boothby to Cynthia Mosley, 28 September 1925, Boothby Papers File 20/675; Review of Nicolas Mosley, *Party Games*, File 41/740; Robert Boothby to Cynthia Mosley, 5 September 1925, Boothby Papers File 20/674.
7. Robert Boothby to Oswald and Cynthia Mosley, 23 December 1926, Boothby Papers File 14/687, note Mosley's response, 25 December 1926, in which he claimed that the near future rested with 'the energy and discipline of metal hard natures'. For Boothby and socialism see his letter to Cynthia Mosley, 2 August (1925?), Boothby Papers File 20/673. Willie Graham Labour Member for Central

Edinburgh served under Snowden at the Treasury. Mugwumps originally were defectors on anti-corruption grounds from the US Republican Party in the 1880s; in the British context the term was applied to the Liberals who shifted to Labour during and after the 1914–18 war. For Lloyd George see Boothby to Harold Macmillan, 4 July 1969, (copy), Boothby Papers File 13/558. Robert Boothby to Oswald Mosley undated but May 1930, Mosley Papers OX/M/D/4/1. Robert Rhodes James, *Bob Boothby A Portrait* (London, 1991), Chapters 3, 4.

8. Sampson, *Macmillan: A Study in Ambiguity*; Horne, *Macmillan 1894–1956*; D.R. Thorpe, *Supermac*; for Stanley see entry in *ODNB*, Volume 52 pp. 233–5.

9. For Elliot see entry in *ODNB*, Volume 18 pp. 187–90, Colin Coote, *A Companion of Honour: The Story of Walter Elliot* (London, 1965); Nicolson Diary, 15 February 1930, Macmillan reported in Nicolson Diary, 2 July 1930. Macmillan wrote to Nigel Nicolson concerning this comment and asking for it to be omitted from the published version. 'It is only because the average reader will have quite forgotten Sir Oswald Mosley's position at that time which was constitutional and Parliamentary and will only recall his later developments. I have nothing to be ashamed of, but I think the casual reader might be surprised.' Harold Macmillan to Nigel Nicolson, 17 May 1965 Nicolson Papers.

10. *The Times*, 27, 28 May 1930, see the handwritten draft in Macmillan Papers c 359, b/192. For letters in support of Macmillan see Gerald Barry, 30 May 1930, E. Remnant of the *English Review*, 4 June 1930 in Macmillan Papers c 457/15, 149.

11. Ball (ed.) *Headlam Diaries*, p. 193, 26 September 1930; Robert Boothby to Oswald Mosley, 18 May 1930 in Rhodes James, *Bob Boothby*, pp. 103–4. For sceptical assessments see Simon Ball, 'Mosley and the Tories in 1930: The Problem of Generations', *Contemporary British History* 23:4 (2009) 445–60. Richard Carr, 'The Right looks Left? The Young Tory Response to MacDonald's Second Labour Government', in Shepherd, Davies and Wrigley (eds.), *Britain's Second Labour Government*, pp. 185–202.

12. Tom Jones Diary, 26 October 1930; Middlemas (ed.), *Whitehall Diary*, pp. 274–5. John Strachey to Aneurin Bevan, 17 October 1930, Strachey Papers Box 1, note also Bevan's reply 20 October 1930 cited above. Terence O'Connor was a lawyer who had been Conservative Member for Luton 1924–9 and had won a by-election in Central Nottingham 27 May 1930. *Weekend Review*, 25 October 1930, for tri-partite symposium. The third participant was the Progressive Liberal lawyer, Kingsley Griffin.

13. HC Deb Volume 244 Columns 67–81 for Mosley, specific references at Columns 75, 80–81; for comment see *Weekend Review*, 1 November 1930.

14. HC Deb Volume 244 Columns 57–67, Elliot; 81–9, Stanley; 234–40, O'Connor; 578–89, Boothby.

15. HC Deb Volume 244 Columns 109–19, Brown; 169–74, Strachey; 754–62, Bevan; 137–43, Phillips Price; 536–45, Cocks.

16. HC Deb Volume 244 Columns 226–34, Maxton; 397 for text of ILP amendment; 422 for Jennie Lee's comment; 737–48, Frank Wise arguing for international co-operation on reorganisation and rationalisation. Dalton Diaries, 28, 29 October 1930, noted that Mosley had links with Beaverbrook but was aloof from the Maxtonites – Pimlott, *Political Diary of Hugh Dalton*, pp. 124–5.

17. HC Deb Volume 244 Columns 576–7, Morley; 773–81, Owen.

18. HC Deb Volume 244 Baldwin references to 1903 at Column 809, Democracy, 810.
19. Williamson, *National Crisis and National Government*, Chapter 4; Viscount Bridgeman to J.C.C. Davidson, 2 November 1930, in Rhodes James (ed.), *Memoirs of a Conservative*, p. 351; Neville Chamberlain to Hilda Chamberlain, 14 February 1931, Neville Chamberlain Papers NC18/1/726.
20. Mosley Manifesto in *Observer*, 7 December 1930; for a summary, see Thompson, *Political Economy and the Labour Party*, pp. 87–91.
21. McShane and Muggeridge had spoken in the Debate on the Address a few weeks earlier, HC Deb Volume 244 Columns 429–432, 30 October, Columns 91–100, 29 October 1930, respectively. McShane had supported the ILP amendment; for Muggeridge see *Dictionary of Labour Biography*, Volume 5 (London, 1979), pp. 159–62. Lovat Fraser's retrospective justification of his support in the context of the BUF's Olympia meeting is at HC Deb Volume 290 Column 2000, 14 June 1934.
22. M. Phillips Price, *My Three Revolutions* (London, 1969), pp. 263, 265.
23. *Birmingham Town Crier*, 12 December 1930, 14 June 1930 for the six day comment.
24. Paul Davies, *A.J. Cook*, 175–6; *New Leader*, 19 December 1930.
25. MacDonald Diary, 7 December 1930; Dalton Diary, 7 December 1930; Pimlott (ed.), *The Political Diary of Hugh Dalton*, p. 134; *New Leader*, 5 December 1930.
26. *New Leader*, 19 December 1930; *Birmingham Town Crier*, 19 December 1930.
27. J.M. Keynes, 'Sir Oswald Mosley's Manifesto', *The Nation and Athenaeum*, 13 December 1930.
28. Amery Diary, 17 December 1930, in Barnes and Nicholson (eds), *The Empire at Bay*, p. 144.
29. *The Times*, 11 December 1930.
30. *The Times*, 17 December 1930; for Horne and Buchan see the entries in *ODNB*, Volume 28 pp. 149–51, Volume 8 pp. 449–56.
31. See memorandum marked 'Private and Confidential' in Beaverbrook Papers C/254; Mosley had commended the 'Caesarian tradition' rather than 'the Napoleonic' following the Smethwick by-election. Mosley to Boothby, 25 December 1926, Boothby Papers file 4/678. On the memorandum see Williamson, *National Crisis and National Government*, pp. 146–9.
32. Harold Macmillan to Lord Lloyd (copy), 14 November 1930, Macmillan Papers 458/200.
33. Letter from Macmillan, *Weekend Review*, 27 December 1930.
34. Oswald Mosley to Harold Macmillan, 24 June 1931, enquiring about the credibility of a putative New Party candidate, Macmillan copy reply 29 June, 'Do let us meet again sometime', Macmillan Papers c 466/216; Macmillan to Edward S. Morris, 9 December 1930, Macmillan Papers c 459/183; for enthusiasm for Beaverbrook see copy letter to Lord Lloyd, 5 March 1930, 'I cannot help feeling delighted at Max Beaverbrook's triumphs' c 456/133; Devonshire's comment is in letter 25 October 1929 c 862, 243–6. Horne, *Macmillan*, p xii for gardens comment.
35. Robert Boothby to Oswald Mosley in Rhodes James, *Bob Boothby*, pp. 105–7; Boothby Papers, File 14/683.
36. *Smethwick Telephone*, 17 January 1931; *Birmingham Town Crier*, 16 January 1931; for Birmingham Borough Party hostility see Executive, 29 December

1930, 28 January 1931; PLP Minutes, 27 January 1931. Dalton Diary, 28 January 1931, in Pimlott, *Political Diary of Hugh Dalton*, p. 139, *New Leader*, 23 January, 6, 13 February 1931.

37. HC Deb Volume 248 Columns 695–91 for Mosley; Thomas comment at Column 736; note in previous day's debate Brown, Columns 493–8; Wise Columns 516–23, 11–12 February 1931.

38. *A National Policy* (London. 1931); Beatrice Webb Diary, 1 March 1931, in Cole (ed.) *Beatrice Webb's Diary*, pp. 267–8.

39. Robert Boothby to Oswald Mosley, 30 January 1931, with reply, Boothby Papers File 14, 684–5. Excerpt of Boothby letter in Rhodes James, *Bob Boothby*, p. 108.

40. Gerald Barry Diary, 2 February 1931, Barry Papers/1. The Mosley Manifesto had been assessed sympathetically in *Weekend Review*, 13, 20 December 1931. Mosley presented his views *Weekend Review*, 24, 31 January, 14 February 1931.

41. Paul Corthorn, 'W.E.D. Allen, Unionist Politics and the New Party' *Contemporary British History* 23:4 (December 2009) 509–26.

42. Skidelsky, *Oswald Mosley*, pp. 242–5; for Bevan see Foot, *Aneurin Bevan*, pp. 128–34; Allan Young's hope was expressed in a letter 28 February 1931, p. 132, footnote 4; for Brown's explanation see his autobiography *So Far...*(London, 1943), pp. 156–9. The Bevan–Strachey contrast is in Strauss Transcript.

43. Beckett's political journey can be traced in his unpublished autobiography.

44. Letters to MacDonald from John Strachey, Robert Forgan, both 24 February 1931, W.J. Brown, 4 March 1931, MacDonald Papers 1310.

45. Catlin's question was posed in a letter to Philip Noel-Baker, 24 March 1931, accompanied by a copy of a letter to Mosley, 20 March, Baron Noel Baker Papers NBKR 2/3; see also Sir George Catlin, *For God's Sake Go: An Autobiography* (Gerrards Cross, 1972), pp. 73–86, where Catlin states that his letter to Mosley received no response; Ian Mikardo, *Backbencher* (London, 1988) pp. 45–7.

46. Beatrice Webb Diary, 25 February 1931, Mackenzie (ed.), *The Diary of Beatrice Webb*, Volume 4, p. 239; 1 March 1931, Cole (ed.) *Beatrice Webb's Diaries*, p. 268.

47. *New Leader*, 6 March 1931; Beatrice Webb Diary, 25 February 1931, Cole (ed.), *Beatrice Webb's Diaries*, p. 267.

48. *Smethwick Telephone*, 28 February 1931; *Birmingham Town Crier*, 6 March 1931.

49. Ben Shaw and George Shepherd to MacDonald, 28 February , 2 March 1931, respectively, MacDonald Papers 381, Dalton Diary unpublished, 15 March 1931; for the local response to Strachey see Birmingham Borough Labour Party Meeting, 12 March 1931, Special Executive 17 March 1931; *New Leader*, 10 April 1931.

50. Frank Wise to C.P. Trevelyan, 3 March 1931, Trevelyan Papers MS 142; also Howell, *MacDonald's Party*, pp. 46–7.

8 Rejections

1. Nicolson Diaries 26 January, 11 September 1931, Norman Rose *Harold Nicolson* (London, 2005) Chapter 10; for Joad see *ODNB* Volume 30, pp. 132–4. For the

New Party see Matthew Worley, *Sir Oswald Mosley and the New Party* (London, 2010).

2. Pelling, *Social Geography of British Elections*, p. 256.
3. A.J.P. Taylor, *Beaverbrook* (London, 1972), Chapter 3; for Ashfield, see entry in *ODNB* Volume 52, pp. 162–3.
4. See entries in *ODNB* Volume 20, pp. 898–9 de Frece; Volume 54, pp. 786–8, Tilley.
5. Howell, *Respectable Radicals*, pp. 15–16, p. 255, for Bellamy.
6. *Ashton Reporter*, 28 March 1931.
7. *Ashton Reporter*, 18 April 1931 for Gordon's biography,
8. *Ashton Reporter*, 4 April, no Liberal candidate; 18 April, Broadbent; 25 April 1931, Liberal Association.
9. *Ashton Herald*, 25 April, 1 May 1931; *The Times*, 27, 28 April 1931.
10. *Ashton Reporter*, 18 April, start of Young's campaign; 25 April, Manchester New Party split.
11. This verdict on Young is in John Beckett unpublished autobiography, Chapter 17; Nicolson Diary, 27, 28 April 1931, some passages in Nigel Nicolson, *Harold Nicolson Diaries and Letters 1930–1939* (London, 1966), pp. 70–71. Maureen Stanley, wife of Oliver Stanley, Peter Eckersley formerly chief engineer at the BBC, Bruce Lockhart, diplomat and writer, author of *Memoirs of a British Agent*.
12. Jack Jones, *Unfinished Journey* (London, 1937), pp. 253–9; for Jones see Dai Smith, *Aneurin Bevan and the World of South Wales*, pp. 126–9.
13. *Ashton Reporter*, 1 May 1931.
14. John Strachey and C.E.M. Joad 'Parliamentary Reform: The New Party's Proposals' *Political Quarterly* 2:3 (1931); for the contemporary context see Ronald Butt, *The Problem of Parliament* (London, 1967), Chapter 4.
15. Select Committee on Procedure on Public Business, *Special Report* 1930–31 (161)VIII 203. paragraphs 3284, 3271, 3272.
16. Nicolson Diary, 5–7, 10 June 1931; Jones, *Unfinished Journey*, pp. 263–4; for a contemporary, albeit diplomatic, assessment see John Strachey, 'The Progress of the New Party', *Weekend Review*, 20 June 1931.
17. Nicolson Diary, 12 June, industrialists; 22 June, miners; 23 June, William Randolph Hearst. For Horner rumour see Nina Fishman, *Arthur Horner A Political Biography 1894–1944* (London, 2010), p. 221.
18. Williamson, *National Crisis and National Government*, pp. 258–9.
19. Nicolson Diary, 1, 4–13 July 1931; HC Deb Volume 254 Columns 2141–7 for Mosley, 8 July 1931.
20. HC Deb Volume255 Columns 481–740.
21. Nicolson Diary, 17, 22 July 1931. For Strachey's maiden speech see HC Deb Volume231, Columns 957–61, 5 November 1929. For fruits of the three MPs' visit see Aneurin Bevan MP, E.J. Strachey MP and George Strauss MP, *What We Saw in the Soviet Union* (London, 1931). Strachey's memorandum 'The New Party and Russia' is Included with Nicolson Diaries see also Strachey 'The New Revolution in Russia' *Weekend Review*, 18 October 1930.
22. Nicolson Diary, 22–23, 26 July 1931. Thomas, *John Strachey*, Chapter 7; Newman, *John Strachey*, pp. 40–47.
23. John Strachey, *The Menace of Fascism* (London, 1933), pp. 161–4; Aneurin Bevan to John Strachey, 29 July 1931, Strachey Papers, Box 1; Robert

Boothby to Oswald Mosley, 10 June 1973, in response to the publication of Hugh Thomas's biography of Strachey, Boothby Papers File 14/713.

24. Nicolson Diary, 21 July 1931, in Nigel Nicolson, *Diaries 1930–1939*, pp. 81–2.

25. *The Times*, 3 August 1931; *Derbyshire Times*, 8 August 1931.

26. Aneurin Bevan to John Strachey, 29 July 1931, Strachey Papers Box 1; Williamson, *National Government and National Crisis*, Chapters 8–9; Marquand, *Ramsay MacDonald*, Chapters 25–6.

27. Oswald Mosley to Harold Nicolson, 16 August 1931, from Cap d' Antibes, Nicolson Diary, 20 August 1931 and copy letter to Mosley, 20 August; TUC Research Department Memorandum, 17 August 1931, TUC Archive MS 292/420/2.

28. Dalton Diary (unpublished) 28 August 1931, Sankey Diary, 28 August 1931, Sankey Papers c 285.

29. Williamson *National Crisis and National Government* Chapter 10.

30. Nicolson to Mosley 21 August 1931, Diary 26 , 31 August 1931, Mosley to Nicolson 4 September 1931, all in Nigel Nicolson (ed.), *Diaries 1930–1939* pp. 88–90.

31. HC Deb Volume 256 Column 24, MacDonald, 40, Henderson, 55, Maxton. 8 September 1931.

32. HC Deb Volume 256, Columns 72–82, Mosley, 'bankers' palace' reference at Column 76; for Amery see Barnes and Nicolson (ed.) *The Empire at Bay*, diary entry 8 September 1931, p. 199, his actual speech at Columns 107–13; on General Powers, HC Deb Volume 256 Columns 156–60 ; Nicolson Diary 9, 11 September for optimism, 12 September 1931 for wet Trafalgar Square rally.

33. HC Deb Volume 256, Columns 1208–11, 18 September 1931; Nicolson Diary 21 September 1931 in Nigel Nicolson (ed.) *Diaries 1930–1939* p. 91.

34. HC Deb Volume 256 Columns 1299–1304, Henderson, 1345–50, Addison 21 September 131; Williamson *National Crisis and National Government* Chapter 12; Andrew Thorpe *The British General Election of 1931* (Oxford, 1991), pp. 146–8.

35. Mosley's contribution to the Gold Standard debate is at HC Deb Volume 256 Columns 1320–23, compare with Strachey Columns 1375–9; Nicolson Diary 11 September, 1, 2 October 1931; the Memorandum 'Some Notes on the future of the New Party,'25 September 1931; For Mosley seeking a deal with the National coalition see Neville Chamberlain to Hilda Chamberlain 26 September 1931 NC18/1/756.

36. Williamson, *National Crisis and National Government*, pp. 433–45 for Liberal choice; Campbell, *Lloyd George: The Goat in the Wilderness*, Chapter 11.

37. *Dumfries and Galloway Standard*, 3, 10 October 1931.

38. Skidelsky, *Oswald Mosley*, pp. 272–80; *Staffordshire Sentinel*, 17, 24, 31 October 1931; *ODNB* Volume 13, pp. 318–19, for Copeland.

39. James Lees-Milne, *Another Self* (London, 1970), p. 97.

40. *Dumfries and Galloway Standard*, 21 October 1931; for Merthyr, *Western Mail*, 13, 14, 21, 22, 24 October 1931; *Merthyr Express*, 17, 24 October 1931.

41. The Birmingham debacle owed more to a dramatic rise in the Conservative vote than to Labour decline. See Boughton, Thesis, p 17.

42. Harold Macmillan, *Winds of Change: 1914–1939* (London, 1966), p. 263.

43. *Staffordshire Sentinel*, 31 October 1931.

9   Options

1. Press cutting in Mosley Papers B/3/; note also Harold Laski on Mosley's options after his parliamentary resignation speech, *Daily Herald*, 30 May 1930.
2. For a comparison of Mosley and Joseph Chamberlain see A.K. Chesterton, *Oswald Mosley: Portrait of a Leader*, (London n.d.), pp. 54–5.
3. R.J. Scally, *The Origins of the Lloyd George Coalition: The Politics of Social Imperialism 1900–1918* (Princeton, NJ, 1975); Skidelsky, *Oswald Mosley*, especially Chapter 1; Cannadine, *The Decline and Fall of the British Aristocracy*, especially pp. 547–9.
4. Frank Gray's *The Confessions of a Candidate* was published in 1925; see the entry in *ODNB* Volume 23, pp. 424–5; C. Fenby, *The Other Oxford* (London, 1970).
5. For Keynes's views see 'The End of Laissez-Faire' (1926), 'Am I a Liberal?' (1925), 'Liberalism and Labour' (1926) in *Essays in Persuasion* (London, 1932); Peter Clarke ,*The Keynesian Revolution in the Making: 1924–1936* (Oxford, 1988); Robert Skidelsky, *John Maynard Keynes: The Economist as Saviour 1920–1937* (London, 1992) Chapters 7, 8; D.E. Moggridge, *Maynard Keynes: An Economist's Biography* (London, 1992), Chapter 18.
6. George Bernard Shaw to Oswald Mosley, 25 October 1931, Mosley Papers XO MD/4/2.
7. Nicolson Diary, 11 December 1931.
8. Nicolson expressed his own opposition to Mosley's choice in a letter to Forgan, 15 April 1932, Nicolson Papers.
9. For Allen see *ODNB* Volume 1, pp. 835–7.
10. The shift in his politics 1931–43 can be followed in his autobiography *So Far*, especially pp. 216–19, 243–55; the book, published in 1943, is dedicated to the conservative historian Arthur Bryant.
11. Robert Boothby to John Strachey, 7 November 1932, Boothby Papers File 20/1093; Newman, *Strachey*, Chapters 3–4.
12. See Dai Smith, *Aneurin Bevan and the World of South Wales*, Chapter 8.
13. Macmillan, *Winds of Change: 1914–1939*, p. 500; see also references pp. 263, 378.
14. Rhodes James, *Boothby*, Chapters 6–11, the Czech affair is discussed in Chapters 8, 11; p. 332 for post-election celebration. Strachey had won in Dundee, Boothby had retained East Aberdeenshire.
15. Kevin Morgan, *The Webbs and Soviet Communism* (London, 2006), pp. 167–9 for Guild Socialists and Italian fascism; see also C. Keserich, 'The British Labour Press and Italian Fascism' *Journal of Contemporary History* 10:4 (1975) 579–90. For Dalton see his *The Fateful Years: Memoirs 1931–1945* (London, 1957), pp. 31–5; Pimlott, *Hugh* Dalton, pp. 214–15, with diary comment at 215. For comparisons and the argument that any thorough distinction between fascism and other positions is mistaken see Zeev Sternhell, *The Birth of Fascist Ideology: From Cultural Rebellion to Political Revolution* (Princeton, NJ, 1994), and his earlier work *Neither Right nor Left: Fascist Ideology in France* (London, 1986). On strategies for stabilisation see Charles S. Maier, *Recasting Bourgeois Europe: Stabilization in France, Germany and Italy in the Decade after World War 1* (Princeton, NJ, Second Edition, 1988).
16. *The Greater Britain* (London, 1932).

17. *The Greater Britain*, pp. 78–81.

18. *The Greater Britain*, p. 16.

19. For Marconi affair see Bernard Wasserstein, *Herbert Samuel: A Political Life* (London, 1992); for Amritsar see entry on Edwin Montagu, *ODNB* Volume 38, pp. 717–20.

20. *The Greater Britain*, p. 150.

21. Michael Mann, *Fascists* (Cambridge, 2004); Macgregor Knox, *To the Threshold of Power 1922/33: Origins and Dynamics of the Fascist and National Socialist Dictatorships*, Volume 1 (Cambridge, 2007); Gramsci's comment is in 'Italy and Spain' originally published in *L'Ordine Nuovo*, 11 March 1921, translated in Quintin Hoare, *Antonio Gramsci: Selections from Political Writings, 1921–1926* (London, 1978), pp. 23–4.

22. Tom Stannage, *Baldwin Thwarts the Opposition, the British General Election of 1935.*(London 1980). The Communist victory in West Fife owed much to conflict within the Scottish mining unions, where the left could make credible claims to be more effective and more democratic, and Labour was identified with conservative officialdom. See Stuart Macintyre, *Little Moscows: Communism and Working-Class Militancy in Inter-War Britain* (London, 1980). This local analysis can be complemented by Thomas P. Linehan, *East London for Mosley: The British Union of Fascists in East London and South-West Essex, 1933–40* (London, 1996).

23. For a detailed presentation of Baldwin in rural Essex addressing a Conservative gathering in July 1935, see memorandum by R.A. Butler in Williamson and Baldwin (eds), *Baldwin Papers*, pp. 335–43. The contrast with Mosley at Olympia just over a year earlier is revealing. The strengths and limitations of Mosley's style can be considered in the context of Jon Lawrence, 'The Transformation of British Politics After the First World War' *Past and Present* 190 (2006) 185–216.

24. Ira Katznelson, *Fear Itself. The New Deal and the Origins of Our Time* (New York, 2013); for Keynes's comment on Roosevelt *New York Times*, 31 December 1933, see Skidelsky, *Keynes*, p 492, for comment on Mosley, p. 478.

25. TUC Research Department memo, 17 August 1931 TUC Archive MS 292/420/2.

26. George Orwell *Homage to Catalonia* (Harmondsworth, 1974) pp. 220–21.

27. Diane Mosley to Unity Mitford, 18 August 1938, in Charlotte Mosley (ed.), *The Mitfords'Letters: Letters Between Six Sisters* (London, 2008), p. 135.

28. Lord Citrine, *Men and Work The Autobiography of Lord Citrine* (London, 1964), p. 210. Arthur Horner, *Incorrigible Rebel* (London, 1960), pp. 107–8, adds Lansbury to make a quartet. See also Nina Fishman, *Arthur Horner: A Political Biography*, Volume I, *1894–1944*, p. 213.

Select Bibliography

Unpublished Primary Sources

Personal Papers

Clifford Allen Papers, University of South Carolina Library
Gerald Barry Papers, British Library of Political and Economic Science
Beaverbrook Papers, Parliamentary Archives
John Beckett Unpublished Autobiography, Labour History Archive and Study Centre, People's History Museum, Manchester
Boothby Papers National Library of Scotland
Cecil of Chelwood Papers, British Library
Neville Chamberlain Papers, University of Birmingham, Cadbury Research Library
Citrine Papers, British Library of Political and Economic Science
Dalton Diaries, British Library of Political and Economic Science
George Lansbury Papers, British Library of Political and Economic Science
E.M.H. Lloyd Papers, British Library of Political and Economic Science
Ramsay MacDonald Papers National Archive
Ramsay MacDonald Papers, University of Manchester, John Rylands Library
Macmillan Papers, Bodleian Library, University of Oxford
Maxton Papers, Mitchell Library, Glasgow
Mosley Papers, University of Birmingham, Cadbury Research Library
Nicolson Papers, Balliol College Archive, Oxford
Baron Noel-Baker Papers, Churchill Archive, Churchill College Cambridge
Passfield Papers, British Library of Political and Economic Science
Marion Phillips Papers, Labour History Archive and Study Centre, People's History Museum, Manchester
Ponsonby Diaries, courtesy of Lord Ponsonby
Rennie Smith Diary, Bodleian Library, University of Oxford
Sankey Papers, Bodleian Library, University of Oxford
Stansgate Diaries, House of Lords Record Office
John Strachey Papers, courtesy of Elizabeth A. Qaghi
George Strauss, Transcripts of Interviews, Nuffield College Oxford
J.H. Thomas Papers, Kent County Record Office, Maidstone
C.P. Trevelyan Papers, University of Newcastle Library
John Ward Papers, Labour History Archive and Study Centre, People's History Museum, Manchester
Wilfrid Whiteley Papers, Borthwick Archive, University of York

Papers of Organisations

Birmingham Borough Labour Party, Birmingham Central Library Archives
Birmingham Conservative and Unionist Association, Birmingham Central Library Archives

Doncaster Borough Labour Party, Doncaster Archives
Labour History Archive Study Centre, People's History Museum, Manchester.
Labour Party National Executive Minutes
Minutes of Parliamentary Labour Party, People's History Museum, Manchester
Lancashire and Cheshire Miners' Federation Minutes, National Union of Mineworkers, Lancashire Area, Leigh
Trade Union Congress Archive, Modern Record Centre, University of Warwick
Transport and General Workers' Union Archive, Modern Record Centre University of Warwick

Government Records

Retirement Pensions 1929 CP 366(29), CP 341(29), CAB 24/207/32.
Mosley Memorandum 1930 CP 134930), CP145(30), CAB 24/211/44.

Published Primary Sources

Parliamentary Papers

Hansard House of Commons Debates, Fifth Series, Select Committee on Procedure on Public Business *Special Report* 1930–31 (161)VIII.203.

Political Parties, Published Reports

Independent Labour Party Conference Reports; Labour Party Conference Reports.

Contemporary Political Statements

A National Policy (London, 1931)
Aneurin Bevan MP, E.J. Strachey MP, and George Strauss MP, *What We Saw in Russia* (London, 1931)
Arthur Cook and James Maxton, *Our Case for a Socialist Revival* (1928).
Independent Labour Party, *The Living Wage* (1926).
J. Johnson, 'Birmingham Labour and the New Party', *Labour Magazine 1931*, 534–6
J.M. Keynes, 'Sir Oswald Mosley's Manifesto', *The Nation and Athenaeum*, 13 December 1930.
Labour Party, *Labour and the Nation* (1928).
(Sir) Oswald Mosley, *Revolution By Reason: An Account of the Birmingham Proposals together with an analysis of the financial policy of the present Government which has led to their great attack on wages.*(1925).
———*The Greater Britain* (London, 1932).
John Strachey, *Revolution By Reason* (London, 1925).
John Strachey and C.E.M. Joad, 'Parliamentary Reform: The New Party's Proposals', *Political Quarterly* 2 (3) 1931.

Newspapers and Periodicals

Ashton Herald
Ashton Reporter
Birmingham Post
Birmingham Town Crier
Daily Herald

Derby Mercury
Derbyshire Times
Dumfries and Galloway Standard
Durham Advertiser
Durham Chronicle
Harrow Gazette
Harrow Observer
Manchester Guardian
Merthyr Express
New Leader
Railway Gazette
Smethwick Telephone
Staffordshire(Evening) Sentinel
The Mineworker
The Times
Weekend Review

Secondary Sources

Books

Oliver Baldwin, *The Questing Beast* (London, 1932).

Simon Ball, *The Guardsmen. Harold Macmillan, Three Friends and the World They Made* (London, 2005).

Stuart Ball, *Baldwin and the Conservative Party. The Crisis of 1929–1931* (New Haven, CT, 1988)

——— (ed.) *Parliament and Politics in the Age of Baldwin and MacDonald: The Headlam Diaries, 1923–35* (Cambridge, 1992).

John Barnes and David Nicolson (eds), *The Empire at Bay The Leo Amery Diaries, 1929–1945* (London, 1988).

Hester Barron, *The 1926 Miners' Lockout. Meanings of Community in the Durham Coalfield* (Oxford, 2010).

Michael Bentley, *The Liberal Mind 1914–29* (Cambridge, 1977).

Huw Beynon and Terry Austrin, *Masters and Servants: Class and Patronage in the Making of a Labour Organisation: The Durham Miners and the English Political Tradition* (London, 1994).

Robert Blake, *The Unknown Prime Minister the life and times of Andrew Bonar Law* (London, 1955).

R.J.B. Bosworth (ed.), *The Oxford Handbook of Fascism* (Oxford, 2009).

S.V. Bracher, *The Herald Book of Labour Members* (London, 1924).

Fenner Brockway, *Inside the Left* (London, 1942).

Gordon Brown, *James Maxton* (Edinburgh, 1986).

W.J. Brown, *So Far* (London, 1943).

Alan Bullock, *The Life and Times of Ernest Bevin* Volume 1 *Trade Union Leader 1881–1940* (London, 1961).

Ronald Butt, *The Problem of Parliament* (London, 1967).

John Campbell, *Lloyd George the Goat in the Wilderness* (London, 1977).

——— *Aneurin Bevan and the Mirage of British Socialism* (London, 1987).

David Cannadine, *The Decline and Fall of the British Aristocracy* (New Haven, CT, 1990).

Richard Carr, *Veteran MPs and the Aftermath of the Great War: The Memory of all That* (Farnham, 2013).

'Cato', *Guilty Men* (London, 1940).

Sir George Cattlin, *For God's Sake Go* (Gerrards Cross, 1972).

A.K. Chesterton, *Oswald Mosley Portrait of a Leader* (London, n.d.).

Winston Churchill, *The Second World War* Volume 1 *The Gathering Storm* (London, 1948).

Lord Citrine, *Men and Work: The Autobiography of Lord Citrine* (London, 1964).

Peter Clarke, *Lancashire and the New Liberalism* (Cambridge, 1971).

———— *The Keynesian Revolution in the Making, 1924–1936* (Oxford, 1988).

Catherine A Cline, *Recruits to Labour: The British Labour Party 1914–31* (New York, 1963).

Margaret Cole (ed.), *Beatrice Webb's Diaries, 1924–1932* (London, 1956).

Colin Coote, *Companion of Honour The Story of Walter Elliot* (London, 1965).

———— *Editorial: The memoirs of Colin Coote* (London, 1965).

Maurice Cowling, *The Impact of Labour 1918–24: The Beginning of Modern British Politics* (Cambridge, 1971).

———— *The Impact of Hitler: British politics and British policy, 1933–1940* (Cambridge, 1975).

Hugh Dalton, *The Fateful Years: Memoirs, 1931–1945* (London, 1957).

Paul Davies, *A.J. Cook* (Manchester, 1987).

Lewis M. Debney (ed.) *The Portable Edmund Wilson* (Harmondsworth, 1983).

Bernard Donoughue and George Jones, *Herbert Morrison: Portrait of a Politician* (London, 1973).

Stephen Dorril, *Blackshirts! Sir Oswald Mosley and British Fascism* (London, 2006).

John Dos Passos, *USA* (Harmondsworth, 1966).

D. Faber, *Speaking for England Leo, Julian and John Amery – the Tragedy of a Political Family* (London, 2005).

C. Fenby, *The Other Oxford* (London, 1970).

Nina Fishman, *Arthur Horner: A Political Biography, Volume 1, 1894–1944* (London, 2010).

Michael Foot, *Aneurin Bevan, 1897–1945* (London, 1962).

Martin Gilbert (ed.), *Plough My Own Furrow: The Story of Lord Allen of Hurtwood, Told Through His Writings and Correspondence* (London, 1965).

———— *Winston Spencer Churchill Companion,* Volume 5 Part 2 *The Wilderness Years, 1929–1935* (London, 1981).

Ray Ginger, *The Bending Cross. A Biography of Eugene Debs* (New York, 1949).

Frank Gray, *The Confessions of a Candidate* (London, 1925).

Adrian Gregory, *The Last Great War. British Society and the First World War* (Cambridge, 2008).

Roy Gregory, *The Miners in British Politics, 1906–14* (Oxford, 1968).

A.M. Gollin, *Proconsul in Politics: A Study of Lord Milner in Opposition and in Power* (London, 1964).

Ewen Green, *Ideologies of Conservatism: Conservative Political Ideas in the Twentieth Century* (Oxford, 2002).

Mary Agnes Hamilton, *Arthur Henderson* (London, 1938).

Kenneth Harris, *Attlee* (London, 1982).

Peter Harris, *The IRA and Its Enemies. Violence and Community in Cork, 1916–1923* (Oxford, 1998).

Quintin Hoare (ed.), *Gramsci, Selections from Political Writings, 1921–1926* (London, 1978).

Patricia Hollis, *Jennie Lee, A Life* (Oxford, 1997).

Alastair Horne, *Macmillan, 1894–1956* (London, 1988).

Arthur Horner, *Incorrigible Rebel* (London, 1960).

David Howell, *A Lost Left. Three Studies in Socialism and Nationalism* (Manchester, 1986).

—— *Respectable Radicals: Studies in the Politics of Railway Trade Unionism* (London, 1999).

—— *MacDonald's Party Labour Identities and Crisis 1922–1931* (Oxford, 2002).

Robert Rhodes James, *Memoirs of a Conservative: J C C Davidson's Memoirs and Papers 1910–37* (London, 1969).

—— *Victor Cazalet, A Portrait* (London, 1970).

—— *Anthony Eden* (London, 1986).

—— *Bob Boothby, A Portrait* (London, 1991).

James Johnston, *A Hundred Commoners* (London, 1931).

Jack Jones (Labour MP), *My Lively Life* (London, 1928).

Jack Jones, *Unfinished Journey* (London, 1937).

Raymond A. Jones, *Arthur Ponsonby: The Politics of Life* (London, 1989)

Ira Katznelson, *Fear Itself: The New Deal and the Origins of Our Time* (London, 2013).

David Kennedy, *Freedom from Fear: The American People in Depression and War, 1929–1945* (Oxford, 1999).

J.M. Keynes, *Essays in Persuasion* (London, 1932).

Michael Kinnear, *The Fall of Lloyd George the Political Crisis of 1922* (London, 1973).

—— *The British Voter* (London, 1981).

Macgregor Knox, *To the Threshold of Power 1922/33: Origins and Dynamics of the Fascist and National Socialist Dictatorships* Volume 1 (Cambridge, 2007).

James Lee-Milne, *Another Self* (London, 1970).

D.M. Leeson, *The Black and Tans: British Police and Auxilaries in the Irish War of Independence* (Oxford, 2012).

Robin Leleux, *A Regional History of the Railways of Great Britain* Volume IX, *The East Midlands* (Newton Abbot, 1984).

Fred Leventhal, *The Last Dissenter: H.N. Brailsford and His World* (Oxford, 1985)

—— *Arthur Henderson* (Manchester, 1990).

Alison Light, *For Ever England: Femininity, Literature and Conservatism Between the Wars* (London, 1991).

Thomas P. Linehan, *East End for Mosley: The British Union of Fascists in East London and South-West Essex* (London, 1996).

Desmond Macarthy (ed.), *H.H.A.: Letters of the Earl of Asquith to a Friend* Second Series (London, 1934).

Stuart Macintyre, *Little Moscows: Communism and Working-Class Militancy in Inter-War Britain* (London, 1980).

N. and J. Mackenzie (eds) *The Diary of Beatrice Webb*, Volume 3 *1905–1924, The Power to Alter Things* (London, 1984).

—— Volume 4 *1924–1943, The Wheel of Life* (London, 1985).

Ross McKibbin, *The Evolution of the Labour Party 1910–24* (Oxford, 1974).

—— *Ideologies of Class Social Relations in Britain 1880–1950* (Oxford, 1990).

—— *Classes and Cultures England 1918–1951* (Oxford, 1998).

—— *Parties and People: England 1914–1951* (Oxford, 2010).

Harold Macmillan, *Winds of Change 1914–1939* (London, 1966).

Charles S. Maier, *Recasting Bourgeois Europe: Stabilisation in France Germany and Italy in the Decade after World War 1* (Princeton, NJ, second edition, 1988).

Michael Mann, *Fascists* (Cambridge, 2004).

David Marquand, *Ramsay MacDonald* (London, 1977).

—— *The Progressive Dilemma* (London, 1991).

Peter Marsh, *Joseph Chamberlain, Entrepreneur in Politics* (New Haven, CT, 1994).

Arthur Marwick, *Clifford Allen: the Open Conspirator* (Edinburgh, 1964).

Timothy W Mason, *Social Policy in the Third Reich: The Working Class and the 'National Community'* (Oxford, 1993).

—— *Nazism Fascism and the Working Class,* edited by Jane Caplan (Cambridge, 1995).

Billie Melman, *Women and the Popular Imagination in the Twenties: Nymphs and Flappers* (London, 1988).

Keith Middlemas (ed.), *Thomas Jones: Whitehall Diary* Volume II *1926–30* (London, 1969).

Ian Mikardo, *Backbencher* (London, 1988).

Donald Moggeridge, *Maynard Keynes: An Economist's Biography* (London, 1992).

—— (ed.), *The Collected Writings of John Maynard Keynes* Volume XX (Cambridge, 1981).

David Montgomery, *The Fall of the House of Labor: The Workplace, the State and American Labor Activism* (Cambridge, 1987).

Kenneth O. Morgan, *Consensus and Disunity: The Lloyd George Coalition Government, 1918–1922* (Oxford, 1979).

—— *Michael Foot: A Life* (London, 2007).

—— and Jane Morgan, *Portrait of a Progressive: The Political Career of Christopher, Viscount Addison* (Oxford, 1980).

Kevin Morgan, *The Webbs and Soviet Communism* (London, 2006).

—— *Bolshevism,Syndicalism and the General Strike. The Lost Internationalist World of A A Purcell* (London, 2013).

Charlotte Mosley (ed.), *The Mitfords' Letters: Letters Between Six Sisters* (London, 2008).

Nicholas Mosley, *Rules of the Game: Sir Oswald and Lady Cynthia Mosley, 1896–1933* (London, 1982).

Sir Oswald Mosley, *My Life* (London, 1968).

C.L. Mowat. *Britain Between the Wars, 1918–1940* (London, 1955).

Allan Nevins and Frank Ernest Hill, *Ford: Expansion and Challenge, 1915–1933* (New York, 1957).

Michael Newman, *John Strachey* (Manchester, 1989).

Nigel Nicolson (ed.), *Harold Nicolson, Diaries and Letters 1930–39* (London, 1966).

George Orwell, *Homage to Catalonia* (Harmondsworth, 1974).

John Paton, *Left Turn* (London, 1936).

Henry Pelling, *Social Geography of British Elections 1885–1910* (London, 1967).

G.A. Phillips, *The General Strike: The Politics of Industrial Conflict* (London, 1976).

Ben Pimlott, *Hugh Dalton* (London, 1985).

—— (ed.), *The Political Diary of Hugh Dalton, 1918–1940, 1945–1960* (London, 1986).

Martin Pugh, *Hurrah for the Blackshirts! Fascists and Fascism in Britain Between the Wars* (London, 2005).

Neil Riddell, *Labour in Crisis: The Second Labour Government, 1929–31* (Manchester, 1999).

Daniel Ritschel, *The Politics of Planning: The Debate on Economic Planning in Britain in the 1930s* (Oxford, 1997).

Keith Robbins, *Sir Edward Grey: A Biography of Lord Grey of Fallodon* (London, 1971).

Norman Rose, *Harold Nicolson* (London, 2005).

Nick Salvatore, *Eugene V. Debs, Citizen and Socialist* (Urbana, IL, 2007).

Anthony Sampson, *Macmillan: A Study in Ambiguity* (London, 1967).

R.J. Scally, *The Origins of the Lloyd George Coalition: The Politics of Social Imperialism, 1900–1918* (Princeton, NJ, 1975).

Jon Schneer, *Ben Tillett: Portrait of a Labour Leader* (London 1982).

———— *George Lansbury* (Manchester, 1990).

G.R. Searle, *Country Before Party Coalition and the Idea of 'National Government' in Modern Britain, 1885–1987* (London, 1995).

Robert Self, *Neville Chamberlain A Biography* (Aldershot, 2006).

———— (ed.), *The Austen Chamberlain Diary Letters 1916–1937* (Cambridge, 1995).

————*The Neville Chamberlain Diary Letters*, Volume 2 *The Reform Years* 1921–27 (Aldershot, 2000).

———— *The Neville Chamberlain Diary Letters*, Volume 3 *The Heir Apparent 1928–33* (Aldershot, 2002).

John Shepherd, *George Lansbury: At the Heart of Old Labour* (Oxford, 2002).

Jim Simmons, *Socialist Evangel* (Birmingham, 1971).

Robert Skidelsky, *Politicians and the Slump: the Labour Government of 1929–31* (London, 1967).

———— *Oswald Mosley* (London, 1975).

———— *John Maynard Keynes The Economist as Saviour 1920–1937* (London, 1992).

———— *Interests and Obsessions Historical Essays* (London, 1993).

Dai Smith, *Aneurin Bevan and the World of South Wales* (Cardiff, 1993).

Lord Snell, *Men Movements and Myself* (London, 1938).

Snowden, Philip, Viscount, *An Autobiography* (2 vols. London, 1934).

Tom Stannage, *Baldwin Thwarts the Opposition: The British General Election of 1935* (London, 1980).

Zeev Sternhell, *Neither Right nor Left: Fascist Ideology in France* (London, 1986).

———— *The Birth of Fascist Ideology From Cultural Rebellion to Political Revolution* (Princeton, NJ, 1994).

John Strachey, *The Menace of Fascism* (London, 1933).

A.J.P. Taylor, *English History 1918–1945* (Oxford, 1965).

———— *Beaverbrook* (London, 1972).

Hugh Thomas, *John Strachey* (London, 1973).

Noel Thompson, *Political Economy and the Labour Party* (London, 2006)

Andrew Thorpe, *The British General Election of 1931* (Oxford, 1991).

D.R. Thorpe, *Supermac: The Life of Harold Macmillan* (London, 2010).

Ernest Thurtle, *Times Winged Chariot* (London, 1953).

Charles Townshend, *The British Campaign in Ireland 1919–21: The Development of Political and Military Policies* (Oxford, 1979).

Frank Trentmann, *Free Trade Nation: Consumption and Civil Society in Modern Britain* (Oxford, 2009).

J. Tringham (ed.), *A History of the County of Stafford* Volume X *Tutbury and Needwood Forest* (Woodbridge, 2007).

John Turner, *British Politics and the Great War Coalition and Conflict 1915–1918* (New Haven, CT, 1990).

John Vincent (ed.), *The Crawford Papers. The Journals of David Lindsay twenty seventh Earl of Crawford and tenth Earl of Balcarres* (Manchester, 1986).

Graham Walker, *Thomas Johnston* (Manchester, 1988).

Bernard Wasserstein, *Herbert Samuel: A Political Life* (London, 1982).

Egon Wertheimer, *Portrait of the Labour Party* (London, 1929).

Raymond Williams, *The Country and the City* (London, 1973).

Philip Williamson, *National crisis and National Government: British Politics, the Economy and Empire, 1926–1932* (Cambridge, 1992).

—— *Stanley Baldwin: Conservative Leadership and National Values* (Cambridge, 1999).

—— and Edward Baldwin (eds.) *Baldwin Papers: A Conservative Statesman* (Cambridge, 2004).

Ellen Wilkinson, *Peeps at Politicians* (London, 1930).

Trevor Wilson, *The Downfall of the Liberal Party 1914–29* (London, 1966).

—— (ed.), *The Political Diaries of C P Scott, 1911–1928* (London, 1970).

I.S. Wood, *John Wheatley* (Manchester, 1990).

Matthew Worley, *Sir Oswald Mosley and the New Party* (London, 2010).

Chris Wrigley, *Arthur Henderson* (Cardiff, 1990).

—— *Lloyd George and the Challenge of Labour: The Post-War Coalition, 1918–1922* (Hemel Hempstead, 1990).

Kenneth Young (ed.), *The Diaries of Sir Robert Bruce Lockhart* Volume 1 *1915–1938* (London, 1973).

Works of Reference

Dictionary of Labour Biography, Volumes I–XIII (London, Basingstoke, 1972–2010).

Oxford Dictionary of National Biography (Oxford 2004).

F.W.S. Craig, *British Parliamentary Election Results, 1918–1949* (London, 1969).

—— *British Parliamentary Election Results, 1885–1918* (London, 1974).

William Knox (ed.), *Scottish Labour Leaders* (Edinburgh, 1984).

Articles and Chapters in books

Simon Ball, 'Mosley and the Tories in 1930: The Problem of Generations', *Contemporary British History* 23:4 (2009) 445–60.

Stuart Ball, 'The National Government 1931: Crisis and Controversy', *Parliamentary History* (1993) 184–200.

Michael Bentley, 'Liberal Politics and the Grey Conspiracy of 1921', *Historical Journal* 20 (1977) 461–78.

David Cannadine, 'Politics, propaganda and art: the case of two "Worcestershire lads"', *Midland History* (1977) 97–122.

Richard Carr 'The Right Looks Left? The Young Tory Response to MacDonald's Second Labour Government', in John Shepherd, Jonathan Davies and Chris Wrigley (eds.), *Britain's Second Labour Government, 1929–1931: A Reappraisal* (Manchester, 2011), pp. 185–262.

D.H. Close, 'The Realignment of the Electorate in 1931', *History* 67 (1982) 393–404.

Paul Corthorn, 'W.E.D. Allen, Unionist Politics and the New Party', *Contemporary British History* 23:4 (2009) 509–526.

P. Coupland, '"Left Wing Fascism" in Theory and Practice: The Case of the British Union of Fascists', *Twentieth Century British History* 13:1 (2002) 38–61.

John Farr, 'The Conservative Basis for the Formation of the National Government in 1931', *Journal of British Studies* 19 (1980) 142–64.

Cristopher Howard, 'Expectations Born to Death: Labour Party Expansion in the 1920s', in J.M. Winter(ed.), *The Working Class in Modern British History: Essays in Honour of Henry Pelling* (Cambridge 1975).

David Howell, '*The Sheik*, A Valentino in Real Life: Sir Oswald Mosley and the Labour Party, 1924–1931', *Contemporary British History* 23:4 (2009) 425–43.

David Jarvis, 'Mrs Maggs and Betty. The Conservative Appeal to Women in the 1920s', *Twentieth Century British History* 5:2 (1994) 129–152.

——— 'British Conservatism and Class Politics in the 1920s', *English Historical Review* 440 (1996) 59–84.

C. Keserich, 'The British Labour Press and Italian Fascism, 1922–5', *Journal of Contemporary History* 10:4 (1975), 579–90.

Jon Lawrence, 'The Transformation of British Politics after the First World War', *Past and Present* (2006), 185–216.

Ross McKibbin, 'Arthur Henderson as Labour Leader', *International Review of Social History* 23 (1978) 79–101.

Sian Nicholas, 'The construction of national identity: Stanley Baldwin, "Englishness" and the mass media in inter-war Britain', in M. Francis and I. Zweiniger-Bargielowski (eds), *The Conservative Party and British Society 1880–1990* (Cardiff 1996) 127–46.

Adrian Oldfield, 'The Independent Labour Party and Planning 1920–26', *International Review of Social History* (1976) 1–29.

Nicholas Owen, '"MacDonald's Parties": The Labour Party and the Aristocratic Embrace 1922–31', *Twentieth Century British History* 18:1 (2007) 1–53.

Martin Pugh, 'Class Traitors': Conservative Recruits to Labour, 1900–30', *English Historical Review* 113 (1998) 38–64.

Daniel Ritschel, 'A Corporatist Economy in Britain? Capitalist Planning for Industrial Self-Government in the 1930s', *English Historical Review* (1991) 41–65.

——— 'Why was There no Keynesian Revolution under the Second Labour Government? A reassessment of Sir oswald Mosley's Alternative Economic Agenda', in John Shepherd, Jonathan Davies and Chris Wrigley (eds.), *Britain's Second Labour Government, 1929–1931: A Reappraisal* (Manchester, 2011), pp. 55–84.

Bill Schwarz, 'The Language of Constitutionalism: Baldwinite Conservatism', in *Formations of Nations and Peoples* (London 1984) 1–18.

Robert Self, 'Conservative Reunion and the General Election of 1923: A Reassessment', *Twentieth Century British History* 3 (1992) 249–73.

J.O. Stubbs, 'Lord Milner and Patriotic Labour 1914–18', *English Historical Review* (1972) 717–54.

Duncan Tanner, 'Class Voting and Radical Politics: The Liberal and Labour Parties, 1910–1931', in Jon Lawrence and Miles Taylor (eds), *Party, State and Society: Electoral Behaviour in Britain since 1820* (Aldershot 1997) 106–30.

——— 'Political leadership, intellectual debate and economic policy during the second Labour Government 1929–1931', in E.H.H. Green and Duncan Tanner (eds), *The Strange Survival of Liberal England: Political Leaders Moral Values and the Reception of Economic Debate* (Cambridge 2007) 113–50.

Andrew Thorpe, 'Arthur Henderson and the British Political Crisis of 1931', *Historical Journal* 31 (1988) 117–39.

——— 'The Communist Party and the New Party', *Contemporary British History* 23:4 (2009) 477–92.

J.D. Tomlinson, 'Women as "Anomalies": The Anomalies Regulations of 1931, their Bakground and Implications', *Public Administration* (1984) 423–37.

Richard Toye, '"Perfectly Parliamentary"? The Labour Party and the House of Commons in the Inter–War Years', *Twentieth Century British History* 25:1 (March 2014) 1–29.

Philip Williamson, 'Safety First: Baldwin, the Conservative Party and the 1929 General Election', *Historical Journal* 25 (1982) 385–409.

——— 'Financiers, the Gold Standard and British Politics, 1925–1931', in John Turner(ed.), *Businessmen and Politics: Studies of Business Activity in British Politics 1900–45* (London 1984) 105–29.

——— 'A Bankers' Ramp? Financiers and the British Political Crisis of August 1931', *English Historical Review* (1984) 770–806.

——— 'The doctrinal politics of Stanley Baldwin', in Michael Bentley (ed.), *Public and Private Doctrine: Essays in British History Presented to Maurice Cowling* (Cambridge 1993) 181–208.

——— 'Baldwin's Reputation: Politics and History 1937–1967', *Historical Journal* (2004) 127–68.

Matthew Worley,' What was the New Party? Sir Oswald Mosley and Associated Responses to the "Crisis" 1931–2', *History* 92:1 (2007) 39–63.

——— 'Who Makes the Nazis? North West Experiences of the New Party, 1931–2', *North West Labour History Journal* 32 (2007) 7–16.

——— 'A Call to Action: New Party Candidates and the 1931 General Election', *Parliamentary History* 27:2 (2008), 236–55.

David Wrench, 'Cashing-In: The Parties and the National Government, August 1931–September 1932', *Journal of British Studies* 23 (1984) 135–53.

Unpublished Theses

John Boughton 'Working Class Politics in Birmingham and Sheffield, 1918–1931' (Ph.D. thesis, University of Warwick, 1985).

M. Burrows, 'The Left Wing Road to Fascism: An Investigation into the Influence of Socialist Ideas upon the Political Ideology of the British Union of Fascists' (Ph.D. thesis, University of Sheffield, 1998).

Michael Hart 'The Decline of the Liberal Party in Parliament and in the Constituencies, 1914–31' (D. Phil thesis, University of Oxford, 1982).

C.J. Howard 'Henderson, MacDonald and Leadership in the Labour Party, 1914–22' (Ph.D. thesis University of Cambridge, 1978).

K.W.D. Rolf 'Tories, Tariffs and Elections: West Midlands in English Politics 1918–1933' (Ph.D. thesis, University of Cambridge, 1974).

Index

245

Printed and bound by CPI Group (UK) Ltd, Croydon, CR0 4YY